Interviews with Top University Teachers:

How to Build Quality Teaching, Inspire Your Students, and Create More Time for Research

Interviews with Top University Teachers:

How to Build Quality Teaching, Inspire Your Students, and Create More Time for Research

Timothy Falcon Crack

PhD (MIT), MCom, PGDipCom,
BSc (HONS 1st Class), IMC

Published by: Timothy Falcon Crack, P.O. Box 6385, Dunedin North, Dunedin 9059, New Zealand.

Cover images: MIT Buildings 10 (front) and 6 (rear), Fall 2014. See Davis (1939) for a discussion of the bronze bas-reliefs on the travertine walls in Building 6.

First edition, Third Printing, February 2022.
ISBN: 978-1-99-115540-5

Typeset by the author.
www.KelleySchool.com
timcrack@alum.mit.edu

Contents

Preface

My goal is to help university teachers to build quality into their teaching. Quality teaching should inspire students and meet learning objectives, while exploiting teaching efficiencies that create more time for research. These outcomes should improve job satisfaction and prospects for career success. Teachers can use this book to improve their own outcomes; Administrators can give this book to new teachers to build quality teaching from Day 1.

Most of us have colleagues who are outstanding university teachers. They win teaching awards, and are praised by administrators, academic colleagues, and students alike. Tautologically, they are outstanding because they behave *differently* from other teachers. We do not, however, sit in their classrooms, or sit beside them in their offices when they prepare a course or a class. So, unless they mentored us as teachers, we often do not know exactly what they do to make themselves stand out from their peers. Even the students of outstanding teachers do not necessarily know exactly what their teachers are doing, because they see only the tip of the spear. That is, they see them in the classroom or during office hours, and not during the other 85% of their working week. So, how can we know what outstanding university teachers do? The obvious answer is to ask them.

I contacted a select group of outstanding university teachers in the United States, United Kingdom, Australia, Israel, and New Zealand (hereafter, N.Z.). I asked these teachers a series of questions about their teaching, and I interwove their thoughtful responses with reflections upon my own 30 years of award-winning university teaching.

Note the following: most of my reflections are given in the present tense, although I retired recently; all references appear at the end of the book; quotes from my interviewees, quotes from the literature, and stories are usually presented using a double-indent and a **sans serif** font; and, key points are indicated with a key (🗝), or large key $\left(🗝 \right)$, in the margin, depending upon importance.

I have edited down some interviewees' responses. I have also taken the liberty of minor editing to account for punctuation, spelling, grammar, tense, etc., while retaining original voice and intent. I did not, however, change U.K., Australian, or N.Z. English to American English.

When I interviewed university teachers, I told them that I would not attach their names to their comments. There were two reasons for this. First, I wanted the interviewees to feel free to disclose things that they might not wish to have associated with their names (e.g., how a disability that they have not disclosed to their employer affects their teaching, or how they responded to a challenge that was unfairly foisted upon them by their boss, etc.). Second, I suspect that many readers think of themselves as falling into categories based on ethnicity, sex, disability, etc. I do not want, for example, a young male teacher to naively think that advice from an older female teacher does not, or could not, apply to him. So, although I do identify some comments as coming from interviewees based upon some categorizations, I do so only when the comment relates directly to the impact of that categorization upon their teaching. Otherwise, with a few exceptions, I do my best to obscure identifying characteristics of my interviewees, sometimes even using pseudonyms (e.g., "Prof. Mustard," "Prof. Plum," etc.) to help to tell a story.

Most of the teaching tips given here are culled from face-to-face classroom instruction. Nevertheless, the majority of these tips carry over to remote/online teaching. Many of the teaching tips are "purely mechanical," in the sense that you don't need any special skills or abilities to implement them, yet they improve student satisfaction and the efficiency of your teaching, leaving you with better teaching evaluations and more time for research.

> When asked, "What are the three most important things you do (or do not do) as a teacher that make you a great teacher?," one modest interviewee wrote, "I do not feel that I was trained for that or was taught the appropriate tools. I am sure that I will get better with time."

> A more senior interviewee wrote, "Be patient, teaching evolves over time, and as long as you intend to improve, you will improve, but not all at once."

Like many things in life, it is easy to wander aimlessly into poor teaching evaluations and inefficient teaching. To aim for good teaching evaluations and efficient teaching, however, requires a deliberate/intentional strategy. The advice in this book is designed to be part of that strategy. I provide specific guidance to help with the training that my modest interviewee did not get, and appropriate tools to accelerate the improvement in your teaching referred to by my more senior interviewee.

This collection of tips, advice and parable-like stories would not have been possible without the contributions of many outstanding teachers. I thank Tom Arnold, Nicola Beatson, Alex Butler, Scott Chaput, Paul De Lange, Olena Onishchenko, Mike Osborne, Helen Roberts, Anindya Sen, Sharon Tal, Meredith Tharapos, Geoff "Tank" Todd, and Craig Wisen. I also thank Professors "Sage," "Scarlett," and "Peacock," who wish to remain anonymous (which is not surprising, given their comments). A special vote of thanks goes to Scott Chaput, Olena Onishchenko, and Mike Osborne, whose ideas changed the format of this book.

I also thank the many talented teachers, communicators, and presenters whose actions shaped my classroom approach, both consciously and unconsciously. The usual disclaimers apply: Any errors are mine, and any views expressed are mine (even the ones I disagree with).

Invitation to Contribute

I invite you to send me e-mails with queries, corrections, and constructive criticism. If you have some gem of an idea that you think will add value, please let me know! I revise my books frequently, and I will be happy to include any contribution that adds value, no matter how small. If I use your material, I will thank you in the next edition and send you a free copy.

I am especially interested in hearing from anyone who may be under-represented here. For example, more input from teachers in the humanities or medical fields may be valuable.

Finally, if this book improves your teaching (e.g., you have more confidence in the classroom, happier students, better teaching evaluations, or more time for research), then please leave a positive review on `www.Amazon.com`, so that others can hear about your success. Search for this book on Amazon's Web site and click on the box labeled, "Write a customer review." Thank you!

`www.KelleySchool.com`
(Online documents, Errata, links to Amazon, etc.)
`timcrack@alum.mit.edu`

Chapter 1

Introduction

As a university teacher, you likely had success at school and at university. If you had unusual curiosity, studied very hard, and got excellent grades, then that makes you different from 90% of your students! They are distracted by parties, alcohol, drugs, and sex; how can you compete with that? You and your class may be a low priority until an exam or another significant assessment appears on the horizon. Then, briefly, you have their undivided attention. To grab and hold your students' attention the rest of the time, you need a deliberate strategy with solid foundations.

1.1 Infrastructure

Flesh without a supporting skeleton will get the attention of your audience for the wrong reasons! You likely know that "supra" means above or over, as opposed to "infra," which means below or beneath. It makes no sense to discuss tips to raise your teaching skills above those of your peers without first providing a brief, but solid, philosophical infrastructure to support these tips. Therefore, let me begin by reviewing, albeit briefly, eight thoughtful approaches that have served as the philosophical foundation for my teaching career.

1.1.1 Deming Approach

Given my age, and his, I was lucky to watch the late W. Edwards Deming give a presentation at my undergraduate University when I was about 20 and Deming was about 85. Deming was a famous U.S. operations researcher who had a significant influence on the recovery of the manufacturing industry in post-WWII Japan.[1] Deming's *14 Points for Management* include "Cease dependence on inspec-

---

[1] Deming got his PhD at Yale in 1928 and published more than 170 research articles. For example, we cite Deming and Birge (1934) in Crack, Osborne, Crack, and Osborne (2021).

tion to achieve quality. Eliminate the need for inspection on a mass basis by building quality into the product in the first place" (Deming, 2018 [1982]).

The admin boffins (Chapter 6) at your university are, however, almost certainly using teaching evaluations to identify weaknesses that they wish to fix. This is the wrong way to attack the problem. Instead of them trying to fix a process that is broken, they should be insisting that you build quality into your product from Day 1. "Inspection does not improve the quality, nor guarantee quality. Inspection is too late. The quality, good or bad, is already in the product. As Harold F. Dodge said, 'You can not inspect quality into a product.'" (Deming, 2000 [1982], p. 29).

So, my "Deming approach" to teaching a new course has always been to put in as much effort as is needed to create a well-structured course on Day 1. This does not mean that I have all the lecture materials produced in advance (I may still be keeping only two weeks ahead of my students as we walk through the semester), but it does mean that I have the content mapped out and I know what I will be doing and when and how.

The alternative approach to this (which many teachers seem to follow) is to teach a relatively poorly structured/delivered course the first time you face it, and to improve it a bit the second time, and a bit more the third time, etc. This slow-and-painful approach means that your teaching (and evaluations) may be initially half-heartedly poor, and then only slowly improve over time. Meanwhile, you put the other half of your efforts into research (or administration or engagement) slowly over time. This is often referred to as a course getting "bedded in," an analogy to planting a garden and watching it grow into what you want.

Allowing a course to bed in over several successive semesters means, essentially, that a different course is being taught each time. This can produce pass/fail rates that vary notably over time, typically trending up or down. This inconsistency may attract the unwanted attention of the admin boffins. See the example discussed in Section 6.2.

I choose, instead, to set aside other obligations and to expend most of my teaching preparation effort up front in one big burst. Once the course is up and running, I can then devote more time to research. In subsequent semesters I can take the course "off the shelf" with little effort, and otherwise focus on research, rather than on improving a poorly-built course.

1.1.2 Whitehead/Chicago Approach

Alfred North Whitehead[2] wrote, "Whatever be the detail with which you cram your student, the chance of his meeting in after-life exactly that detail is almost infinitesimal; and if he does meet it, he will probably have forgotten what you taught him about it. The really useful training yields a comprehension of a few general principles with a thorough grounding in the way they apply to a variety of concrete details.

"In subsequent practice the men will have forgotten your particular details; but they will remember by an unconscious common sense how to apply principles to immediate circumstances. Your learning is useless to you till you have lost your textbooks, burnt your lecture notes, and forgotten the minutiae which you learned by heart for the examination. What, in the way of detail, you continually require will stick in your memory as obvious facts like the sun and moon; and what you casually require can be looked up in any work of reference.

"The function of a University is to enable you to

---

[2]Whitehead is perhaps best known for his three-volume *Principia Mathematica*, co-authored with his former student Bertrand Russell (Whitehead and Russell, 1910/1912/1913). It is an attempt to distill mathematics down to logic.

shed details in favor of principles. When I speak of principles I am hardly even thinking of verbal formulations. A principle which has thoroughly soaked into you is rather a mental habit than a formal statement. It becomes the way the mind reacts to the appropriate stimulus in the form of illustrative circumstances. Nobody goes about with his knowledge clearly and consciously before him. Mental cultivation is nothing else than the satisfactory way in which the mind will function when it is poked up into activity" (Whitehead, 1923, pp. 17–18).

Whitehead's words show their age only insofar as he refers to the students as "men." Otherwise, they serve as an important foundation for motivating current university teachers.

In 1990, when applying to U.S. graduate schools, I received a document from the University of Chicago Graduate School of Business that quoted part of the above Whitehead extract, and then went on to state, "Essentially, the Chicago philosophy holds that it is wasteful and inefficient for the university to try to provide a pale substitute for business experience. What the university can do well is develop the student's critical, analytical, problem-solving, and decision-making capabilities; it equips the student with the basic knowledge and analytical tools to cope in our constantly changing business environment." Two-dozen years later, the University of Chicago was still using exactly the same language (University of Chicago GSB, 2004, p. 14). Since then, I have included this quote in many business school course syllabi.

Eison (1990) bemoans the fact that students will recall so little of the factual content of their classes (he quotes 8%). In response, he recommends teaching less, but doing it well. Personally, I do not see this as a problem. I'd be perfectly happy with 8% of facts retained, presumably the most important, because I am training their "critical, analytical, problem-solving, and decision-making capabilities," not their memory banks.

> One interviewee wrote, "Let students watch me struggle to solve problems that may or may not have a solution. Teach them how to think and not what to think." He gave a quote that he attributed to Socrates: "I cannot teach anybody anything. I can only make them think."

> For a complementary but not contrary view, one interviewee gave the following quote: "I've learned that people will forget what you said, people will forget what you did, but people will never forget how you made them feel." This

quote has been attributed to several different people, including Carl W. Buehner (in 1971) and Maya Angelou (in 2003) (See Seales, 2017).

1.1.3 Emerson's Self-Reliance

Ralph Waldo Emerson's 50-paragraph 1841 essay "Self-Reliance" argues that to be yourself, to be a fully functioning individual, you must avoid giving in to conformity for the sake of conformity: "A foolish consistency is the hobgoblin of little minds, adored by little statesmen and philosophers and divines" (Emerson, 1841, para. 14). He argues, in the words of his day, that "Whoso would be a man must be a nonconformist."

Let me go one step further and argue that if you wish to be an exceptional teacher, then a *necessary* condition is that you be a non-conformist; conformity is mediocrity. Non-conformity is not, however, a *sufficient* condition for being an exceptional teacher. For example, in Section 2.3, I give an example of one of the worst teachers we ever hired. He was certainly a non-conformist! (Was this non-conformity a comfort to him on his one-way trip to the airport after only three weeks in the job?)

Emerson writes about non-conformity with respect to your own history of behavior and non-conformity with respect to other peoples' behavior (i.e., non-conformity in the time series and in the cross section, respectively).

The advice in this book, from me and from my interviewees, is designed to allow you to be intelligently and successfully different from your past self and from others. At the risk of being self-deprecating, however, note that Emerson also argues that you should "trust thyself," and toss laws, idolatries, customs and books (including this one) "out of the window"! (Emerson, 1841, paras. 3, 34)

Quotes from Emerson's essay appear throughout this book. For example, I mention him in Section 6.2, when I point out that short-sighted boffins often value conformity and will question you if you choose to do anything that sets you apart: "For nonconformity the world whips you with its displeasure" (Emerson, 1841, para. 11).

1.1.4 Student-Centered Approach

My students are my clients, but it is certainly *not* my job or my goal to give them what they want. (See Section 6.1 for discussion!) I tell the students that my goal is "to give every student every opportunity to master the material" (I stole this statement from Prof. Richard L. Ratliff, who was an inspirational accounting teacher at the University of Otago in N.Z. in the 1980s).

My goals for my students are, however, far deeper than simply mastering the material. I want to build lifelong learning skills in my students. I want to give them a core foundation of knowledge that they need in order to operate in the real world. I want to build their critical thinking skills and show them how to acquire wisdom. These are difficult/lofty goals. Some students will not show much interest in this until after they graduate, but a little rubs off on everyone.

> When asked, "What are the three most important things you do (or do not do) as a teacher that make you a great teacher?," one interviewee wrote, modestly, "I'm not a great teacher; I can't be because I feel daunted by the task of teaching a subject I don't fully understand. I'm always aware of glossing over problems that I can't address because there is too little time, because the students may not have the background to follow if I try to explain a problem, and because I don't fully understand the problem myself. But I hope that I inspire the students to want to continue to study the subject.

Inspiring students to study more, it seems to me, is a lesser objective than aspiring to deliver masterful, erudite lectures, but it is a most important objective. Why? I inform them that each subject is huge, the results of decades, sometimes centuries of effort by thousands of people, that the percentage of the subject that their tutors can cover in the allotted contact time is miniscule. They are now at University, so they must become self-directed learners. So, what is my objective, as their teacher? I tell them at the beginning that my task is to give them a roadmap; an imperfect roadmap because I don't know it all. The roadmap will not just cover the dry subject in the texts; it will also include the personalities, the fights and debates, and the open questions demanding an answer.

My intention is to inspire them to leave the lecture hall or the seminar room, rush to the library, explore the literature, and read more. If they do that, then they don't need to worry about passing the exam. Passing will be a by-product of getting stuck into the subject. I'm not sure I convince everyone."

My University conducts a *Survey of Graduate Stu-*

dent Opinions each year. They contact recent graduates and ask them about their experiences. Oddly, the admin boffins rarely share the results with the teaching faculty. This action seems to be two steps removed from the Deming approach I mentioned previously (i.e., they are trying to inspect quality into the product, but not sharing the results of the inspection!). I saw the most recent survey (at the time of writing the first edition). There are 28 faculty in my Department. I was mentioned very positively and in some depth 12 times. Two of my colleagues were mentioned once each, just in passing. My remaining 25 colleagues were not mentioned at all. I think that the fact that the students who graduated and left rated me highly indicates that although my goals were lofty, I achieved some success with them. I firmly believe that the time I spent building critical thinking skills and lifelong learning skills in my students is reflected in these graduates' opinions.

1.1.5   Oppressive Labels I

Some academics label themselves (or are labeled) a "good researcher but not a good teacher," or vice versa. These labels are *oppressive* if you act upon them; they keep good people down.

Good research is just one form of good teaching. (What else are you doing in your research if not teaching?) So, if you are a good researcher, then you are already a good teacher. It is just that *classroom* teaching may require a change of gears. For example, research-informed teaching (discussed further in Section 2.2.1) is one way to bridge the gap between publishing in journals and teaching in a classroom. Many of my other purely mechanical tips will also help you to successfully change gears.

1.1.6 Oppressive Labels II

Pedagogy researchers once thought that it was beneficial to match the method of instruction to a student's sensory learning styles (i.e., visual, auditory, reading/writing, or kinesthetic) (Dunn, Beaudry, and Klavas, 2002; Fleming and Baume, 2006). Even at that time, however, there was widespread disagreement about the advice that should be offered to teachers and teacher educators, and a lack of rigorously controlled experiments and of longitudinal studies to test the claims of the main advocates (Coffield, Moseley, Hall, and Ecclestone, 2004, p. 140).

Subsequent rigorous investigation has, however, revealed no evidence at all of any benefit to matching methods of instruction to students' learning styles (Massa and Mayer, 2006; Snider and Roehl, 2007; Pashler et al., 2008; Riener and Willingham, 2010; Rogowsky, Calhoun, and Tallal, 2015; Willingham, Hughes, and Dobolyi, 2015; Husmann and O'Loughlin, 2019; Furey, 2020).

For example, Rogowsky et al. (2015, p. 76) found that "there were no statistically significant results that showed that individuals with stronger auditory learning style preferences had higher listening comprehension aptitude than reading aptitude or, conversely, that individuals with stronger visual word learning style preferences had higher reading than listening aptitude."

Could it be, however, that teaching and learning are distinct enough that learning styles are irrelevant in your classroom but are relevant when your students study the material on their own time? Husmann and O'Loughlin (2019) tested students in anatomy courses and found that the majority of students did not match their study methods with their preferred learning style, and that those who did match study methods to learning style did not perform differently from those who did not match them.

Nevertheless, student learning styles stubbornly

remain a popular idea and a misguided pedagogical priority (Rogowsky et al., 2015; Willingham et al. 2015; Furey, 2020).

Confirmation bias (e.g., seeing someone who professes to be a visual learner and who also excels at geography) could explain the stubborn adherence to sensory learning styles theories (Riener and Willingham, 2010; Willingham et al. 2015).

Paying attention to debunked learning styles theories is costly because it diverts attention away from dimensions that differ from person to person and *do* affect learning (Furey, 2020). These dimensions include ability, background knowledge, and interest (Riener and Willingham, 2010).

These learning styles theories are *oppressive* because students may act upon their labels (Furey, 2020). For example, they may avoid effective methods of study that are inconsistent with their label, they may avoid subjects that appear inconsistent with their label, and they may apply their preferred method of study in inappropriate circumstances (Coffield et al. 2004, p. 137; Furey, 2020).

Although sensory learning styles are unimportant, "the optimal instructional method is likely to vary across disciplines" (Pashler et al., 2008, p. 116) (e.g., a literature course likely involves more reading than diagrams, and a geography course likely uses more maps than a literature course).

Random differences between students' responses means that "a particular student will sometimes benefit from having a particular kind of course content presented in one way versus another" (Pashler et al., 2008, p. 116). Beware of confirmation bias, however, because this response to instructional manipulation is not true in general.

The bottom line is that sensory learning styles do not matter for your teaching or for your students' learning, and mistakenly assuming that they do may be harmful to your students. Instead, I use a multi-modal "eclectic" approach (Snider and Roehl, 2007). That is, where possible, I explain things verbally, write the words on the blackboard, draw a diagram, and have the students perform hands-on experiments. (Compare this with the military "EDIP" approach discussed in Section 3.4.) Do not confuse an eclectic approach with an attempt to capture students with different preferred learning styles; I follow and recommend the eclectic approach because, in my experience, overlapping reinforcement of instruction is *good pedagogy for all students.* (See also Section 3.3.2 for a discussion of "chalk and talk" combined with other approaches.)

You should also encourage students to take notes. They should be hand-written rather than typed on a laptop (Mueller and Oppenheimer, 2014; Stephens, 2017). The active processing involved in "generative" hand-written note taking (e.g., summarizing, paraphrasing, concept mapping) aids understanding and retention, whereas laptop users tend to take a non-generative/verbatim record involving shallow cognition (Mueller and Oppenheimer, 2014). See also Wittrock (1990) who discusses reading and writing as generative processes.

1.1.7 Lincoln Approach

I created and taught an introductory corporate finance course (Crack, 2018). Half the students in this course have such poor numeracy skills, however, that they fear the course's math content. So, I try to assuage their fears with Abraham Lincoln's words appearing in the box on p. 18. His words apply to *you* too: If my teaching advice is overwhelming, or you fear that implementing it will *consume* time allocated to research, rather than *create* it, then you need to jump right in and embrace it now. You can begin by picking, say, 10 tips suited to your teaching style, and then adopt others over time.

The Lincoln Approach

Many non-finance majors are fearful of the mathematics in this class. Let me turn to President Abraham Lincoln's words. When the Civil War was almost over, and the South was nearly defeated, Abraham Lincoln was advised to *destroy* the South. He refused to do so and replied with something like "Do we not destroy our enemies by making them our friends?" That is, rather than destroy the Southerners, he thought they should be embraced. After all, once they have been embraced as friends, they are destroyed as enemies.

Abraham Lincoln's words apply surprisingly widely. For example, I often need to master a new finance topic, a new mathematical technique, a new piece of software, etc. At first I may feel that I am facing an enemy, but I jump into the new challenge and I embrace it. I wallow around in my ignorance for a little while. Soon I begin to see some patterns. Shortly after that, some concepts begin to gel, and then, after some honest work, I master the material, destroying my "enemy."

I invite you to follow the Lincoln Approach: Set aside your fears or prejudices, jump in and embrace the material, and make your enemy your friend!

1.1.8 Truth Will Out

My final philosophical foundation is about grades. When you assign a grade, you pass judgement on work performed. Your judgement can impact the timeline of a student's degree completion and alter his or her employment prospects. So, it is important to get it right.

You must fail students some of the time. Students do not, however, like spending time and money to earn a fail. So, you will get students visiting your office, telephoning you, sending you emails, complaining to your boss, etc., when you fail them.

We spend a great deal of time focused on promoting student success. It is important, however, to not overlook the mindset required for handling student failure. Their failure is usually their own fault, but it is *you* who triggers the news of it.

Giving every student every opportunity to master the material (see Section 1.1.4) goes hand in hand with including as many instances of and as many forms of assessment as possible, within reason. For example, I often use four lengthy assignments, each made up of many sub-questions of different style and difficulty, a multiple-choice midterm exam with 50 questions and a multiple-choice final exam with 75 questions, where the exam questions also vary in style and difficulty.

I also try to build in opportunities for "extra credit." For example, my mid-term exam might be worth only 10% of the overall grade, but if a student does better on the final exam than they did on the mid-term exam, then the mid-term exam grade is erased and replaced by the final exam grade in the weighted-average calculation. (I do this only if the final exam re-examines students on material that was already examined in the mid-term exam.) This provides students with flexibility to not study for (or to not even sit) the mid-term exam, and to make up for it later. This form of extra credit is often called "plussage" in N.Z.

In my mind, I figure that the "Truth will out" (Shakespeare, 1596). That is, after so many opportunities for success, and with early warnings given to underperformers, if any student comes out of my course at the end of the semester with a fail, then, barring exceptional personal circumstances, I am confident that they *earned* their fail. It's not like a course with a single exam worth 100% of the course grade (see the example in Chapter 11).

Instead, my assessment is like a series of statistical experiments where a "Law of Large Numbers" (Feller, 1971) kicks in to average out randomly good or bad results, and to yield an accurate assessment of the student's true underlying innate ability.

> "The voyage of the best ship is a zigzag line of a hundred tacks. See the line from a sufficient distance, and it straightens itself to the average tendency" (Emerson, 1841, para. 16).

1.2 Teaching Styles

Your teaching style is an amalgam of attitudes and actions, some generated wholly from within yourself but some borrowed from without. The end result is unique, like your fingerprints or your gait.

What you borrow from others is a function of your personality type. Thus, some of the advice collected here will not apply to you because your personality type means you simply cannot use it. For example, in Section 3.3.5, I point out that introverts and extroverts can have completely opposite views on how to behave in the classroom, but conditional upon who they are, they are both right. For the most part, however, the more mechanical advice collected here can be used by *anyone* to improve their teaching performance.

When I started surveying university teachers, I was at first surprised to find that every person I contacted wrote something that neither I nor any other interviewee thought to mention. In some cases, the teachers I interviewed told me about things that I already do in the classroom, but which I had overlooked in my original notes for this book. It was very much a case of "to-morrow a stranger will say with masterly good sense precisely what we have thought and felt all the time, and we shall be forced to take with shame our own opinion from another" (Emerson, 1841, para. 1). In these cases, my advice and the advice of my interviewees are in concert, and are not presented separately. In other cases, the teachers I interviewed had wonderful comments that I am happy to adopt, but which would never have occurred to me. In other cases still, the teachers I interviewed advised me to do the complete opposite of what I have been doing very successfully for 30 years. In the latter case, my advice and the advice of my interviewees' are typically presented one after the other for contrast.

Should I use the *nom de plume* "Janus" to present diametrically opposed advice? No, Emerson would tell you to take only the advice that suits *you as an individual in your circumstances*: Different advice suits different personality types; different employers have different cultures; different class sizes demand different approaches; and, different audiences have different needs. My choose-what-suits-you dictum is a common theme here.

I recognize also that different disciplines have different approaches to teaching. For example, in financial economics, we use face-to-face lecturing; interactive small-group tutorials; practitioner guest speakers; case-based student presentations, individually or in groups; interactive computer lab sessions; in-class demonstrations of software; in-class viewing of videos; individual and group assignments; occasional field trips; and, mid-term and final exams. I have used all of the foregoing at one time or another. Most of my advice applies to face-to-face lecturing, interactive small-group tutorials, mid-term exams, final-exams, in-class demonstrations of software, and individual and group assignments.

Students in other disciplines at my University, however, dissect cadavers, perform dentistry work on patients, sit in on hospital visits with attending physicians, travel to Antarctica to perform hands-on research, etc. Similarly, when I arrived at MIT for my PhD, the physics students had just put a satellite into orbit, and they had an operating nuclear reactor on campus just a few blocks from my apartment. Much of my advice applies, however, regardless of these discipline-specific differences.

1.3 Levels of Understanding

For any given topic, there are at least three levels of understanding. For example, I read a book written by a Vietnam War helicopter rescue pilot (Mason, 1983). Mason explains, with diagrams, what the different controls in a Bell Iroquois UH-1 (originally HU-1) "Huey" helicopter do, where they are, and how to use them to fly a helicopter. I have peered into a Vietnam-War-era Huey on the ground at a U.S. military base and seen these controls first-hand. I also used to work with a Vietnam War helicopter rescue pilot and we talked about some of his extraordinary experiences. So, I have a low level of understanding. I am confident that I have just enough book learning to be able to *crash* a Huey almost immediately with near certainty, if I could even get it off the ground in the first place!

The next level of understanding would be for me to take 150 hours of lessons and to learn the hands-on basics of how to fly a Huey. This would give me a middling level of knowledge. I could then speak to you with confidence of what it is like to fly a Huey. I would not, however, be qualified to be an instructor. To become an instructor, I would need tens of thousands of hours of flying experience and practical personal exposure to recovery from extreme events. For example, I have read about how to recover from "mast bumping" (it is counterintuitive), and what to do if the engine fails (autorotate!), but even after 150 hours of instruction, I am unlikely to have the firsthand experience of these events that the best instructors have.

So, there is the base level of understanding that you obtain when someone else explains something to you, there is the middling level of understanding brought about by limited personal experience on the job, and there is the high level of experience needed to be an instructor, based on deep personal experience, including personal practical exposure to extreme events.

The first time that you teach a class, even if it is in the specialist area of your PhD, you really have only the second, middling, level of understanding. It takes years of teaching to achieve the third level of understanding. For example, the first time I taught my final-year investments class, I had never bought a stock and I gave my students a base level of understanding by following closely the textbook used by the previous year's instructor. Thirty years later, however, only 15% of that original course content remains, and I try to give my students a base-to-middling level of understanding, supported by 30 years of a mix of personal and professional investing experience and 30 years as an instructor. I am also the author of their 700-page textbook. You cannot achieve this level of understanding on Day 1 in a new course. So, be patient; If you take your craft seriously, you will eventually become an instructor-level instructor.

The first time you teach a class, you lack some knowledge and experience. After teaching a class 10 times, however, almost every question that can be asked will have been asked. Nowadays, my class often laugh when I answer questions; They think it is funny that I have an answer prepared to 99% of questions that arise, no matter how esoteric.

1.4 Why Teach?

Eison (1990) implores you to ask yourself "Why do I want to teach?" A good answer to this question is part of your *raison d'être*; without it, you may crash and burn in this demanding profession.

In my case, my experience in my area means that I have had the opportunity to construct some unusually thoughtful/clear answers to student questions, even difficult questions. Nevertheless, 1% of student questions push me toward some extreme that I am unfamiliar with. (I do not necessarily tell the students this, but I am learning the material too, it is just that I am learning it at a *much higher level* than they are.) I look forward to both the routine questions that I have prepared unusually good answers to and the 1% of questions that push me to an extreme. I enjoy the former because I like building useful things (e.g., explanations for students, useful research papers, helpful books, tree houses, brick walls, etc.). That is, I am a builder of useful things, both tangible and intangible. I enjoy the latter 1% of extreme questions because I am insatiably curious and like to learn new things. These two traits are two of the main reasons why I am a teacher. What are *your* reasons for teaching?

1.5 We Are Not Alone

Good teaching is a group effort! Good teachers share more than just knowledge, passion and a lifelong love of learning; they also share teaching techniques.

> One interviewee wrote, "I think being able to discuss teaching with peers, even in an informal setting, is what makes a set of great teachers as opposed to one simply trying to make himself or herself into a great teacher. As with a lot of things in life, it is much more difficult to do it alone."

> Another wrote, "Ask for help if you need it. Most staff members want you to succeed and will find time to help you. If you ask."

Appendix A contains the survey instrument that I sent to university teachers. In it I say that I am seeking responses because I do not want "to limit myself to my own narrow world view," and because "I don't know what I don't know." Similarly, in the box on p. xvi (at the end of the Preface), I encourage you to share additional teaching tips with me so that I can incorporate them here to improve this book. In addition to that, I encourage you to share this book and my teaching tips with your colleagues.

Chapter 2

Preparing for Class

Note that I use the label "professor" throughout this book to refer to any university teacher. You should not take this literally to mean only a teacher with that rank.

2.1 Tangible Environment

2.1.1 Your Room

At least 10 days before your first class of the semester, go to your room and test that you can operate all electric, electronic, and physical systems. Do not assume that because you could use them last semester, you will be able to use them this semester. (The break between semesters is a prime time for the IT folks or the electricians or builders to get access to institute significant changes.)

Bring a checklist of the things that you need to test and anything else that goes with that. For example, I bring software that I plan to use (Excel files, Matlab code, etc.), pdf files I plan to show, and videos I intend to view, and I make sure that I can get them all up and running. Can you control the sound system, the microphones, and the lights? Do you know who to call if something goes wrong with the facilities mid-class?

It is all well and good to go to your classroom and test out the equipment before your first class, but you also need to be aware that once you put 100, 200, or 500 bodies into a room, those bodies make sound (even when they are not talking) and they absorb a lot of sound too. So, if you take a buddy with you and put him in the back row of an empty classroom, he may be able to hear you clearly when your voice is low, and you may conclude incorrectly that you do not need to use a microphone. Once the room is full, however, he might not be able to hear a thing you are saying. So, you need a loud voice, projected well, and/or a microphone.

Story (Squeeze Them In): The admin boffins tried to force me into breaking my 622-person class into two streams, so that I would have to teach twice as many hours. The largest classroom on campus seated only 549 persons. So, they reasoned that it would be impossible for me to fit 622 persons into *any* classroom.

After many years of teaching first-year students, however, I knew that a significant proportion of them would not attend class on any given day (because of their debauched distractions and their subsequent hangovers). So, I assured the administrators that they would fit.

It turned out that there was only one hour during my 50 hours' teaching in that room that semester when a single student arrived and walked away, not being able to find a seat. The student did not identify himself to me at the time, but did complain to my boss. There were, in fact, dozens of spare seats in the lecture theater, but they were not on the ends of the aisles. I told my boss that if the student had made himself known to me, I would have asked folks to slide into the middle, making room. After that, I paid more attention, and a couple of times I asked students to raise a hand if there was an empty seat beside them, and then I directed late-comers to those seats.

There are many arguments for small-group teaching being more effective than large-group teaching. In this case, however, even my smaller groups would have been enormous, so it made more sense to squeeze them all into one room.

There have been several occasions where a university has assigned me a room to teach in, and I have walked over to look at the room and it is simply not suitable. For example, I need a whiteboard or a blackboard, and it does not have one, or it has screens that pull down for the projector, but they cover the whiteboard/blackboard when pulled down. Perhaps it is a 10-minute walk from my office, and even longer from the other side of campus. In that case, I will get soaked on a windy/rainy winter's day, my students will be straggling in late because of the long walk from their last class, and they will want to leave early because of the long walk to their next class.

As soon as room assignments are posted, go and see your assigned room. If it is no good for you, then ask for a different one. Tell the admin boffins what you want, and be specific. To them, it is no more than shuffling a name in a spreadsheet, but to you it might make a world of difference. If you ask for a new room, the worst that they can say is "No."

If you are teaching a small group in a small room with movable furniture, then never accept someone else's layout as being what is best for you. If the furniture is not where you want it, then ask the students to help you move it to a layout that serves better as a catalyst for interaction and learning.

For example, when teaching a small group (of about 15), I decided that tables in a rectangle or a circle worked best, because everyone could see everyone else's faces, improving interaction and improving learning. The desks in my room were, however, always arranged in rows. So, I asked the students to help me to create the physical environment I wanted, to facilitate interaction and learning. They were happy to help me move the furniture, and happy to help me move it back again at the end of class. Many hands make light work; With their help, it took less than a minute's set-up and the same to put it back again. After a few classes, I did not even have to ask for help; the students would move the furniture at the beginning and end of class, without being asked. Any class time lost to furniture rearrangement is more than made up for with improved interaction and better learning.

Let me add that the above physical actions are very visible. I mention several times in this book, that being *seen* to be taking actions sends a subconscious message to the students that also improves the *intangible* environment in the classroom (Section 2.2). Eison (1990) similarly mentions the importance of demonstrating a *visible* concern for your students (I take this to mean both their learning, and their general welfare).

2.1.2 Gearing Up

Halmos (1974), using another skeleton reference, says, "The organization of a talk is like the skeleton of a man: things would fall apart without it, but it's bad if it shows. Organize your public lecture, plan it, prepare it carefully, and then deliver it impromptu, extemporaneously."

When I was first a professor, I rented a house that belonged to a retired professor. He had a full-sized blackboard in his basement that I used to practice my lectures. I spoke each word out loud and drew every diagram, sharpening my lecture until I was happy. As I got older, and I knew the material more thoroughly, however, I would read through the material I was going to discuss, and the only things

I would practice were drawing diagrams and using spreadsheets or other software. One interviewee described this practice as "extremely important."

If you use PowerPoint slides, then be sure to print your slides to a pdf file and to bring both sets of slides with you. This is because sometimes PowerPoint slides display oddly on other computers. You might not discover it until you are standing in front of 500+ people. If you printed to a pdf file beforehand, however, then you can switch to the pdf files when the PowerPoint goes awry.

Always bring a backup thumb/USB drive to class with you. In addition, email your files to yourself in advance or use a cloud-based service, so that if the system is down, you can still access your files.

If you plan to show a YouTube video, then back it up to your thumb drive first. That way, if you meet a download issue (which has happened many times to me!) you can switch to the backup on the thumb drive. To save any YouTube video, just put "ss" in front of the "youtube" part of the URL (i.e., "http://www.ssyoutube...") and follow the instructions. The folks at that link will tell you that the free download is of "low quality" and try to sell you something else, but the free download is fine.

Thumb drives are small and insignificant in appearance, by design. I frequently find other professors' thumb drives left behind in the computers in the classrooms I teach in. So, I always bring my thumb drives to class in a small brightly-colored box (which I used to keep 3.5-inch floppy disks in 20 years ago). Each drive is attached to a lanyard. I shut the box over the end of the lanyard as soon as I plug the drive into the computer, and the colorful box is highly visible on the top of the desk at the front of the room. This technique has always stopped me from leaving the drive behind when I leave the classroom. You could tie the lanyard to a bright pink toy elephant, or something similar.

Story (Stop Talking!): One day I arrived ten minutes before class to find (viewing through the peephole in the door) that the previous class was still in session.[1]

My 500+ students were already starting to assemble outside the doors. I gave the teacher a couple of extra minutes to wrap up, but he

---

[1]Hint: When leaning in to peep through the peephole in a big heavy classroom door, first wedge your foot at 45 degrees against the base of the door. Otherwise, the door can fly open, pushed by students hurrying to leave, and you can get whacked in the head. It happened to me once; once was enough!

showed no sign of stopping. So, I stepped into the classroom, and stood there looking at him and his 500+ students. He kept going. I pointed at my watch, and he still kept going. Someone, not a student, eventually got up to tell him to wrap it up.

His 500+ students were late for their next class, and my 500+ students started my class with me late. I had had similar problems previously, but usually only for a minute or two. I apologized to my students, and I told them it was beyond my control. In fact, that was not true.

I told the Department scheduled in that hour that over 1,000 people were inconvenienced. It turned out that this was a guest speaker who did not know that he had to end 10 minutes before the hour. After that, I took control by making up and printing a page stating in large bold font "**NOTE: CLASSES FINISH 10 MINUTES BEFORE THE HOUR. SO, PLEASE STOP TALKING 10 MINUTES BEFORE THE HOUR TO ALLOW YOUR STUDENTS TO LEAVE AND THE NEXT CLASS TO ARRIVE.**" I taped it to the top of the front desk, using enough clear tape that even with repeated books and papers and laptops sliding over it, the page would not be damaged and the words would not be obscured.

I subsequently brought this note and a roll of sticky tape with me to the 10-days-before-class-starts lecture room visit for every course I taught. I never had a problem with interlopers again! Sometimes I would turn up at a room I had not used in two years to find my notice still there, having helped out many others in the interim. So, I strongly recommend that you print out a similar piece of paper and tape it to the front desk in any room in which you teach.

2.1.3   On the Day

There have been many times when I arrived in a classroom on the day to find it boiling hot, or smelling like a badger's den. I wanted to open the doors for some fresh air, but there was nothing available to prop the doors open with.

Commercially-made door stops are too small to work with the big doors in my lecture theaters, and the door stops supplied by the University are often missing (stolen or lost). I tried putting a chair in the doorway, but it is a tripping hazard and may breach the fire code. So, in my home workshop, I cut a couple of wooden door wedges/chocks from a piece of pine. They are about eight inches (20cm) long and 2 inches (5 cm) high. I put them in the box I carry to every class, and I use them often. These door stops also helped during the early stages of the COVID-19 pandemic in 2020, before we went into a full lockdown, because I propped open my lecture theatre doors, thereby stopping 100+ students from all touching the same door as they arrived or left the classroom.

If my class starts at 2PM, then I aim to get to my class 10 minutes prior to 2PM, to get set up and then answer the odd question or two. To achieve this goal, I aim to walk out of my office door "10 minutes prior to 10 minutes prior." I wear a suit and tie to teach, but I don't wear it to commute. So, about an hour before I leave for class, I put a do-not-disturb sign on my office door. This gives me time to suit-up, and gives leeway for unexpected events that take time away from final class prep.

Be sure that new faculty know when they are supposed to start talking in class! It is on the hour at my University. I have, however, seen new faculty *leave their office* on the hour to go to class. In that case, some of the students will have already left the classroom by the time the teacher arrives; they will assume that the class must have been cancelled. Of course, at some schools, classes start at times other than on the hour.

If you teach a small class or a small seminar (or hold a small meeting), for goodness' sakes leave the door open if at all possible! (It's not always possible.) Why put an extra barrier in the way of a student (or a colleague) joining the group?

I have been in many small-group seminars/meetings where the organizer closed the door and I got up and opened it, and then some late arrival came in and added value. Often they were just passing by and not even intending to join us, but then they got curious when they saw/heard us.

Sometimes I have arrived on time (or even a little early) to small seminars where I did not enter because the door was closed already and I did not wish to disturb the session. Kiwis (i.e., New Zealanders) have an awful habit of starting a meeting early if they can. This applies to social events, scheduled festival activities, business meetings, etc. I have stopped my colleagues doing this on many occasions, and then had folks arrive on time or even slightly early, who would have felt like they arrived late had I allowed the meeting to start early.

Note also that in small-group settings the air can quickly get stale in a small room, especially if there are smokers in the room or if it is a hot stuffy day. Closing drapes or blinds can keep temperatures down, but darkness can be sleep-inducing. So, leave the door open if you welcome a breath of fresh air from people or from Mother Nature!

2.1.4 Syllabus & Notes

I usually write the abstract for a research article *after* having written the rest of the article, because only then do I grasp the research paper in its entirety. However, I usually draft my course syllabus *before* doing any of the real course preparation work. The final version may change, but my draft syllabus guides my course structure.

> One interviewee wrote that you should prepare "from the time you draw up a course syllabus. Start with what you want the students to learn and work from there. Speak with those who taught the pre-requisites (don't just read syllabi) to find out what was covered, as you will be using this as a foundation. You should link prior learning to new material to improve understanding. Speak with those whose courses

use your course as a pre-requisite to ensure students learn what is needed to succeed at the next level. This also helps you to find out if anything has been missing in prior versions of the course. Speak with people who taught your course before. They may be able to supply you with a wealth of information to save you from reinventing the wheel: past course syllabi, past assignments, past exams, spreadsheets, resource material, issues to watch out for, pointers to which material the students find most challenging, etc. Once you have your objectives and constraints, structure the order of material to build up to where you want the students to be at the end. Often, this is not in the same order as the material in the textbook."

When inheriting a course, especially a topics-based course, be aware, however, that some instructors may have chosen topics to suit their narrow research interests or abilities. Their course might not fit you any better than their clothes would fit you! Look closely; You may need to cut some topics out and replace them with favorites of your own.

One instructor wrote, "Teach your course, not someone else's. It's just too damn hard."

What topics will you choose and in what order? Have you chosen topics that build upon themselves and relate to other topics naturally as you walk through the semester? Have you found resource materials for each of your topics? Do you know how you will assess the material? Do you have a lesson plan for each class? These questions are much more important than your syllabus, *per se*. (In fact, given proper preparation, you could teach your class without a syllabus at all. The syllabus is, however, an important tool for helping you to *construct* your course, and informing others of its content.)

> One interviewee wrote, "I write my syllabi with a mind to *causing* students to learn, mindful of the unintended consequences that any policy may create. Along those lines, I take pains to make sure that some students do not get unfair advantages (or disadvantages) relative to others. All this is unrecognized by students, but it is critical to the learning outcomes."

For a big first-year class, my syllabus contains a day-by-day schedule of topics. For an advanced class, however, I list topic headings without a dated schedule. That's because the advanced material is complicated, and even after teaching it 15+ times,

I cannot predict exactly how long it will take to cover. Also, some years I get a cohort of particularly weak (or particularly strong) students, and some topics take longer (or shorter) than expected. This relative strength/weakness can be exasperated by the vagaries of staffing in the prerequisite courses (but any consistent weakness in preparation needs attention). Also, because I am teaching a financial markets course, I want the liberty to devote significant time to significant market events. So, I do not want a schedule I cannot keep to.

> One interviewee wrote that consistency is all important, and that "students form their expectations based on the course syllabus. No radical changes (like sudden topic drops or additions) should be made during the semester. It will confuse the students."

I carry printed notes into the classroom. For low-level classes, they are a printout of PowerPoint slides; for high-level classes, they are a printout of my textbook. I annotate the notes with comments: "stop here to draw diagram on board," "stop here to display prop," "stop here to show Excel sheet", "stop here to show business news video," "stop here for quiz with a small prize," etc. I record in my physical notes where the class started and I date-stamp it and write down the week of the semester. For example, "Start Wed May 1, Week 11." I also record where the half-time break (discussed in Section 3.2.2) occurred with "$\bullet\frac{1}{2}$" in the margin (the bullet is easily picked up by the eye). I record where the class ended with, say, "End Wed May 1, Week 11." Each year, I print out new notes, and I copy my annotations over from the last year, adding new items as I adopt new explanations, new material, or new props, etc. Then, the next time I teach the same class, I have that detailed annotated and scheduled plan already in my hand before going to class. It tells me that I need to practice that diagram, get that prop, have that Excel sheet ready, check that the video is still on YouTube, and make sure that I bring the prize to class. After the fact, it allows me to tell students exactly which pages of the book or notes were covered on exactly which dates. It also allows me to track my progress relative to the previous year.

As mentioned previously, I bring printed notes to class. They are annotated slides, or annotated pages from my textbook. I put a sticky note with a checklist on my handheld notes. It says, "mike, BlackBoard, notes," and then what files I need to download, and what quiz questions we will start the class with. "Mike" means check that the microphone is properly plugged into the recharging device to get a boost before I start (previous teachers often fail to insert it properly or at all), and remember to put it on my lapel before I start teaching, "BlackBoard" means get my BlackBoard web page up and running, and "notes" means to get my slides/notes/book on screen. I devote the 10 minutes before class to checking off those items as I get the room set up. If a student wants to talk to me during my setup period, I tell them to "Please wait until I have the classroom set up for the whole class. If I have free time after that, then I will take your question." It would be foolish to stop to speak to a single student and then end up starting late and inconveniencing 500+ students.

2.2 Intangible Environment

2.2.1 Learning Goals

My University requires that my course syllabus contain "Learning Goals;" I emphasize these in the first two classes. Let me give this list from my latest class, accompanied by my verbal explanations, shown here in square brackets. (My explanations pre-empt questions from students who wonder why the topics are included; they also help me to establish the intangible learning environment.)

- To dig into capital markets finance and get our hands dirty with data and real-world issues. [Unlike lower-level classes, we dig into the issues and the data and demonstrate that real-world implementation of even the simplest notions are detailed and messy.]

- Loosely speaking, to learn the names of things and the size of things. [Students who interview for jobs have to be able to hold a conversation with a potential employer. Once employed, you have to be able to talk to colleagues or clients.]

- To improve capital markets quantitative critical thinking skills, and data analysis skills. [Much of finance deals with numbers. It is easy to distort the truth with numbers. So, skepticism and critical thinking are vitally important. Being able to analyze numbers is a step in the direction of being able to avoid being scammed, being able to invest and build wealth, and being able to explain complex financial topics to non-specialists in terms that they will understand.]

- To gain empirical knowledge of financial markets. [There are many simple results that hold in financial markets. It is important that these be included in the foundations of your financial knowledge so that you understand how to respond to financial market events and misleading financial market news headlines.]

- To grasp a big picture understanding of portfolio construction, investment styles, and transaction cost issues. [The big picture is important because we have time to look at the details in only a few of the main cases.]

- To understand key issues surrounding the choice of active versus passive investing from both the manager and investor perspectives. [This is a major theme in the course; When is it worth our time and effort to try to beat passive markets?]

- To improve data handling skills and spreadsheet construction. [Vital for any business major.]

- To separate practitioner wheat from academic chaff. [Academic-oriented publications that have no practical application should be outed as such, and students must be able to read any piece of academic work and pull out the practitioner applications—if there are any.]

- Time permitting, to discuss 10 cutting-edge current practitioner techniques, results, products, or trends. [Whether they survive and thrive or fizzle and fail, these topics are job interview fodder and water-cooler conversation at any employer you want to work for. Knowing about these issues could get you a job or keep you a job.]

When I first taught U.S. MBA students, they would always ask me "Why are we doing this?" That is, "Why are we spending our valuable and limited time studying this topic?" If you do not have a good answer, then it should not be in the class. For the most part, these queries have led me to include applied topics in my classes, and to include theory only when needed to support the applied topics. The students appreciate it because they are being given useful tools. Nowadays, my students no longer ask me why we are studying any topic because I anticipate their question by telling them why it matters up front.

Undergraduate students typically do not care that you just published a theoretical paper in the top journal in your field. They care whether they can learn something they find interesting in your class and whether you and your class help them to graduate and get a job—without infringing too much upon their social lives. So, when changing gears from editing a theoretical research paper in the morning to standing in front of an undergraduate class in the afternoon, you need to appreciate the different needs of your different audiences.

> Halmos (1974) says that you are talking only "to attract the listeners to your subject and to inform them about it; and remember that less is more." Eison (1990, p. 22) says, "Teach less, better."

So, you should resist the temptation to share too much information about your research with your students. Bring your research into the classroom (i.e., research-informed teaching) only when, where, and how it makes sense to do so.

> **Story (Mining Bitcoin):** I "flatlined" my fast PC at close to 100% CPU for one solid year on a computationally intensive research project (Crack, McAlevey, and Sen, 2020).
>
> I told the students that in the winter months I did not need to heat my office because my PC was giving off so much heat that it felt like

I was mining bitcoin! They found that story more interesting than my key research finding (i.e., required sample sizes for Student-t tests of the mean with non-normally-distributed financial returns data).

I advertise my advanced class as a "capstone course." A capstone (or "keystone") is the uppermost wedge-shaped stone at the apex of a stone archway. On the one hand, it is supported by the other stones, but on the other hand, if you remove it, the other stones collapse. My capstone course assumes the knowledge of 10 courses that my students are supposed to have completed before sitting in my classroom. I realize however, that the "great summer brain flush" took place, and many of my students never really understood a third of what they were taught anyway. So, I re-teach some basic finance, accounting, algebra, calculus, probability, statistics, economics, numerical techniques, etc. I cover only the topics that we need later and which past experience reveals them to be weak on.

2.2.2 Ethics, Cheating, & Boundaries

Your students come to you with spontaneity and instinct. Emerson labels this primary wisdom as *intuition*, arguing that all later teachings are *tuitions* (Emerson, 1841, para. 21). The distinction between *intuition* and *tuition* is worthy of deep consideration because some students' primary wisdom easily admits dishonesty, lying and cheating. Sometimes this behavior comes from ignorance, sometimes from stupidity, but in a few cases, it is born of a deep instinctive dishonest nature ("Yes, Virginia, there are truly bad people in this world; Incomprehensible though it may be to our little minds.").

If you teach at a university, you will catch your students cheating. In nine out of every ten semesters, I send students to the Dean's Office for further action. The cheats used to offend me. Now, however, I view their cheating as part of the fabric of university life. Prosecuting cheats is part of my job, just like taking out the garbage is part of my job at home; no drama or offence is called for.

Many professors are, however, afraid to prosecute cheats for fear of getting roasted on their teaching evaluations. Let me discuss two ways to reduce this risk, and then one strong reason why you should prosecute cheats even if it does mean getting roasted.

The first way to reduce the risk of getting roasted on your teaching evaluations is to be clear up front about expectations and consequences. You can say, "Here is the social contract. If you breach the contract, the consequences are that I do not hand back your exam/assignment. I send you to the Dean's Office to be investigated. This could take more than a month. All grades are withheld until these issues are dealt with. Then I apply whatever penalty the Dean requires me to apply, that is, if you are still a student at the University by that stage." If the contract is clear, then most students will not complain when they are caught and prosecuted.

To further make my intentions clear, I put the following three quotes on my course syllabus.

⊛ U.S. Air Force Academy: "Character is one's moral compass—the sum of those qualities of moral excellence which compel a person to do the right thing despite pressure or temptations to the contrary."

I also like "Character teaches above our wills. Men imagine that they communicate their virtue or vice only by overt actions, and do not see that virtue or vice emit a breath every moment" (Emerson, 1841, para. 15), but I have not used it on a syllabus because it is slightly too deep and the wording is out of date.

⊛ U.S. Air Force Academy Honor Code: "We will not lie, steal, or cheat, nor tolerate among us anyone who does."

⚷ ⊛ West Point Cadet Honor Code: "A cadet will not lie, cheat, steal, or tolerate those who do."

I take at least one of the three quotes from above and repeat it at the top of every assignment I hand out. I also include specific examples of academic dishonesty from past semesters in my syllabus (like the student who hired a master's student to do his homework for him; no, that's *not* OK).

Story (Occupy Wall Street): I got a shock when I moved from being a practitioner in the financial markets in the City of London to being an academic in N.Z. I left behind an ethical, moral business that treated its employees and clients with respect, and stepped into a university system that often did none of these things. During the "Occupy Wall Street" movement in 2011–2012, I had to explain to my students that the most ethical/moral place I ever worked was at the world's largest institutional asset manager, and that they should not believe all that they were hearing in the news at that time.

At one point in the movie *Journey to the Center of the Earth* (based on the Jules Verne book of the same name), the intrepid explorers reach the center of the Earth, and their compass spins. In a meeting with our Vice Chancellor, I described this scene, and I told him that this was what my students' *moral* compasses look like when they arrive at our University.

The second way to reduce the risk of being roasted for your anti-cheating policy is to make credible claims that increase the likelihood in students' eyes that they will be caught if they cheat. For example, I tell my students that unlike many instructors, I have reached the top of the academic promotion scales. So, I cannot be promoted any further. Also, it is unlikely that I will be demoted, given that some of my colleagues have behaved in truly awful, immoral and unethical ways and still kept their jobs, or were even promoted. So, reprisal (in the form of dishonestly-negative teaching evaluations from students I prosecute) cannot harm me. I also tell the students that I catch cheats in nine out of every 10 semesters, and that in a recent semester I sent one-third of the class to the Dean's Office to explain themselves (only a few ended up being prosecuted, because it is often only one student who cheated in group work, but I do not mention that).

A strong reason for prosecuting cheating students *regardless* of the consequences for you teaching evaluations is that *it is the right thing to do*. If a student at my University repeats a low-level cheating action, the penalty increases in severity to reflect the severity of this repeated action. If you choose to ignore cheating, or to only slap a student on the wrist when they can be prosecuted, then you risk failing to contribute to the identification of a serious pattern of ethical breaches by an instinctively dishonest student—which is part of your job. (Be sure to also see the two "Repeat Offender" stories about *faculty* members in Section 11.2.)

> **Story (Cheating Housemate):** All spreadsheets sent to me by students get saved to the same non-university email account, which is searchable. A student, let me call her "Samantha," sent me a spreadsheet that contained an answer that did not quite fit the question I had asked that year. The student's calculation inexplicably used a sample size day count that applied the previous year, but not that year. Some text in the spreadsheet seemed uniquely expressed. So, I searched my email account for that unique text, and up popped a spreadsheet

sent to me one year earlier by another student, let me call him "Bob." I entered Samantha's name into the online student management system and her semester address popped up. I entered Bob's name into the online student management system and his address popped up. Hey presto! Samantha and Bob were one year apart in the same degree program and living at the same address. *Duh!* Is that circumstantial information enough to convict on? No, probably not. If you tell Samantha that you know she used Bob's spreadsheet, she will likely admit it if she is not horribly bent, or deny it if she is.

If your students were at university only for the academics, you would not be competing with all their debauched distractions. Fortunately, you have an opportunity to intersperse your academics with distractions of your own (like my bottom-of-the-hour changes of pace, described in Chapter 3). You can speak into their lives in ways they will remember long after the academic minutia have evaporated without a trace. You can point out why cheating, lying, and stealing are bad things, and why altruism and charity are good things. (This can be a difficult case to make when leaders in your institution are not necessarily modeling these characteristics.)

Story (To the Full Extent): A student handed in a spreadsheet that was not his own work. We accused him of cheating. He denied it and counter claimed that his instructor was the one who was unprofessional and unethical, and the student was appalled to be accused of such behavior, blah, blah, blah.

Unbeknownst to the cheat, the spreadsheet contained hidden details that told us who had built the spreadsheet (a well-known practitioner who I know), and when it had been built (with the year, month, day, and time down to the 1/100th of a second). My practitioner friend's web site contained a spreadsheet that the student had stolen and built upon, which had an identical creation date (to the same 1/100th of a second). The creation date was years before the student was even born! So, his protests of innocence were ridiculous.

The moral of the story is that when "The lady doth protest too much, methinks" (Shakespeare, 1599–1601), you are likely dealing with a future white-collar criminal, not just a student who gave in to a moment's temptation. A slap on the wrist is not sufficient. You must prosecute to the full extent of the law.

Suppose a single student cannot attend your exam because of a conflict on the day. If the student asks to sit your exam a day *earlier* than your other 100+ students, then you should say, "No." It is much better that a single student sits it one day *later* than the others. The reason is simple. If one student sits your exam a day early, and that student cannot be trusted, then he or she can pass inside information about the exam contents to dozens of your other students, and you won't be sure which students got the illegal inside information (a one-to-many information flow). If, however, your single student sits the exam *after* everyone else, then the worst that can happen is that dozens of students pass information to your single student (a many-to-one information flow). In that case, you now know exactly whose exam script you need to look at very carefully and you need only compare exam performance with prior performance for that single student (looking for anomalies).

> **Story (A Peeping Tom):** I wanted to up-
> load the front page of an exam to BlackBoard
> because it described the count of questions on
> the exam, calculators they could bring, etc. Un-
> fortunately, it also contained a sentence that
> identified some exam content. So, I highlighted

that sentence black and printed the document to pdf. It looked like the sensitive information was redacted, but when I passed my mouse cursor over the black highlighting, my words were revealed like a photographic negative.

In a class of 120+ students, I deduced that at least one student would figure it out, and then the cat would be out of the bag. What to do? I changed the sensitive text to read, "Hey! Stop peeking under here!" and then I blacked it out again, and then printed the cover page to a pdf file for student distribution, and added a note to accompany the file saying that some sensitive text had been blacked out. A day later, I was in a classroom just before a small group tutorial was about to start and a good student sitting there answered a cell phone call and started laughing. He explained that his buddy had just looked under the blacked-out text and read it to him over the phone. The moral of the story is that even your good students may discover poorly-hidden secrets.

For your bad students, however, no boundary is sacred. For example, I stepped out of my U.S. office for a minute and returned to find an MBA student sitting in my desk chair behind my desk, going through my desk drawers. He said he was looking for a handout he had missed (I now keep all sensitive stuff in my office locked up at all times). Another U.S. MBA student spoke to me for a minute and then dropped foul-smelling trash in my office garbage can. I told him to fish it out and take it away with him; he was visibly annoyed. Another sat on a secretary's desk near my office and picked up her phone to make a phone call without even asking. She told her professor boss, who walked out of his office, took the phone from him mid-call, slammed it down and told him to get out. Another who had made a mistake on an assignment I graded wrote me a lengthy letter arguing that he had discovered that I was wrong (no I wasn't), that he should be given 100%, why his skills were superior to those of his classmates, and why I should not tell anyone else about the error of mine that he had discovered, because he alone deserved compensation for it. Etcetera.

Finally, although it seems obvious, do not steal your colleagues' work or your postgraduate students' work. Do not put your name on their publication unless you did enough work to have earned that co-authorship. For example, supervision alone does not guarantee co-authorship. Similarly, do not add your name to a thesis committee if you did not supervise. Doing so is intellectually dishonest. Yes, these admonishments are based on experiences in universities I worked. (See also Section 11.7 for the story of Prof. Plum who was booted off a thesis committee.)

2.2.3 Engagement & Respect

If you want to be a good teacher, you need to engage with your students, and treat them with respect. If they feel respected then they will, subconsciously, be more inclined to attend class, engage with you, learn and grow, and evaluate you positively.

For the first 20 years or so of my teaching career, I memorized the names and faces of all the students in any class that was smaller than about 150 persons. I printed out a class list and consulted it while going for a walk or sitting on the bus or subway. I asked my wife to test me on it when we were out walking. I would ask her to give me a Christian/first/given name and I would give her the corresponding surname, and vice versa; give me a face and I will give you a name, etc. It meant that no student could hide anonymously in my classroom. In larger classes (e.g., 500+ students), however, I memorized only the names of students who interacted with me regularly, and a few extras (to their surprise if I called upon them). The best way to remember students' names is to *use* them. I ask my students to forgive me, however, if I make mistakes while learning and using their names.

My students usually study several courses from my Department at the same level as my course. So, I use email to co-ordinate with the other instructors just before the start of the semester so that as far as possible we do not have mid-term exams on the same day, or big assignments due the same day. (If you do this, be sure to take the time to *tell* the students that you did it. They like to hear that you thought about their welfare, and did something about it in an organized fashion. It creates an atmosphere of mutual respect.)

When co-ordinating dates, make sure that you do not have big assignments due or exams scheduled on a Monday; students often need help the day before, and you typically cannot hold extra office hours on a Sunday. Similarly, look at the timing of the semester and do not have big assignments due or exams scheduled in the second half of the week before they go on Spring Break, etc. Students often like to get away a little early for these breaks. It is not just because they are lazy; Sometimes the flights are all booked up for the Friday or the weekend, and they have no choice but to leave on Wednesday or Thursday.

2.3 Recruitment Environment

Failures and successes in recruiting can have a significant impact on planned and unplanned individual teaching loads. So, let me tell you some recruiting stories with lessons.

One semester I was asked to attend the big (500+ students) first-year class because there had been multiple complaints about our newest recruit. He was hired when I was away, and I had not met him or even seen a picture of him. I sat in the big lecture theater with the 500+ students and waited for him to arrive.

A calm well-dressed guy turned up early and started to put his presentation on the projector, but his slides said, "Biochemistry," when I was expecting them to say, "Corporate Finance." Someone interrupted him and told him he was in the wrong room. Darn, that guy arrived early, appeared calm, was well dressed, and looked well prepared! He ran off to find his room, looking somewhat alarmed.

Our guy did not even arrive before he was due to start talking. I watched the clock tick and I was getting ready to get up, walk to the front, talk to the class, and maybe take over, when he sauntered in late, looking disheveled, like he had just woken up after sleeping off a hangover under a bridge.

The new guy did not use the projectors or the whiteboard. He just talked. He told the students that he had 16 years' of experience teaching this material (he said that at least a half-dozen times in the allotted 50 minutes); I am not sure why he kept repeating it. He asked the students very simple questions, promising them brownies (i.e., chocolate cookies) later in the semester for correct answers. When someone answered, he said, "Let's give this person a round of applause," which fewer than half the students did, and only half-heartedly.

He presented only some of the material that was in the course content (and which higher-level instructors were relying upon him to cover). He kept repeating low-level material unnecessarily. He played some games throwing screwed up paper balls into boxes. The games made no real sense and did not seem connected to the course content in any obvious or logical way, although he said that they were. He could not operate the classroom lights, the computer, the projectors, the microphone, the speakers, or anything. It was basically a total shambles. It was like someone had just dropped in randomly off the street to give an off-the-cuff talk on a topic they used to know about, but without having done any recent preparation, and figured that being fashionably late was OK.

> **Story (Playtime):** Playing games in the classroom is absolutely fine, as long as they make sense. After winning several teaching awards, I was invited to a colleague's class to watch her teach and to give feedback. During her class she played a game using lottery tickets and asking people to bid for them. I misunderstood, and I bid a small amount for something that I thought had some value. She complained to me afterwards that I had *ruined* her classroom game. Only when she explained did I fully understand what the game was even about, and what point she was trying to make. So, it was her fault, not mine, for not making it clearer. Your games must be simple enough and clear enough that everyone understands their purpose and their connection to the class content.

Continuing, I went to talk to the new guy in his

office after class, and he told me he was late to class because he could not find the lecture theater (they used different rooms on different days), and he did not use the IT system because he did not know how it worked. As I talked to him, I could not get him to stay on any one topic for more than about 30 seconds. I attended two weeks of his classes. After repeated meetings with him, and one-to-one coaching, I struggled to lift his performance in the classroom to what I would call, "mediocre."

He made a point of emailing the whole Department several times to tell us what *we* were doing wrong in our teaching. He lasted a total of three weeks with us, and pissed off everybody he met. He left thinking that we were not good enough to be his colleagues. He was not the least bit embarrassed about giving the worst classroom performance we had seen in living memory; he thought he did fine.

The new guy had to pay back the removal expenses we paid on his behalf, because he did not stay in the job long enough for those costs to vest. It was a complete waste of time and effort on everybody's part. The only good thing, at the end, was that I was wondering how we were going to terminate him, but he left of his own accord, saving us some administrative effort.

One strong piece of advice comes from this story: Don't let your department make recruitment decisions without seeing the candidates give a *mock lecture* in addition to a research seminar. Two weeks before the campus interview, give the candidate two or three teaching topics to pick from. Choose important self-contained topics that would normally appear in your first-year classes, and tell the academic audience in advance that they should ask first-year questions. We have done this for several years now, and it is amazing what a mock lecture reveals about the candidate that is different from what a research seminar reveals.

Story (Overconfidence): We hosted a job candidate who claimed to be such a great teacher that he never made a mistake in the classroom. Contrary to his claim, however, I counted 10 mistakes during his mock lecture. Don't make impossibly arrogant statements to your audience; you look like a fool! Job candidates are at their best during the interview; it is downhill from there. So, we asked ourselves, "If he shows this much arrogance during the interview, what will he be like on the job?" You can guess the outcome of the interview.

In similar vein, one interviewee wrote, "Don't think you are the smartest person in the room and definitely never ever say that. It will turn students against you from the start. It is quite possibly untrue as well, especially in large classes. You are likely to be the most knowledgeable person in the room on the topic, but that doesn't make you the smartest. Quite a few people confuse these things."

Here is a recruiting story that ended abruptly. The guy could teach and was doing research, and publishing, but...

Story (Stitching Mailbags): ...his CV said he had worked at Morgan State University in the U.S. for a couple of years. In fact, although he was hired by Morgan State, unbeknownst to us, he never arrived with them. He had stolen the identities of people he studied with, and a neighbor, and used credit cards in their names to rack up $114,241.74 in debt to finance a lavish lifestyle. He had been arrested for this identity theft and fraud, faced a federal grand jury, and was sentenced to 16 months in a federal penitentiary. So, although he said he was at Morgan State, in fact, he was stitching mailbags or making license plates. Once his name was on our Web site, someone outed him.

He was more surprised than I was when I bumped into him using our photocopier late one evening a few days later (he had told everyone that he was overseas at a conference, but, in fact, he was in town and coming into the office in the late evenings). I asked him to come to see me the next day. He asked if it was about the masses of pornography he had been caught downloading a few weeks earlier. (He even tried to claim on his expense account for an external disk drive to store it!) I said, "No, it is something else," and I left it at that.

I was annoyed to get an email from him two hours later with his resignation, because I was planning to "terminate with extreme prejudice" the next day. He fled the country immediately, without paying back his non-vested removal expenses.

The moral of the story is that we were too trusting; We failed to call up previous employers to confirm that our candidate worked for them as stated on his CV. Don't make the same mistake!

Let me finish with an unusual recruiting story.

Story (Cheap Rent): "Dr. Peripatetic" came to us with a strong record of research and teaching. He had moved around a lot, which raised some red flags. We figured, however, that the worst-case scenario was that we would be renting his skills for two years before he moved on again; That's not uncommon in geographically-remote N.Z.

When Dr. Peripatetic arrived, we granted him two weeks in our "Executive Residence" (a University-owned hotel, a block from the Business School). We figured that this stay, along with his prior online searches, would be enough time for him to secure rental accommodation.

At the end of two weeks, however, the manager of the Executive Residence contacted us to say that he was on the verge of calling the Police because our new recruit refused to leave. Huh?

Dr. Peripatetic explained to us that when conducting his online search of rental costs, he had mistakenly assumed that the *weekly* rents he was seeing quoted were *monthly* rents. So, he had just discovered that his rent would be *four times* what he had budgeted for, and he was balking at paying this.

Nevertheless, he managed to find somewhere quickly and he moved out of the hotel. We noticed, however, some irregularities at work. He had clothes and towels hanging up to dry in his office. One colleague found him sitting at his desk in boxer shorts and a T-shirt. His suitcases were in his office. (You can guess where this story is headed.)

We asked Campus Security to check the record of his swipe card access to the building. Sure enough, his pattern of entry to the building suggested that he was living in his office! He admitted it. Fortunately, one of our PhD students helped him to get into some new modestly-priced graduate student accommodation that had just opened up a few blocks from campus.

The moral of the story is this: When I was a rookie on the academic job market in the U.S., each of the half-dozen schools I flew out to made the effort to put me in touch with a real estate agent. That person showed me what I could get, and for how much money, if buying or renting. It was really informative to have that information in hand while interviewing and long before any offers were made. If we had done this with Dr. Peripatetic, I suspect that he would have spent his two years (yes, he stayed two years) somewhere else. So, be sure to offer this simple real estate service to your job candidates to help set expectations.

We had similar real estate issues when we hired an IT admin wizard. He had to ask for a raise when he arrived from the U.S. because housing costs are so much higher in N.Z. that in the U.S. For example, in mid-2021, the median home price in N.Z. was NZD820K (USD586K), which is about 67% higher than the median U.S. home price of about USD350K at the same time (NAR, 2021; REINZ, 2021).[2] Note, of course, that high rents go hand in hand with high home prices.

Although housing cost information is freely available online, *pushing* this information out to job candidates can help to set your candidates' expectations in advance, and can help you to avoid unexpected administrative headaches; it also creates a positive impression in your candidates' minds.

---

[2]This affordability problem is compounded because median household income is about 20% *lower* in N.Z. than in the U.S. For example, in 2019, median household income was about NZD82.5K (USD57.2K) in N.Z. but was about USD68.7K in the U.S. (USCB, 2020; MER, 2021). In my academic field, the U.S.-N.Z. salary disparity is *much* worse!

Chapter 3

Inside the Classroom

To stand in front of a classroom full of students is an unnatural act. You have seen many others do it before you, when you were a student, but doing it yourself for the first time can be a challenge. The preparation discussed in Chapter 2 is vital, but there is more to it than that. Standing in a classroom and presenting material to your students places you at the tip of the spear. Your choice of behavior in the classroom can make or break your students' impression of you (and their assessment of you), because this is where they see you most.

3.1 What is Your Job?

3.1.1 ...To Profess

A professor's job is to *profess*; it is that simple. To profess means to state openly that you hold some particular view, belief, feeling, opinion, etc. You must profess in the classroom, in your research, in your office, in the hallways, in admin meetings, etc. You must profess even when others (published authors, textbooks, colleagues, students, etc.) disagree with you. You must, however, justify your views logically; this requirement distinguishes you from many of the admin boffins on campus. To profess takes wisdom, knowledge, experience, confidence, and some measure of wit.

3.1.2 ...To Render Down

A professor's job is to render complex ideas down to a digestible simplicity. Fortunately, I have dyslexia. It has been a companion for more than half a century. I compensate by reading things six times, reading them backwards and forwards, holding a ruler under the text I am reading, covering words or parts of words with my fingers as I read, etc. I need to break things I read down into smaller ideas, and link them logically behind the scenes, often doing much more work than the writer intended. This is true with words, with numbers, with algebra and calculus, etc. I am often working things out "from first principles" whereas other people might just understand them immediately.

> One interviewee wrote that having a "beginner's mind" contributes to being a good teacher. "I always try to understand why students get confused if they ask me questions. I have also found that in most of the cases, only strong students *ask* questions. If strong students have gotten something wrong, then the chances the rest of the class is confused are high. If I see that students consistently misunderstood something, I try to revise this material in the next lecture, making sure I explain it clearly."

I draw many diagrams and I build many interactive Excel spreadsheets to help students to build intuition and understanding. For example, I needed a diagram, like a Venn diagram, to show how the major theories in my field are related to each other. I searched for this diagram online without success and ended up drawing it myself (Crack, 2020a, p. 559). In another case, I wanted to demonstrate that high t-statistics in an OLS regression can co-exist with a lousy R^2 and awful predictive ability. So, I built a simple Excel spreadsheet where the students need only click on a few "spinners" to alter the data-generating process and the degree of uncertainty in the residuals and see the impact of these in a simple graphical and numerical display. The bottom line is that simple targeted teaching tools can assist very much with student understanding, but you may have to build them yourself.

My students often write on their evaluations of my teaching that I am good at explaining complex ideas. I think that my ability to explain things is a consequence of my dyslexia; it gives me the "beginner's mind" mentioned in the interviewee's comments above. For example, I recently showed students how to "read" complicated integral calculus formulae, of the sort often used in theoretical finance. They had previously been trained in integral calculus at school and university, but were following only mechanical rules without the behind-the-scenes understanding. I showed them how to *understand* what they were reading. One day, not long after instructing my class in these techniques, I entered a classroom to find a physics lecture just ending. The professor was about to erase some integral calculus on the board; I asked him to please leave it there, and then I explained it to my incoming finance class in the terms we had just learned.

3.1.3 ...To Create Knowledge

Butler (2017) says, "PhD students are PhD students because they are extraordinarily good students and they're really good at learning. Though, that's not the job for academics. The job is not the learning, the job is creating knowledge, and the transition from being a consumer to a producer of knowledge is scary, and it is the road that has very few signs or roadmaps to help them get down." So, when teaching and/or supervising PhD students, accept that you need to guide students from learning to creating.

> One interviewee wrote, "With my PhD students, I treat them as being ignorant of the unwritten rules of the academy. How can they possibly know them already if they are unwritten?"

> Another interviewee wrote, "A philosophy lecturer asked some questions that I was embarrassed to realise I couldn't answer. 'What is

knowledge and how do we know what we know?'
Even with a first degree in hand, I didn't have a
clue about the generic nature of what I'd studied and what I was hoping to teach, and I didn't
have a clue about how we knew it was worth
studying and teaching, and about how we knew
whether it was true or not.

"I started to read, but it was haphazard. Then
a fortuitous event happened. Karl Popper came
to give a lecture. It was standing room only; I
arrived an hour early and only just got a seat
at the back. Popper's lecture addressed the
philosopher's questions directly. I was riveted.
From then on, I read with direction, starting
with Popper's works and then going from one
book/paper/author to another. The pursuit has
never stopped. I've developed views about using scientific method / epistemology as an aid
to learning; I drop these views into my lectures
from time to time. I shan't bore you with the
views here, just stress that I think a knowledge
of scientific method(s) is important for effective
learning.

"Don't forget method; learn from the great
thoughts and thinkers of the past; stand on
some shoulders."

3.1.4 ...To Tutor

A professor's job is to be a tutor. I was a student in a class at Harvard Business School (HBS) with Prof. Robert C. Merton. My student peers and I all knew that Prof. Merton would win the Nobel Prize very soon because of his extraordinary body of work. The class was held in a fancy classroom on the finely manicured HBS campus in Boston, across the river from Cambridge. The desks in the classroom were spotless, elegant, solid wood tables with a fine cherrywood inlay. We sat on $500 black Italian-leather padded swivel chairs with gas lifts (they would probably cost $1,000 each today). A little old man (who dressed like he had just stepped out of the 1940s) came into the classroom each day before Prof. Merton arrived. He had a bucket of steaming hot water and a cloth and he wiped the chalk off the blackboards to make them spotlessly clean. The heat of the water guaranteed that the boards dried before Merton arrived a few minutes later. I always dressed up by putting on a collared shirt and a tie to go over from scruffy working class MIT to Merton's class at fancy HBS. Merton always wore a dark suit and a conservative tie. The experience could not have been more luxurious or with a finer professor. I felt blessed.

Prof. Merton made a statement on the first day of class that I have never heard any other instructor say: "There is no teaching assistant in this class. *I* am the teaching assistant. Come to me with your questions." I figure that if it was good enough for Merton (now a Nobel Prize winner) to say, then it is good enough for a relative nobody like me to say, and I do so in each advanced class that I teach.

3.1.5 ...To Teach History

As an undergraduate mathematics student, I loved hearing history lessons from my teachers, though they were few and far between. As a PhD student, sometimes I would get into the elevator in my building only to have three Nobel Prize–winning professors step in there with me, on their way to lunch (I took a particular interest in my shoes at these times). I was fortunate to have been taught by, talked with, or attended seminars by an unusual number of Nobel Prize–winning professors in my field. So, when discussing the material in class, I can bring it to life with personal anecdotes about the history of and the creators of that material.

One interviewee wrote, "Economics, for me, right from the beginning, and through a succession of teachers, was a subject about weighty, important matters, delivered by people who were passionate about it, who had been at the centre of things, who could talk about the fights and debates because they'd known or met some of the personalities, and the subject combined maths with logic and words to achieve meaningful, useful outcomes. I loved it.

"All the above means that I've tried to give my students a sense of the history of the subject, an introduction to the personalities, why they did what they did, what battles they fought, a sense of how long it takes to thrash out problems, that a good problem can occupy someone for a lifetime.

"Perhaps most important, I try to impress on students that the subject is live, that there are open questions that need answering, that my greatest hope is that one of them should proceed to take up one of the challenges and do something about it. That's the flavour of what I received from my earliest teachers, and that's what I've tried to give back. In other words, it's not just about the stuff that's in the textbooks (which is often rather dry), it's also about the huge amount of human baggage that accompanies it, all the stuff that journal editors force us to delete.

"Inspire your students; it's not just about what's in the textbook; don't forget the human stuff."

3.1.6 ...To Act *In Loco Parentis*

Finally, you are acting *in loco parentis* (i.e., in the place of the parent). Many of your students are away from home; some of them for the first time. I argue, in Section 4.8, that your *duty of care* extends well beyond the academic sphere. You can handle some minor student personal issues directly, but more difficult issues may require that you direct students to mental health services, pastoral services, chaplaincy, etc. I give two awful stories in Section 11.2, where professors (including me) failed in their duty of care to their students.

> Regarding online teaching, one interviewee wrote, "Use all of the tools available to you, including people. Remote students can have special circumstances that need to be addressed by a Dean of Students and not solely by yourself. Further addressing challenging situations with the appropriate authorities usually leads to the best solutions."

3.2 Mechanics of Presenting

> When asked what I had failed to ask about, one interviewee wrote, "I would like to name the five deadly sins in teaching: running class late; trying to teach without making any notes; ignoring questions from the audience; never asking students questions; and, cancelling classes."

> Another wrote that I should have asked, "What is the single worst thing a teacher can fail to do that will have a very negative impact on teaching evaluations?" The answer supplied was "To go to class unprepared or semi-prepared and to not be able to answer legitimate questions from students on material that the teacher is discussing."

3.2.1 Nerves

Glossophobia, fear of public speaking, is the U.S.'s biggest phobia (Ingraham, 2014). I have several tips for getting around classroom nerves. First, and most importantly, I prepare carefully, so that I know what I am talking about. ("Prepare, prepare, prepare," one interviewee said.) Second, I try to anticipate questions by stepping back and looking at my teaching materials from an arm's length and with an independent and critical eye. (I do this for research seminars too.) If I can see a point where an obvious question might arise, then I make sure that I have the answer ready, making me "bulletproof." (This becomes less of an issue after you have taught a class several times, because the questions often arise in the same areas or because you already changed your presentation to pre-empt the anticipated questions.) Third, I walk in knowing that if I get a question I cannot answer, then I can simply say, "I do not know, but I will find out." (Which you then have to follow through on relatively quickly or the students lose respect for you.) If you are very senior, you can say, with a theatrically unsteady voice, "I used to know the answer to that question," but don't use that more than once in a semester. Fourth, I dress up for class and I put on a performance. (See further discussion in Section 3.3.5.) Fifth, I start every class with a big smile and a loud-and-growing-louder, "Gooood Afternoon! Welcome back to FINC302, Applied Investments!" That start gets their attention, quietens them down, and gets me launched into the class, like a sprinter leaving the starting blocks. Eison (1990) says that acting confident can help you to feel confident. In my words, *confidence* 🔑 *begets confidence.* Note that I always say the course number and course name because of the number of times I have said that only to see one or two people get up and walk out because they are in the wrong room! Many of my other tips about class preparation and class delivery also help with nerves because they prepare you to be in the classroom. Sixth, I aim to enjoy myself (which distracts me from feeling nervous). I tell stories about being a practitioner, I collect odd stories from the popular press, I explain things better than the students were expecting me to, and I ask them challenging questions, etc.

As mentioned in Section 1.4, each semester roughly 1% of questions from students are ones that I cannot immediately answer. I actively invite these questions. Half of these exceptional questions are asked in the classroom, typically by outstanding students. The other half come from relatively untalented students who found one thing that piqued their interest. So, they drag their knuckles to my office door in search of the secret of fire. I praise them for asking me such a good question. Unfortunately, some of them are punching so far above their weight that they are simply not interested in my answer once they find out how complex it is. They ask, "Do I need to know this to pass the exam?" No, they don't, and there the matter rests for them. For me, however, most of these questions become a page or two (or 10) in one of my textbooks; some become a future assignment for other students; and, some have become research publications.

One interviewee wrote, "Although you should be confident with the subject matter that you teach, be careful to not become complacent." I think this is especially true when you have taught the same course many times. Recall the modest teacher I quoted in Section 1.1.4, who said he felt daunted by the task of teaching a subject he did not fully understand.

3.2.2 Timing

Timing is everything.

I carry a box to class. It is all about timing, though at first glance, this might not be obvious. My box contains spare marker pens or chalk, a spare laser pointer (the classrooms are often out of the basic supplies, stolen by students or other professors), spare batteries, door stops, an overhead projector pen, a pen and pencil, a calculator, my textbook, a bottle of water, a mug, etc. These are things I use in class every day; I do not want to get to a classroom without basic supplies, and then consume time looking for them in nearby rooms, etc.

I tape the official University room booking sheet to the front of my box. It is helpful when I get half-way across campus and suddenly wonder which room I am in today. (Recall the wrong-room story on p. 64.) There is also a checklist in my box, telling me what to bring to class. The checklist has many times saved me from going to class without something vital. Leaving something behind is not much of a problem if you teach in the same building as your office, but if it is a 20-minute round trip to your office, then forgetting something vital means either that you have to go back for it (and you lose class time), or you go without (and you potentially lose class content, to be made up at another time).

When I am opening up my teaching materials on the computer during the 10-minute window at the start of class, I load up `www.Onlineclock.net` (or something similar), and I display a large digital clock on screen. I leave it ticking as I write notes to one side of the board, recharge and then put on my microphone, move any furniture that is in my way, write that day's start-of-class quiz question(s) on the board, etc. A few minutes before the start of class, the clock is the only thing on screen. Nineteen times out of 20, when the clock ticks over the hour, I begin talking. The clock shows my students the time in a clear fashion, and emphasizes that disciplined punctuality is important and expected.

> One interviewee wrote, "being disorganized is the first thing that kills an inexperienced teacher. A teacher is first of all a 'manager.' Students expect that all lectures, tutorials, and assignments are on-time."

I had a wonderful senior colleague who was kind to me and generous with his time. He was an outstanding teacher and deeply knowledgeable about business. He made it clear to his students in advance that he would not tolerate lateness to class under any circumstances. So, if a student arrived late to his lecture, he would silently collect his papers, pick up his jacket and put it over his shoulder, and walk out the door. After the first couple of times it happened, there were no more late arrivals. The peer pressure of walking in late, and thereby terminating the class for all of one's peers, was enough to stop this happening.

I think my colleague took his punctuality discipline too far. Students may have only 10 minutes to get from one class to the next, their previous class may have been on the far side of campus, their previous instructor may have gone over time, they may have been busting to go to the toilet between classes, they may have an injury (e.g., a broken leg), or they may be slowed by a temporary or permanent physical disability. So, I tell my students in the first few classes that I always start on time, but that if they must arrive late, I understand (for the above reasons), and that they must enter as quietly as possible and with as little disruption as possible. I think that this is a better approach than my former colleague's theatrical "exit stage left" approach.

Your students are usually most attentive and most ready to learn during the first 15 minutes of class. So, never cover administrative material at this time, not even in the first class of the semester. I won't even go through my course syllabus until part-way through my second class. My first week of classes uses attention-grabbing examples that introduce words and concepts that we will use throughout the entire semester. These early classes have easy takeaway messages and key points that will be useful in their lives outside of and after university.

The students quickly see that class can be exciting and interesting and also entertaining, and that they need to come to class to see where the emphasis is. It is better to cover course content up front in this attention-grabbing way than it is to cover some boring admin exercise or some pedestrian content that turns them away.

I introduce myself when I cover the course syllabus. This means that I often do not bother to introduce myself until the second class. I do that on purpose to downplay my part in the course and to emphasize that it is the *course material* that counts; I am just a conduit.

One interviewee wrote, "Introductions matter, especially to people from some cultures. So, disclosing some personal information (e.g., about your family and hobbies) may enable your students to establish a better rapport with you, which leads to more trust and respect. It may make you more approachable."

Personally, however, I think that these goals can be achieved for the most part by limiting your introduction to relevant *professional* experience and by telling students that you are often approached and frequently help students in your office hours or by email, etc. See also my discussion on disclosure in Section 4.10.

In a two-hour class, I stop at the bottom of the first and second hours to take a 3-minute change of pace where I do something completely different (e.g., if class runs from 2:00PM to 3:50PM, I stop at 2:30PM and at 3:30PM, when the minute hand on the clock is at the bottom of the hour). It could be material related to that day's topics, but which is non-examinable, or it could be something completely unrelated.

These breaks are opportunities for students to pause, recharge, and regroup. In addition, I always stop completely for 7–9 minutes in the middle of a two-hour class (i.e., starting at 2:50PM in the above example). These longer breaks allow students to get up and walk about, eat, or go to the toilet. They can talk to their classmates and they can ask me questions privately. It also gives me time to run some code, check a spreadsheet, check some stock market prices, etc., often in response to questions in the first hour. Any class time lost to these stoppages is more than made up for by the improvement in the intangible learning environment.

At first, many students will not be expecting bottom-of-the-hour breaks and they may find it odd and look at you like you are nuts. One percent of students will even complain that they do not like these breaks, and they may be quite vocal about it. Give the bottom-of-the-hour breaks enough time to become part of your routine in your classroom, however, and 99% of students will convert, and rave about it on your teaching evaluations. For example, on the very rare occasions where time pressure meant that I did not stop for a break, the students were clearly disappointed. I had trained them and built up their expectations, and then I failed to deliver; So, once adopted, consistency is important.

During my bottom-of-the-hour breaks, I do many things: I tell stories about being a practitioner in London, discuss investing, discuss interviewing for jobs, look at unusual photographs or a funny YouTube video, hold an odd quiz with a prize, listen to an unusual song, show them how to project their voice from their diaphragm without using a microphone, etc. One semester I did nothing but give *handy household hints* (HHH): How to remove mold from bathroom tile grout with no effort; How to undo bolts when suspended upside down under a house working in the dark and likely to get things reversed; How to use a ladder safely; How to tie useful knots; How to remove a very heavy

spherical muddy rock that is in a hole in the ground;
How to spray-paint small items; How to drill holes
without breaking through to the other side of the
wood; How to stop a bathroom mirror fogging; How
to make your soap last longer (from my 1920s/1930s
depression-era parents), etc. The spoken justification for giving HHH was that soon they would be
out in the world, owning their own home, and they
needed to know how to maintain it. In fact, it was
all a diversion. It was a change of pace/focus, and a
chance to recharge their batteries, all of which improved their ability to learn, increased their enjoy-
ment of the course, lifted my teaching evaluations
and led to many positive comments.

In the 10 minutes before class, as students are
filing in, and sometimes during the half-time break,
I play music. I try to pick something that was very
well known in its day, but which the students are
unlikely to know. I often choose music that ties in
with the day. For example, OMD's *Maid of Or-
leans* on May 30th, or U2's *Pride (In the Name of
Love)* on April 4th, Lou Reed's *Perfect Day* when
the weather is perfect, or Sinead O'Connor's *Last
Day of our Acquaintance* on the last day of class,
etc. Sometimes I choose old fashioned music, for
example Vera Lynn's *Wish me Luck as You Wave*

me Goodbye, perhaps for Armistice/Veterans Day.

Let me add that taking scheduled breaks is not just for the students. No matter how high your energy levels, and no matter your level of physical fitness, you may be surprised to find that these breaks give you a revitalizing pause to reconsider and to perhaps execute a mid-journey "course correction." See also the discussion of chalk-and-talk course corrections in Section 3.3.2.

> One interviewee wrote, "I allow the students to refresh themselves by spending a minute or two once in a while reading something on their cell phone. I ask them not to push it and definitely not to ask questions while they are engaged with their cell phone."

Small pauses also matter during teaching. After saying something important, I almost always pause and say it again. If it is numerical or can be summarized in bullet points, then I write it on the board. Then I pause again to give the students time to write it down. See also the quote about powerful pauses from Halmos on p. 112.

> "Pausing between sentences provides an opportunity for non-native English speakers to catch up" (Tharapos, 2019).

A break sometimes triggers an interesting herd-behavior phenomenon. Towards the end of a half-time break, the students think I am ready to resume talking, but in fact, I am just making a note on the whiteboard to talk about later. Noise (chatter and movement) dips in part of the classroom because an observant student sees me do something that they think indicates that I will resume talking. Then noise dips near those people. Then a wave of silence runs over the whole room. This behavioral event has happened in crowded rooms for centuries. It used to be said, until relatively recently, that this silence accompanied an angel passing overhead (the silence is traditionally broken by saying, "*un ange passé*"). So, when this event happens, I mention this old belief to them, which they find interesting.

My two-hour classes often start at 12noon. I tell my students that they should feel free to eat while I talk, if their food is quiet and not stinky. Also, I tell them that they are welcome to eat at half-time. Many of them do bring lunch and eat it then.

For online learning, one interviewee recommended "videos lasting no more than seven or eight minutes, but five is probably best. Those that run longer tend to lose the viewer's interest and lose effectiveness. Five minutes is a good time to focus on one thing. It also allows for splitting examples from theory."

Another recommended "Short sharp bits of digestible information. No long boring rubbish."

If you suspect that time constraints may be an issue in a lecture, Halmos (1974) suggests two approaches to retaining flexibility. First, preselect some material from your class that you can, if need be, "assign as homework" without loss of continuity, if time is pressing (but you may lose the attention of the more competitive students). Second, preselect some "modules" of information from your class that can, especially in the second half of the class, be jettisoned without loss of continuity if time is short.

Never go over time. Ever. If *your* time ends at 3:50PM, then that is when *their* time starts. Going over time is like walking into their student dorm and stealing their stuff. It is an affront.

"To take long, to run over time, is rude. Your theorems, or your proofs, are not all that important in other people's lives; that hurried, breathless, last five minutes is expendable" (Halmos, 1974).

If you are running out of time, then stop and say, "I am running out of time. There is no point in squeezing this into the last few minutes. We will pick up here at the start of next class." If you need this material covered on that day, however, say, "I have run out of time. I will send an email to everyone in the class with a scan of a hand-written half-page note that you need to know for your assignment/exam/project/whatever." Similarly, stopping five minutes early is preferable to starting a new big topic that you cannot meaningfully broach.

Finally, when you are in front of a class, with your heart thumping and your adrenaline pumping, time runs differently for you than it does for your students! For example, in Section 1.1.6, I emphasized the importance of hand-written note taking, but this requires that you *watch* your students when they are copying down material. Do not trust your internal clock. Wait, and do not start talking again until 95% of them are done writing. This could take *three times as long* as you are expecting.

3.2.3 Class Content

I have taught large first-year classes for many years. The largest large class I taught was 622 persons; the smallest large class I taught was about 500 persons. These classes are so large that after a few years of teaching them, I calculated that at any given moment, one student in every 10 at my University of 20,000 students had been a student of mine. This meant I could not walk across campus, or through neighboring streets, without multiple students smiling and saying hello to me. These large classes are required of all business majors. Only 10% of the students in these large classes are, however, majoring in my field. With 90% of students not terribly interested in the subject matter, this means that motivating them and entertaining them is much more important than in a class of mostly majors.

For me, examples of good motivation for non-finance majors include the following: showing them how their retirement savings scheme can turn them into millionaires with little effort as long as they follow a few simple rules; showing them how the banks rob them of money by charging fees; showing them how consumer finance companies rob them of money and mislead them on the interest being charged when they buy a laptop or a car; and, explaining to them how identity theft works and how to choose a strong password. Anything in their personal interest, or that shows them that "The Man" is out to get them and that they need to actively protect themselves gets their attention.

Sometimes my students ask "Why are we doing

calculus (or some other advanced topic)? I won't need this in my first job." There are many ways to answer this sort of question... "First, you might not need this advanced topic in your first job, but you may need it in your second or third job, as I did. Second, the structure of a university degree includes many hurdles that you must jump over before we allow you to don a gown and cross the stage to receive your diploma. This topic is one of those hurdles, and employers want to hire people who have demonstrated the ability to jump over hurdles. Third, when you train for a 26-mile marathon, you do many exercises that are not running. By analogy, mastering this skill is an exercise in learning how to think, and your future preferred employer wants people who can think. So, I am training you for that job. Finally, knowledge of this topic opens doors that will otherwise be closed to you in the future. So, you should study this as a matter of faith; Your enlightenment does not precede your study, it proceeds it." Your discipline-specific words may differ, but the message will be similar.

In lower-level classes you must introduce some of the material that your students will build upon at a higher level. Given the low level, the material must be simplified, but there is no excuse for being untruthful. As a student, however, I had many instructors who simplified their low-level material to the point of untruth. This confused, frustrated, and annoyed me. I had to spend time digging through the literature to sort out their untruths. So, simplify by all means, but do not present untruths.

I make repeated use of real-world examples, both current examples from this week's headlines and notable old examples. It helps students to understand the applications and it reinforces the importance of what we are doing.

> One interviewee wrote, "Giving learning context creates traction. Students can see why the new information is relevant and even how it pertains to their own wellbeing or the wellbeing of their friends and family."

> Another wrote, "Use real world examples and current events. This helps to keep students interested and demonstrates how what you are doing in class affects practice. It also forces you to think about applications."

I cannot overemphasize the importance of bringing a prop or something unexpected to class. I do so in almost every class. Here are some examples to stimulate your imagination.

- I teach financial economics. So, I bring in old local or foreign currency, or an old engraved stock certificate or bond certificate, or gold or silver coins, etc.

- For almost every class, I bring in an important book, and I prop it up on the ledge under the whiteboard for the whole class to see (my impression is that many students no longer read physical books beyond those assigned). I choose key books in the history of ideas in my field, important books for practitioners in my field, and important books on personal finance. I usually pick up the book part-way through class and read some extracts out loud. Sometimes I put it under the document camera and they read it with me.

- Sometimes I stick multiple dollar bills to the whiteboard with sticky tape and I move them around to indicate how a financial transaction works. I put a wide red stripe on one of them so the students can follow it as it moves through the process, perhaps being cut in half at one point (dramatically with big scissors) with the parts heading in different directions. I have also brought in a one-hundred-trillion-dollar bill from inflationary Zimbabwe. I also brought in some rare 1960's paper ticker tape from the New York Stock Exchange (see Crack, 2021b).

- I have also brought in unusual items. For example, I brought in porcupine quills and I asked the students to guess what was in the long/skinny box I was holding. When discussing optimization routines and hill climbers, I brought in a meteorite that was part of the famous Canyon Diablo meteorite that created the massive Flagstaff Arizona crater (see Torgerson, 2010). The students who handled it were amazed by its density.

- Continuing the *in loco parentis* discussion from Section 3.1.6, I have shown the students the Harvard School of Public Health's Healthy Eating Pyramid (HSPH, 2012). If showing anything related to nutrition, however, be sure to choose an unassailable source.

- When discussing "free cash flow" (i.e., money generated by the operations of a business, but over and above the money required to run the business), I brought in two helium-filled balloons that were tied to each other with string. (I needed *two* balloons to get strong and long-lasting lift.) I attached a five-dollar bill to their string with a paper clip. I held the string as I walked along the timeline I had drawn on the whiteboard in the largest lecture theatre on campus, and then I let go of the balloons to illustrate free cash flow leaving a successful business in operation. The five-dollar bill ended up suspended 30–40 feet above my students' heads at the apex of the vaulted ceiling. (Years later, colleagues asked me about the $20 bill or $50 bill that I let go in the classroom. That is, my balloon story got inflated in the re-telling of it by students; pun intended.)

- Wooden nickels were commonly minted/printed for about 100 years in the U.S. They are about 1.5 inches in diameter and one-eighth of an inch thick, often with images and words on them. They were handed out by stores and had some small redeemable value. I found someone in the U.S. who had an 1885 wooden nickel machine. I had him mint some wooden nickels for me with my University's motto on it in Latin and in English, a buffalo, and the old phrase "Don't take any wooden nickels" (look it up if you do not know what it means). I give them out in class sparingly, to recognize particularly outstanding contributions. Some years I give out none. I also give them out to special visitors to my Department. They are worth nothing in real terms, and maybe $1 on `www.eBay.com` or `TradeMe.co.nz`, but the students value them beyond all reason.

- Some props are personal stories. For example, I told my students that self-driving technology existed widely a century ago, but was largely lost. My parents told me that when they were children in the 1920s and 1930s, if someone went to the pub in the neighboring village and had too much to drink, their horse knew the way home. It could avoid other horses, keep its cart to its lane, and, unlike current software, had no problem with falling snow, stationary obstacles, and surprises (e.g., the bridge is out!). Billions of dollars in research is being spent (Baldwin, 2020), just to get back to where we were 100 years ago!

- Sometimes the prop is a goofy YouTube video, or photographs of unusual places or things. Once I noticed that a young woman student had a sewing kit with a big pair of pinking shears in front of her (it was in the Midwestern U.S.). So, I asked her to cut my fancy *Chase Manhattan* credit card in half in front of the class, to make a point about the harmful effects of debt.

- I also brought in a piece of rubber tubing, and used it to illustrate how the calculus symbol for an integral sign evolved. I had planned to draw it on the board, but the physical demonstration worked better.

- I explained that if you sell a house with $500,000 in equity and move countries, your bank will gouge you for a hidden $10,000 in transaction costs on the foreign exchange (FX) conversion. I explained, however, how to keep this fee instead of letting the bank have it, via an online platform for FX trading (Crack, 2020a, p. 218), which I demonstrated. The students had never seen this before. My demonstration also proved to them that some of their textbook knowledge about FX quoting conventions learned in other classes was incorrect in practice. I have also placed stock market trades live in class, looking at the N.Z. Stock Exchange order book, choosing an order type, watching it execute, discussing the commission, and then being allocated a dividend on that stock later in the week. When the check for the dividend arrives in my hands (or my brokerage account) a few weeks later, we discuss taxes on dividends, etc.

- Sometimes the prop is a practitioner, bringing the real world into my classroom. (See, however, discussion of bad visitor outcomes in Section 3.2.4.)

- I offer prizes in class. They encourage students to speak (even humble N.Z. students!). For example, I stick two envelopes to the board with sticky tape. One has a question mark on it and one has "$1" on it. The question-mark envelope has a $3 lottery ticket in it, and the $1 envelope has a shiny dollar coin or crisp dollar bill. I declare that I will allow the student who makes the best comment today to pick between them at the end of class. I have also done it with a box of candy, boxes of Crackerjack (a play on my name), etc. I once had a student contact me 20 years after the event to say he still had and fondly remembered getting an old silver dollar from me in class.

- When someone makes a good comment, I point at the prize(s) and I say, "This is yours unless someone makes a better comment," and so on, until the best of all comments takes the prize at the end of class. Some students choosing between $1 cash or a $3 lottery ticket (with a 99.9% chance of it being worth zero) will choose the $1 cash prize; others choose the lottery ticket. These choices generate interesting conversation.

- Do be aware, however, that if a student actually

wins a \$1M prize, it can ruin their life (e.g., Chan, 2016). This risk also makes for interesting classroom discussion. See also Section 9.2 for discussion of alternative prizes.

- I found a baker who makes fortune cookies for weddings. I created a list of multiple-choice questions about applied investments, rather than his usual wedding-inspired messages. Students who got them as prizes in class were surprised and amused.

- I once gave away a jar of fig jam as a prize in exchange for an answer to a difficult question (...but perhaps you need to be an Antipodean to understand immediately the humor in this).

One interviewee wrote, "I took a course on mythology (Greek/Roman twice a week and Egyptian/Norse and the Bible as Myth one day a week). The professor was very outgoing and filled his lectures with slides from his travels to the places discussed. These brought life to the stories and helped connect them to the real world. With a class of 2,000 he would answer questions."

3.2.4 Second Opinions

Life is short. The most valuable coin you can spend is someone else's time. Nevertheless, some instructors (and nine out of 10 admin boffins I ever met) talk too much while saying little, leaving only the indelible impression that they love the sound of their own voice. An honest second opinion would be helpful in these cases, but who can *you* trust to tell you that you talk too much while saying little? The best person may be a tactless senior colleague with a reputation for brutal honesty; you may need a thick skin.

So, I strongly recommend that you invite a senior colleague to watch you teach and to make notes on your teaching. Alternatively, you can record your class and listen and/or watch yourself in action and engage in some critical introspection.

Halmos (1974) writes, "an annoying mannerism is anything that's repeated more than twice," and he gives verbal, visual (e.g., on the board), and dynamic (i.e., physical action) examples. For example, I had an economics instructor who said, "...the point being..." about every 30–60 seconds in class, every class. It was a running joke among the students. It got to the point where I could not focus on what he was saying, and all I could do was count how many times he said it (*...will he get to 100 today?*). Other instructors say, "ummm" with alarming regularity. Some younger presenters use "like" in the same way. One presenter held a whiteboard marker pen all the time, and would push the cap up a little (with a little squeaky noise) and then click it down (with a loud snap) about every 10 seconds; it is the only thing I can now recall about his classes. One seminar presenter was using overhead transparencies which kept hover-crafting off the top of the projector's platen glass. So, I jumped up and showed him an old trick to stop that: If you brush the back of your hand over the transparency, while pressing down, it squeezes out the air layer, and makes the transparency stick. In his nervousness, he proceeded to repeat that brushing action at least 50 times unnecessarily during his talk. These annoying tics, verbal and otherwise, can be picked up and addressed by a colleague who attends your class, or by your own arm's length review.

Some people adopt these tics because they are nervous. Some people use verbal tics to fill a silence between spoken paragraphs. *Do not, however, be afraid of silences!* You can pause for quite extended periods of time while your students are writing down a diagram, or taking notes, or while you are giving them time to process something important that you said or wrote. It gives the students time to rest and absorb information. Also, quite frankly, silences demonstrate your power in the classroom. That is, although part of your job is to speak, you can *choose* not to. Exercising this option can be used as a subtle control mechanism that shows who is in charge and helps to enforce order; this is more of an issue in large first-year classes. (Your students may outnumber you 500 to one, but you need to maintain order/discipline/respect or your class will descend into a shambles.)

> "Silence is a powerful tool at other times too; the best speakers are also the best non-speakers. A long period of silence (five seconds, say, or ten at most) after an important and crisply stated definition or theorem puts the audience on notice ('this is important') and gives them a chance to absorb what was just said. Don't overdo it, but three or four times during the hour, at the three or four high points, you might very well find that the best way to explain something is to say nothing" (Halmos, 1974).

A second opinion is not just about finding things to fix with your presentation; you also want to know what is good, and worthy of keeping or building further upon. A second pair of eyes may also observe disruptive student behavior that you miss.

Second opinions take different forms. For example, I have invited practitioners into my classroom who do for a living what I am teaching, thereby, in theory, reinforcing my class content. Some of my guests have been outstanding. Some of them have, however, been appallingly ignorant and appeared only upon the recommendation of a (now no longer trustworthy) colleague. The bad ones were so bad that in the last 10 years I have been very selective, and have used only those that I personally know to be outstanding.

Even very good guest speakers always say something that I disagree with; this prompts classroom discussion. I tell the students in advance, however, that I want them to be polite to my guest. So, analysis of any clearly-wrong statements typically takes place after the guest has left. One portfolio manager's presentation was so appallingly bad that the students sat in near silence. One unexpected lesson for the students was that as investors they must be careful about entrusting their money to anyone else to manage, because the hurdle to be a money manager was clearly very low.

3.2.5 Simple Etiquette

I tell my students on Day 1 that, barring physical disability, I expect them to take notes by hand on paper in class. The physical act of writing out notes by hand means that some degree of mental processing goes on. This mental processing aids understanding and retention and does not happen with taking notes using a laptop (Mueller and Oppenheimer, 2014; Stephens, 2017).

I tell the students that their attention levels peak a few minutes after the start of class and then decline steadily, and that this is why we take breaks. After a break, attention levels rise again, though not as high as they were at the start of class (Epigeum, 2011). See further discussion in Section 3.2.2.

I always stop to write things down on the board and to work through numbers. (In a non-numeric field it might be diagrams to show relationships between concepts, or bullet pointed main ideas, etc.). Here are several items of *blackboard/whiteboard etiquette* that students really appreciate.

- When I write on the board, I use a large font. I ask the students in the back row if they can read it (thumbs up for "Yes," thumbs down for "No"); if not, I increase the font size.

- Be sparing in your use of red ink if using whiteboard markers. Red ink does not show up well from the back half of the classroom, unless it is a very wide-tipped pen.

  > One interviewee wrote that about one in 12 men and one in 200 women of Northern European ancestry have the common form of red-green color blindness. He wrote, "When using different-color markers, avoid using red and green on the same graph."
  >
  > Bang (2011) suggests a color palette that contains variability and that can be distinguished between by people with red-green color blindness. Although his subject is computer graphics, his color palette can be applied to choice of different-color markers.

- At the start of class, I write a little list of topics off to the far right on the board. I point at them in the first few classes, but after that I do not point at them; the students know by then that they are the topics for today. It is both to set expectations, and to serve as a checklist to make sure that I do not miss anything out that I intended to cover. I cross them off as I cover them in class.

- I begin writing in the top-left corner of the board and I end up in the bottom right.

- Many instructors erase their blackboard content much too quickly after writing it up. I have even seen instructors or presenters say something out loud, then write that key point on the board, and then *immediately* erase it, for no good reason! It is some sort of weird mental lapse. So, for goodness' sakes leave what you write on the board long enough for all students to copy it down. Moving from top left to bottom right should help avoid the *need* to erase something you just wrote.

- When I am going to draw something big, but which is a *single* item that I want the students to have all on one page, like a table or figure or an important list of points to be compared with each other, I give the students a "heads up." I say something like "This figure is big. You should go to a fresh page and turn your pad on its side, because you will need a full page," or "This proof will take 10 lines, and is easiest to follow if it is all on one page," etc. Sometimes I want to leave a gap above, or to the left of something, so that I can add extra comments after discussion. So, I tell the students to "Please leave a blank line here; we will come back and write some extra comments here." If you do not do this, you frustrate your students needlessly. This is another example of being seen to be thinking about the intangible learning environment.

Story (Whiteboards): For teaching in the large (500+ seats) auditorium, my University supplies only small-tipped pens. They refuse to reimburse any stationery expense unless the item comes from a single preferred stationery supplier, and that supplier does not sell wide-tipped pens. In a classroom with 500+ people, the narrow-tipped pens are almost useless.

So, I paid out of my own pocket to import wide-tipped refillable pens (plus ink) from the U.K., and I use those instead. Subsequent teachers in that room borrowed my pens. If you use a big room, I suggest that you write on the board and then go and sit in the back row to see if you can read what you wrote without straining. (See the disappointing epilogue to this story in Section 6.2.)

When using the overhead projector (whether using physical slides or PowerPoint, etc.), stop and look at what you are projecting. Have you avoided an information overload? For example, some folks recommend no more than six lines per slide, with no more than six words per line. This is called the "6 × 6 rule." The slides are purposefully incomplete, leaving room for you to add value in class. Similarly, ask yourself whether the font is so small that nobody can read the numbers in your tables. If so, then why are you doing that? It is obviously not for the students.

If you are using PowerPoint, be aware that when your presentation is displayed, you only need to hit say, "7 enter" to go to slide 7, or "15 enter" to go to slide 15. It avoids flipping through slides at some enormous rate that looks bad (and might trigger a seizure in a student).

When using a laser pointer, be sure to point with your whole arm, very obviously. Students are looking for, and need, clear visual cues. To the contrary, I have seen presenters "shoot from the hip," with an imperceptible movement of only a fingertip. It's not a lightsaber; we cannot see the beam! Make it plain with clear visual cues! Remember also that when recording lectures for subsequent online distribution, the record of your slides typically does not show the laser pointer's dot. So, you may need to use the mouse cursor instead, or amend your words. Sticking a colored blob on your laser pointer can give a visual and tactile reminder to you to amend your behavior.

As mentioned previously, if I do not know the answer to a question, then I say, "I do not know, but I will find out." This is not a sign of weakness; it is a sign of strength and maturity. Students like to be acknowledged and to be seen to be acknowledged by receiving my reply in class the next time we meet. In the rare case where I cannot answer a question in real time or before the next class, I tell the student that I am working on it, and that it will take some time, so that they do not think I forgot them.

> One interviewee wrote that after being asked a complex question by some engineers in his math class "I was embarrassed to be unable to answer them. It was then that I determined to do something about it and my research began in earnest." This question led to an entire research agenda!

You must not swear, use foul language or tell inappropriate/off-color jokes in the classroom. I have seen many instructors descend into the gutter in the classroom. It lowers the entire tone of the course and with it go your teaching evaluations, and some respect they had for you. There may be some exceptions, but they are few and far between.

> Finally, one interviewee wrote, "Treat students with respect. Don't assume they're all idiots. Most are not and they are there to learn."

3.2.6   Rotated Point of View

Many presenters have it backwards! Let me explain. Suppose I am facing my audience of 500+ students and I want to describe the dramatic decline in U.S. housing prices from April 2006 to March 2012, and the subsequent recovery from March 2012 until January 2018 (St Louis Fed., 2021). So, I stand in front of my audience and I move my hands through the air to describe the decline. Roughly four out of five presenters I have seen will draw it from their own perspective, facing the audience and moving their right hand down and to their right, and then up and to their right, as if they are drawing the line of the plot with a pen on paper suspended in front of them in the air.

Your students get two immediate impressions from this mistake: the conscious and confusing realization that their instructor just drew a picture backwards in mid-air for them, and now they have to do some mental gymnastics to figure out what was meant by this figure that slopes downward and to the students' left and then upwards and to the students' left; and, the subconscious realization that the instructor is self-centered and is presenting this to himself or herself, rather than being student-centered and presenting it to the class.

If you present something backwards and abruptly force the students to do some mental gymnastics to figure it out, then you are disrupting the flow of the class. Whatever be the next 15 words out of your mouth, they are ignored while the students process the rotated picture that was just painted. This is a clear visual manifestation of a disconnect between the instructor's focus and the students' focus, and it creates a negative subconscious impression of the instructor, and a negative impact on your teaching evaluations.

So, when "drawing in the air," I always mentally flip my point of view and place myself in the students' shoes. I ask myself "What do the students see?" and then I draw it from their perspective. It helps that I am dyslexic, because I am not grounded in my own left-right perspective. So, try mentally rotating your point of view, imagining yourself sitting in the audience looking at you waving your arms. From that student perspective, which way do your hands need to move to indicate the picture you are drawing? If you do it correctly, the students will not be aware of any problem, but if you do it backwards, like so many instructors do, you relegate yourself to the ranks of the self-centered, rather than the student-centered instructors.

Similarly, I have seen presenters project a PowerPoint presentation onto the big screen on the wall at the front of the room, but then point their fingers at the little computer screen facing them on the table when they talk. The audience cannot see what is being pointed at. If you mentally flip your perspective, and put yourself in your students' shoes, you cannot make this thoughtless mistake.

3.2.7 Teaching to Present

When I do something in the classroom that will be useful to my students in their own presentations, in class or in their future jobs, I tell them what I am doing. It is just another part of my teaching. For example, when using a laser pointer, or using red ink on a white board, or reverting to a backup when a video fails, etc., I tell them how and why I am doing that so that they understand for their own future presentation purposes.

3.2.8   Struggle of Not?

Sometimes, you do *not* want your students to struggle with a topic. So, you call upon your unique mastery of the material in an area often considered difficult (e.g., when I teach integral calculus to non-math majors using techniques I have seen nowhere else). Other times, however, you *do* want your students to struggle with some task in order to master it and learn a *lifelong skill*.

For example, in a relatively difficult final-year class, I demonstrate Excel spreadsheet skills in the classroom, but I purposely do it so quickly that they get only the general idea, rather than slowly enough that they can copy it down and replicate my steps. In their jobs, the following year, they will need to be able to execute steps in a spreadsheet when they have nothing more than a general idea of how to do it. So, I am trying to reproduce that environment in the safety of the classroom.

It's like the old adage spoken by the character "Max" in *Mrs. Dymond* "...if you give a man a fish he is hungry again in an hour. If you teach him to catch a fish you do him a good turn" (Ritchie, 1885, p. 185). Struggling with the Excel implementation, but knowing that it can be done in only a few keystrokes (because they saw me do it), may be a little frustrating, but this small struggle is something they will face on a daily basis in their jobs. (I do not do this in a first-year class because those green students still need hand holding, but I always do it with students who are about to graduate.)

> When asked what important question I had failed to ask, one interviewee wrote, "What should be the objective function of a college/graduate-level instructor? Without knowing what you are optimizing, how can you be the best teacher you can be? I think the answer should trade off student satisfaction with student learning. The two are not strictly compatible goals."

Epilogue (Excel Struggle): The next sentence spoken by Max after his fish adage in *Mrs. Dymond* is "...But these very elementary principles are apt to clash with the leisure of the cultivated classes" (Ritchie, 1885, p. 185). I was therefore not surprised that a few lazy/entitled students complained to my boss that I went too quickly over the Excel skills in class, and my boss asked me "What are you going to do about it?!" My answer was a calm "Absolutely nothing." I told my boss that this was by design, and although the students might not like it, it was for their own good and they knew it. In other words, "demanding mental effort is painful in the short run, but highly satisfying in the long run... ...respect from students is preferable to their immediate approval" (Browne and Keeley, 1985, p. 78). See further discussion in Section 6.1.

3.2.9 Any Questions?

I always ask, "What are your questions?" not "Do you have any questions?" For an undergraduate class, there is a big difference between these approaches! If you ask, "Do you have any questions?," then quite literally/logically, the answer is "Yes" or "No." It is altogether too easy for the students to answer, "No," because there is then nothing else to be done about it. "No" also saves the students from making themselves stand out among their peers, protects them from shyness, and preserves their humbleness, etc. However, "When students are permitted to answer a question by silence or by uttering a one-word reply, the teacher has little appreciation for what the student's response actually means" (Browne and Keeley, 1985, p. 80).

If you instead ask, "What are your questions?," then this question does not have a simple yes/no answer. Instead, this is a question with no easy out.

They have to perform an internal check and then think for a moment. My approach *presupposes* that they have questions, and encourages a response.

After asking, "What are your questions?," be sure to patiently give them enough time for their mental processing. Ignore your revved-up internal clock, count to 10 slowly or just wait *three times* as long as you think you need to.

Other factors can further delay a response. For example, when I ask N.Z. undergraduate students something, I wait for a response. Then I wait some more. Then I wait a little more. Then a little more. It takes time to get a response out of them because many N.Z. students are humble and do not wish to answer questions that make them appear more talented than their peers. See also Section 2.2.2.

It is also important to resist the temptation to ask and to then impatiently answer your own questions. When I intend to answer my own question, I tell the students in advance that I am going to do so. I do not want them getting into the habit of expecting me to answer my own questions. That would be lecturing masquerading as interaction; Browne and Keeley (1985, p. 79) make a similar point.

Note that if you tell your students to "Please raise a hand if you understand this concept," then you will almost never get 100% of students raising a hand. If I get 80% raising a hand, I am perfectly happy. You should not expect, aim for, or require 100% of students to understand before your continue. Some of the students are thinking about other stuff, did not realize you were discussing something important, daydreaming, or just dim or lazy and headed for a "fail" in your class before they change majors. Invite the stragglers to talk to you at half time, discuss it with their classmates (who said they understand), send you an email any time, or come to your office hours.

If, however, only 25% of students raise a hand to acknowledge that they understand a concept, then ask them where the sticking points are and work on those. Point at successive lines on the board, asking how many understand it, until you find the bottleneck. Sometimes, however, you will need to belay that line of enquiry until the next class (e.g., after confusion about a probability concept, I came to the following class with a wonderful spreadsheet that showed how the concept worked, but it took several hours to build it in my office).

Unlike undergraduates, MBA students are typically older, pay higher tuition, are more mature, and know better the value of a dollar. So, they tend to recognize the opportunity that stands before them. Whether you say, "What are your questions?" or "Do you have any questions?" or even if you say nothing at all, you tend to get the same result: They ask many questions. (See, however, discussion of time-wasting questions in Section 3.3.7.)

Junior students hate me calling upon them in class. They may freeze up, even if they actually know the answer. One way around that is to pick out a group of three. I tuck in my thumb and my little finger and I point with my middle three fingers, and say, "Can one of you three please answer the following question?" Being picked as part of a group reduces their anxiety and increases the chance for an interaction. Another approach is to ask, "Can anyone wearing stripes answer this question?," or, in a classroom with demarcation between sections, "Can anyone on the south side of the room answer this question?" (I point, to help them out.)

Instead of open-ended questions (e.g., "What are your questions?"), you can ask students questions that require lengthier or more complex answers (Browne and Keeley, 1985, p. 80). "Students will think when you require them to do so" (Browne and Keeley, 1985, p. 79). For example, I can ask something like "Why do you think the farmer entered this ridiculously risky financial transaction that wiped out all of his wealth, all his family's wealth, and left him owing an additional \$200,000 to his broker?" (See NBR, 2015). Another example might be "Where have we seen this concept before in this course?" In these cases, you are inviting the students to focus on a specific question, rather than fishing for answers to an open-ended question.

3.2.10 Thoughts Matter

> When asked, "Why did you became a teacher?," one interviewee wrote, "Because I saw a lot of tertiary teachers who didn't care about their students. They didn't put them first. They didn't make them feel valued. I wanted to help students to learn and see how amazing it is to stretch your brain."

Eison (1990) emphasizes that "active teaching" requires engagement and the encouragement of student participation. I have, however, seen many presenters ask a group of students (or faculty) a question that has no sensible answer. For example, the presenter gives out paper handouts, and then asks, "Does everybody have one?" That is the wrong question. What on Earth is the answer to that question? What you should ask is "Who still needs a handout?" This is a simple example, but many other sorts of questions can be asked confusingly. For example, "Has everybody had enough time to copy the diagram from the black board?" "Does everyone understand?" "Can we move on now?" "Are we all done?" None of those questions makes sense. By the time the students figure out what you are actually asking, and how to get your attention with a response, it may be too late to respond.

Story (Active Thinking): When I was a student, I worked such long hours that it was difficult to stay awake in a slow-moving class. So, I adopted an approach to staying awake in the classroom that is perhaps unusual.[1] I describe it to my students as follows: "While I am speaking or writing on the board, or using classroom technology, you need to actively question what is being presented via an internal dialogue with yourself, asking 'Why this?,' 'How

---

[1] I also tell my students that going to the restroom and slapping icy cold water on your face several times using both hands, so hard that it hurts, will keep you awake and alert for another 45 minutes. It is a very effective drug-free alternative to caffeine. I learned about it when doing all-nighters (and double all-nighters!) at MIT.

that?,' 'What does this imply?,' 'How does this link to something similar we saw last week?,' etc. When taking notes, you should translate my words into your own words before writing them down.

"This generative active real-time processing of the information is, in essence, parsing the flow of data I present in order to make it compatible with your own thought patterns and mindset (Wittrock, 1990; King, 1993; Mueller and Oppenheimer, 2014).

"At times, your internal dialogue will generate a question that exceeds the hurdle of confusion necessary for you to raise a hand and ask a question. You won't be the only one with this question, and asking it will help your peers. In my experience, this active approach leads to better learning, retention, and interaction (and it helps you to stay awake!)."

Sometimes students do not know what they do not know. They come to you in your office hours, wallowing around in their ignorance (as in the "Lincoln approach," mentioned in Section 1.1.7), but they do not have the experience or ability (or they are simply too lazy) to identify the patterns they need to see in order to be able to put together a precise enough question for you to answer. If you ask them to reflect upon their problem and to be more precise, then you force them to engage with the material and with you (Browne and Keeley, 1985, p. 80). I often ask a few questions of my own to narrow down where their difficulty is: "Can you explain the connection between this and that?" "Can you sketch a graph of this relationship?" "Can you define this term you are using?" Digging into their thoughts usually whittles their confusion away quite quickly; it also teaches them how to focus their thoughts.

3.2.11   Inviting Deeper Interaction

One of my professors liked to tell us that "attending class is not a spectator sport; you are expected to participate." Chickering and Gamson (1987, p. 4) make the same point. Asking your students questions in class is a routine way to invite student participation. Undergraduates, however, often prefer to keep their counsel. Let me add to the advice in Section 3.2.9 on getting them to engage with you.

Sometimes I invite students to pick a topic from a list, or suggest a better topic, for coverage late in the semester, either in class or in assignments, or both. If competing ideas seem popular, we can take a vote. If the topic is to be at the end of the semester, then it needs to be chosen early enough for me to create exam questions in advance, so as to meet administrative deadlines.

Sometimes I ask my students an unusually difficult question in the middle of a class. I tell the students, however, that I do not want an answer until the next class. Then I remind them at the end of the session that their "homework" is to find me an answer by tomorrow's class. I may promise a small prize for the best answer to come.

"Giving advance notice of questions allows students from high 'uncertainty avoidance' cultures time to prepare well-considered and appropriate responses" (Tharapos, 2018).[2]

---

[2]In high uncertainty avoidance cultures, people are uncomfortable in unstructured situations (Beugelsdijk, Maseland, and van Hoorn, 2015). They prefer formality, ritual, and process, and may be reluctant to question authority figures. Uncertainty avoidance is not to be confused with risk aversion. Beugelsdijk, Maseland, and van Hoorn (2013) rank countries on uncertainty avoidance, putting Argentina, Russia, and Brazil towards the high end (i.e., more formal), N.Z., Australia, and the U.S. in the middle, and China, Norway, Sweden, and Vietnam towards the low end (i.e., less formal).

In final-year classes, I create assignments that challenge my students. I want them to achieve the sense of accomplishment and satisfaction that goes with conquering a difficult task (see further discussion in Section 6.1 and Section 7.2). I tell them that I do not expect them to be able to complete my assignments without asking me questions. I do not know what deficiencies they have in their backgrounds, so I let the assignment questions bring them to light and drive the interaction.

> One interviewee wrote that she uses "hooks" in class. She said, "It is something like Hollywood movies: there is a problem, then the problem is resolved and everyone is happy about it. I try to use this approach in my lectures. For example I can ask students 'Do you know how much interest you are going to pay if you take on a $1,000,000 mortgage to purchase a house?,' and 'Do you know the possible strategies to reduce the amount of interest paid?' I think that the majority of 21-year-old students will be curious to find out the answers to these questions."

⚲ If I communicate high expectations, then the students almost always rise to the occasion (Chickering and Gamson, 1987, p. 4). To meet these high expectations typically requires interaction between students and interaction with me.

For example, I talked to a successful hedge fund manager friend of mine about an assignment I wanted to create for an applied investments class. I wanted to use a particularly complex finance practitioner technique to rebalance a portfolio of stocks. Like me, my hedge fund manager friend had been a college professor in the U.S. before working in the finance industry. He said that it would be *impossible* to give this task to undergraduate business students. He said that I would need software they could not use, high-dimensional non-linear optimization techniques they could not understand, algebra they could not cope with, and proprietary data that were unavailable.

So, I ignored him and spent 10 days one summer creating what I wanted, using only an Excel spreadsheet. I had to distill it down to the essentials, but it works well (both as a learning tool and in terms of fairly consistent N.Z.-market-beating performance). In the lead up to this assignment, we build up skills one at a time in the classroom (optimization, algebra, data handling protocols, Excel skills, etc.). Then when I give the assignment to the students, I tell them that "A successful hedge fund

manager said that this task is impossible at the undergraduate level, and I doubt that you will be able
to complete it without my help." Such a statement
invites and requires interaction.

The above assignment is given as group work
because 90% of undergraduate business students are
incapable of completing it individually, even with
my help. I use groups of 4–6 students. I have done
this with roughly 400 groups of students, and there
were only ever three or four groups who failed to
complete it, almost always because they ignored my
repeated advice and left it to the last minute.

3.2.12 Hard Copy

The first class I was given responsibility to teach
by myself was a final-year investments course of
100+ students, over 30 years ago. I prepared paper
handouts of about six pages for each two-hour class.
The first page was a letterhead with a bullet point
summary of topics, and the remaining pages were
the class notes. (It was the first year that a laser
printer was available in my Department, and I was
the only one exploiting it to the full, with equations
and graphics, etc.)

Since then, I have made a point of putting a
physical paper copy of the core material in my stu-

dents' hands each semester, even if it costs me a couple of hundred dollars out of my own pocket. My students still have plenty of notes to take, based on what I write on the board (explanations, examples, summaries, diagrams, etc.), but they have the *core* material in their hands in the classroom.

In that first class, over 30 years ago, there was no microphone to put on my lapel, no electronic projector to project a computer output onto a screen, no computer in the classroom (indeed, we did not even have computers in our offices when I started as a junior academic). We did, however, have overhead projectors with plastic slides, which I used only rarely, preferring chalk. Nowadays, in that same class (a final-year investments course of 100+ students), my students have my textbook in their hands, I project its pages onto an overhead screen, and I walk through explanations with a marker pen on a whiteboard, while wearing a microphone.

When teaching the big first-year undergraduate class, I always make my PowerPoint slides available in advance. I give them the PowerPoint file, a two-slides-per-page pdf file, and a four-pages-per-slide pdf file (to give them valuable choices). I strongly recommend that they print their choice out in advance, so that they can annotate them.

When I prepare slides for classes, I have two equally important goals in mind. First, quite frankly, these materials are a crutch for me to lean on. I print them out, annotate them, and hold them in my hand in class because they are a roadmap through the material I plan to cover. If you are working 80+ hours a week (and I assume many of you with strong research agendas are), then you are likely so tired that having this roadmap in your hand is especially helpful. Second, the slides are an aid to my audience. Butler, in the context of academic presentations, says that the presentation is for the audience, not the presenter. So, the slides should help the audience to follow along if they are paying attention, or to get back on track if they are not paying attention (Butler, 2020).

There are many benefits to the students having the core material in their hands. They do not have to waste time writing down fundamental material, and can focus instead on writing down the value-added accompanying material that I deliver, explaining what is in their hands. They can pause and ask questions that there would not be time for if they had to write everything down.

Also, if there is a power failure or a software or

hardware glitch (which happens all too frequently!), then I can abandon all electronic means of presentation and just walk them through what is in their hands. I have done this outside the classroom when the fire alarms went off! (We lost only a few minutes of class time; I even had some chalk with me and drew a diagram on a cement wall outside.)

Something will go wrong (hardware, software, electrics, fire alarm, heating, cooling, leakage, etc.). So, you need to be ready for it. By ensuring that my students always have physical pages in front of them, I am ready for many of these failures. As suggested already, slower students can pause on material I have already covered, while faster students can skip ahead. It also means that if an impatient student asks a question about something I am going to cover in five minutes, I can point them at it and they can read it while the rest of us catch up.

3.2.13 Puppy Training 🐾

After getting a puppy, I discovered that many schools of thought exist on the how best to train it. Some people suggest punishing a dog who behaves badly, even using *physical* punishment. More recently, however, physical punishment has been recognized as slowing the rate of learning of the animal because its fear of responding incorrectly to a command (and being punished), means it might not respond at all. Keep that thought in mind while you read the following few paragraphs.

Care must be taken in showing a class what they do not understand (Falk and Konold, 1992, p. 161). It is possible to go too far. For example, suppose that in class I ask students to solve a simple differential calculus problem (indeed, the *simplest* differential calculus problem). Then I call for answers. In a class of 120, I know that I will get 10 different answers from the confident students, with some common answers and some uncommon ones. If I am lucky, one student will give the correct answer (but more often than not it is zero). Then I can show the class the fallacy in their thinking and I can explain why they never understood basic calculus. Then I can explain it more clearly than they have seen it before. Suppose that I then ask a simple probability question. Again, in a class of 120, I know that I will get 10 different answers from the now-slightly-less confident students, with some common answers and some uncommon ones. Perhaps 10 students will know the correct answer. Suppose I then ask a basic question about performing an operation in an Excel spreadsheet, and none of my now-unconfident students can answer it correctly.

By this stage, 95% of the students have been unable to answer three basic questions that they should have mastered at least two or three years ago. A certain amount of embarrassment creeps in among them because of their revealed unconscionable ignorance. If I now ask another simple question, they will be reluctant to answer, because I have altered their self-perceptions, and they fear being wrong and being shown to be wrong. Revealing their demonstrated ignorance has caused them to lose confidence in the simplest topics of their education to date, not to mention the more complex topics. Even if I present this material in the friendliest, most reassuring, most supportive manner, and do not act like an arrogant ass, I will have difficulty getting them to take part in answering classroom questions again. Their reticence may last them the rest of the semester.

The bottom line is that it is best to limit examples where you call for student answers in a large classroom and then demonstrate an all-round lack of knowledge. One way around this is to not *ask* them what they think, but to *tell* them what they think. That is, tell them that "In past years, students have commonly given the following incorrect

answers. We will now debunk them one at a time."
As long as they are not publicly admitting that they
too held those erroneous views, then their ignorance
is not made public and they are not embarrassed by
their ignorance. They will then be happy enough to
take part later in other sorts of classroom question-
and-answer sessions. Another solution is to advertise small-group interactive tutorials as a safe place
for students to make mistakes. 🐾

3.3 Classroom Dynamics

3.3.1 Passion

> One interviewee wrote, "Great teachers love
> what they do. They are not fearful of their stu-
> dents or their opportunity to share knowledge
> and educate the next generation. Great teach-
> ers are good communicators who make learn-
> ing exciting. Their passion for knowledge is ex-
> ceeded only by their need to breathe. They are
> addictive and students truly love attending their
> classes."

The etymology of the word "passion" is interesting.
You likely know that it derives, perhaps 1,000 years
ago, from the Latin word *passio*, meaning *suffering*,

or *that which must be endured.* (Hence the "Passion of the Christ" referring to Christ's sufferings leading up to and including his crucifixion.) Five hundred years ago, "passion" came also to refer to a *consuming emotion.*

"Passion" came up repeatedly with interviewees. One interviewee split passion up into love of the students and love of the subject matter. (I would add love of learning and love of helping others to learn, which are slightly different.) Several interviewees said that when they were students, their most inspiring teachers were visibly passionate about their area, about knowledge, or about their craft. Some interviewees said they themselves loved to, and were unafraid to, share their own passion.

One interviewee wrote, "I bring an energy and enthusiasm to the classroom that many instructors do not. Thinking back to my instructors in college, only a few stand out as seeming to be enthusiastic and excited to be teaching. Having good content is neither necessary nor sufficient."

Another wrote, "A standout memory for me are teachers that genuinely cared about student learning. They never minded being interrupted when I knocked on their door with questions from lectures or tutorials. They were excited about trying to explain key concepts and challenged me to think more about what I was learning and why. They oozed enthusiasm and passion for their craft and their joy of sharing knowledge was contagious."

Another wrote, "I had a linear algebra teacher in college who was thoroughly excited about the topic and his energy ⋆really lifted the class⋆ beyond what most thought they were capable of doing."

Eison (1990, p. 24) says, "energy can carry the day." I certainly bring a high level of energy into the classroom. I am upbeat, happy, joking, intense, serious, professional, curious, coaxing, and business-like, all at the same time. After teaching a two-hour class, I feel about the same as I do after running five miles (eight kilometers).

Eison (1990, p. 24) says, "an instructor's enthusiasm is often contagious; so too is a lack of enthusiasm."

For example, sometimes I am in the middle of a class and I am tired, after working long days for weeks or months on end with no breaks. I begin to feel like the early meaning of "passion" applies (i.e., that which must be endured). My energy level drops a little, my voice lowers a little, or I do not smile as much, or stand up as straight. I know from past experience that if I do nothing, the remainder of the class will be like wading through molasses for all concerned. So, as soon as I am aware if it, I actively counter it: I dig a little deeper, I stand up straighter, I smile more, I raise my voice, I pause and tell a joke or a story, I speak with more enthusiasm. I try to demonstrate some of the consuming emotion that drives my curiosity about my area of interest. Doing so always works, often before the students are even aware of the molasses I actively side-stepped.

3.3.2 Chalk and Talk

I have heard much criticism of chalk and talk. That is, criticism of instructors who do nothing but stand in the classroom and talk and write on the board (e.g., King, 1993; Crouch and Mazur, 2001). Supposedly, chalk and talk is out of date, and a "reversed" or "flipped" classroom (i.e., where student engagement is increased by working though problems live in class) is superior.

A fully reversed classroom may be superior for some instructors, but I have used chalk and talk for 30 years, and I have often had the highest teaching evaluations in my large department (in the U.S. and N.Z.), and I have been nominated for many teaching awards and won many teaching awards and I have been mentioned an order of magnitude more frequently than my colleagues in surveys of the satisfaction of students who graduated.

Some folks, upon hearing that I use chalk and talk, mistakenly equate my approach with a dinosaur-like mistrust of technology and an outdated instructor-focused pedagogy. To the contrary, I exploit modern classroom technology to show textbook pages (or lecture slides) on screen, run Matlab code, use spreadsheets, plot graphs, run simulations, show a short video, etc. There is no shortage of technology in my chalk-and-talk classroom. (I have a PhD from MIT for goodness' sakes!) At the same time, I interact with the students, and we walk and talk through problems together in the classroom. The bottom line is that I almost never use chalk and talk in *isolation.*

Crouch and Mazur (2001) state that in a traditional introductory science course, the students read the textbook after class, if at all. Crouch and

Mazur's "peer instruction" approach, however, requires readings *before* class, so that the instructor can focus on the more difficult parts of the readings *in* class. My approach in my advanced course has been neither of these. Instead, we read the textbook *together in class*. I walk/talk my students through the pages of the text, projected on screen, and we work through concepts and examples on the board or using software (Matlab, Excel, etc.), with additional use of hand-held calculators, etc.

Most years, a single student complains to my boss that "All he does is read his textbook out loud." My rejoinders to that are usually "If all I am doing is reading the textbook, then why does it take us two hours to read six pages?" and "What about everything else we worked through on the board, all the hand-written notes, the software we took out for a spin, the video we watched, etc.?"

Chalk and talk is difficult to do well. For example, I have seen many young presenters who barely even look at their audience while speaking. You cannot use chalk and talk if you cannot read your audience. For me, that would be like driving a car without looking at the road.

Yes, a fully-flipped classroom may be superior for some instructors, especially those lacking knowledge or confidence (Reynolds and Miao, 2014). My experience, however, is that if I am well prepared, organized, cater to my students' needs, am enthusiastic, and hold their attention in class, then chalk-and-talk combined with a focus on generative learning (e.g., via a multi-modal eclectic approach; see Section 1.1.6), is rated as superior to all else. Students like good lecturing (Buchanan and Palmer, 2017)! Conversely, I have seen examples of flipped classrooms and student-led/problem-based learning that were an unmitigated disaster, scarring my Department's reputation for years afterwards.

The bottom line is that you cannot conclude that a particular style of teaching is good or bad any more than you can conclude that a particular flavor of pie is good or bad; it is more about the instructor's preferences, preparation, and implementation, each of which is discussed in this book.

An interviewee with a sciences background was pleasantly surprised to find that his chalk-and-talk style (preferred by him to prepared slides) worked well in a business school context. His students said that it increased engagement and retention because they "need to follow the lecturer in real time." He used the same approach when teaching online, writing on a piece of paper, showing up in real time on screen.

He said that chalk and talk increases his flexibility and interaction with students. For example, he can make "real time course corrections" when his interactions with students in class reveal that the students lack some essential preparation that he must then review before continuing with his planned class content.

For online teaching, another interviewee wrote, "Use a plug-in document camera that is linked to IPEVO software (e.g., Dolan, 2020). It will make writing notes so much easier because you can record your writing on Zoom concurrently with delivering a lecture with slides."

3.3.3 Voices & Audience Tenor

Most people have two voices: a "head voice," and a "diaphragm voice." The head voice is light and high pitched and projected from the back of the throat, but the diaphragm voice is deeper and lower pitched and projected from the gut. I almost always use the diaphragm voice. Sometimes I have taught when I was quite ill, and the head voice was simply not there, leaving me with no choice.

When I first taught, microphones were not available. I would project my voice from my diaphragm and it worked well, even in the largest auditoriums. As I got older, however, the effort required for voice projection was better spent on classroom teaching activities. Lately, I always use a microphone. So, if you find yourself quite tired or hoarse after a class, consider using a lapel microphone; It really does allow you to expend your energies better on moving around the classroom and interacting with students.

If a student with a light voice (often a female) is partway through asking a question in class and another aggressively loud student (often a male) shouts, "We can't hear you!," it is your job to immediately tell the shouting student "Don't you dare shout out at my student. She is talking to me, not you. You do not need to hear her question. It is my job to repeat her question to the class when she is done. It is not her job to speak loudly enough to be heard by you." Then, to the student with the question, "Please forgive the interruption. I want to hear what you said. Please talk to me." If you do not do this immediately then you set a tone of behavior in the classroom that is awful. Students with quiet voices may shy away from asking questions because of the aggressive behavior of other students.

Losing those students' voices in your classroom destroys value. Do not allow it to happen!

Every audience has a tenor (i.e., a prevailing mood or character). Each time your class meets, their tenor will be slightly different. Your students may be in the midst of mid-term exams, and be very tired. They may have just finished your tough assignment, and be feeling beaten up. They may have just come back from Spring Break, and be rambunctious. They may be first-year students and very green, or they may be final-year students or MBA students who are jaded.

I mentioned in Section 3.3.2 that many young presenters barely even look at their audience while speaking, and that for me this would be like driving a car without looking at the road. <u>You must read your audience.</u> You can tell their mood from how they look, how they move, what sort of ambient noise they are generating, how they respond to questions, etc.

If your students are tired, then take a longer break in the middle of class. If they are down, then tell them a funny story or make some *non sequitur* observation. If they are rambunctious, then grab their attention with something that makes them settle down. Sometimes, however, I find that they are behaving oddly for no reason that I can deduce. Then I stop, walk into the room a little and ask, "What is going on?" "Is something happening that has you distracted?" In those cases some weary student explains that there was some social event the previous night, and almost all of them attended, and some of them have not been to bed yet, or something like that; they appreciate me asking.

> One interviewee said, "I try to put myself in my students' shoes to understand what they need. They need to know what is happening in the course, when things are due, etc. Sometimes, they need hand holding, sometimes they don't. Every cohort is different, it is alive and living, and you need to be flexible enough to adjust and also 'read the room'. Sometimes, you can just feel what they need and adjust accordingly."

Many changes in audience tenor can be predicted (e.g., you know they have a big exam that day). Then you can prepare something for them (a joke, a story, a prop, etc.). If, however, you ignore changes in audience tenor, or you turn your back on the students for the whole class, or you stand side-on and never make eye contact, then you risk losing touch with their mood. Then you lose your chance to change your behavior to suit their mood. Then you lose their attention, and it's downhill from there. So, be sure to read your audience every time!

3.3.4 Lost in Translation

The students speak a different language from that of the teacher (Falk and Konold, 1992, p. 155). Your training gives you access to a wide and precise vocabulary, and your age has exposed you to more words than your students. So, part of your job is to teach your students the names of things. Do not be surprised when you mention something that is well known to you and your peers, but your students look at you blankly. If this happens, ask for a show of hands to see who understands.

Story (Staccato Bagels): If you change countries, you may be in for a shock, even if you speak the language fluently. When I first moved to the U.S., I found that Bostonians could not understand my Kiwi accent (even though English is my first language and my parents were both English). Three days in a row I went to a café at the edge of the MIT campus and I ordered the exact same thing. Each day I was served by a different person, got something different, and with a different cost, and never exactly what I ordered. On the fourth day, I tried speaking more slowly and more clearly to the server behind the counter, enunciating my words carefully, politely saying, "please" and "thank you" and smiling, only to have him speak back even more slowly and with aggressively spiteful anger and visceral hateful emphasis on each of his words. His voice was a machine gun staccato: *"Yes! You! Can! Have! Two! Cinnamon! Raisin! Bagels!"* His face was furiously angry. I watched him carefully, but I showed no reaction on my face. (After spending a lot of time on the violent late-night streets of N.Z. in the 1980s, I was naturally poker faced.) I got what I ordered on that fourth day at the café, but the guy behind the counter clearly wanted to kill me. Huh? What the hell was going on, and what should I do about it?

I went out and bought a radio and I listened to late-night local talk shows each evening as I studied. After 4–5 hours of late-night radio talks shows every day for two solid weeks, I was able to make myself understood by almost every Bostonian, and I could understand them too, for the most part (thank you WBZ 1030; I am still a listener!). In order for me to be understood, however, I had to alter my accent and change the emphasis I place on parts of words—in ways a Kiwi never would in N.Z. It was a matter of fitting in as best as possible, and appearing respectful. One lesson from this story is that you may require some voice coaching to succeed in your new country, even if you speak the same language. (Several new staff in my N.Z. academic Department have received voice coaching; It was offered to them privately, so as to not embarrass them.)

Story (In Stitches): This story is aimed at U.S. readers. When I had been in the U.S. for about 18 months, I slipped on ice in downtown Boston while on a 10-mile run. My face scraped over gravel-embedded hard-packed ice as I slid uncontrollably for some distance. I got up and jogged a couple of blocks over to *South Station* to look in the men's room mirror. Thirty seconds later, I saw a kind businessman in the mirror over my shoulder who turned up to hurriedly shove a handful of paper napkins/serviettes at me to wipe up the bloody mess on my face. (He must have seen me jogging through the station looking a bit like something out of a horror movie and grabbed them from a food vendor.) I said, "Thank you. I was worried that I had lost some teeth, but they are OK. Damn it, I am supposed to give a presentation at MIT tomorrow!" He thought that was funny.

I jogged back to MIT, including down the "Infinite Corridor," where two MIT cops bundled against the cold and carrying takeaway coffees did a double-take but said nothing, though I must have looked terrible (the blood splatter stained my white T-shirt permanently).

The next day, after some prompting, I went to the MIT medical facility. The medic was a short skinny man with bad posture assisted by an attractive young female nurse. He kept saying, "Yes, dear" and "No, dear" to her comments. I naively assumed they were an odd romantic couple, but soon figured out that he was just being condescending. I pointed out an obvious lump of gravel still embedded in my face; he disagreed, saying it was coagulated blood. He wanted to give me a local anesthetic before stitching me up. I said, "No, thank you." He said, "Tough guy, huh?" I explained that I was from N.Z. and had never had anesthetic, even for a dozen fillings. After he stitched me up, he said, "You can take *Tylenol* for the pain."

The only time I had ever heard the name *Tylenol* before was in global news stories ten years earlier, where it was reported in N.Z. as a drug that had killed a bunch of people; that was all I knew about it. I said nothing, but after his earlier behavior, I figured that the guy was nuts; No way was I taking some unknown drug that had killed a bunch of people.

Although it is an everyday U.S. drugstore item, 18 months in the U.S. was not long enough for me to know that *Tylenol* is only acetaminophen (paracetamol) and that the "Chicago Tylenol Murders" were terrorist actions that led to the safety seals on drugstore bottles that are now common. Your foreign students face this sort of confusion with common things on a daily basis, both inside and outside the classroom, even after 18 months in your country.

Story (Slow Down/Slang): One of my interviewees experienced difficulty as an English-speaking person studying in a non-English-speaking country. After her experience, she argues that you should spare a thought for your foreign students for whom English is not a first language. For example, perhaps you should speak a little more slowly than usual when you are in class and use local slang only sparingly (or with an explanation).

Given my experiences, I will go one step further than my interviewee and ask you to also spare a thought for *English-speaking* students from other countries, or even from other parts of your *own* country, because they too can have language difficulties. For example, as a student in the U.S., I had problems with American slang phrases. One MIT professor, now at Harvard, was particularly problematic for me because he often used slang phrases. I think that he thought his slang would make his A-level publications kind of folksy.

Of course, language difficulty is a two-way street. For example, I have had foreign students bring a friend with them to my office to act as an interpreter when they speak with me, because their English is so bad.

Putting a written document in my students' hands helps very much with their understanding of my accent (see Section 3.2.12). Writing important points on the board also helps (see Section 3.2.2).

Story (Elocution Lessons): One interviewee, who had childhood speech therapy and elocution tuition paid for by relatives, wrote, "I value their gift of speech more than any of my academic qualifications. Why? Most of my students are non-native speakers of English. Recently the classes have been large, averaging around 300 each and reaching peaks of 600. During all this time, one of the most common pieces of positive feedback from students is that they understand what I'm saying. It's nothing to do with my inspirational finance! Sometimes I get picked up for speaking too fast (usually when I'm high on adrenaline) and I try to be conscious of that. However, neutrality—trying to speak standard English such that nobody knows where I am from, with rounded vowels, clickety-click consonants and moderate pace— seems to be appreciated."

Epilogue (Staccato Bagels): Why would a café assistant be so aggressively rude to me? Are Kiwis that unpopular in the Boston area? Perhaps you figured it out already. It took me two months of exposure to U.S. culture to figure out why the man behind the counter had reacted with such venom. He thought I was yet another racist white person who was talking to him in a slow (and, to him, condescending) manner because he assumed I thought he was a dunce. In fact, I was simply a newly-arrived Kiwi with a strong accent, who had been mis-understood and mis-served the previous three successive days in that same store (and with al-most zero experience of racism). I was tired of being misunderstood (and getting the wrong or-der and paying the wrong price) and I thought that speaking more slowly might help (which it did, although very unpleasantly).

In my life up to that point, I had seen almost no racism in any form. The only exception was on my first day in the U.S., a couple of weeks earlier, when I was looking for a store near my apartment building to get some cutlery and crockery. I took a wrong turn and ended up only one block from where I should have been, accidentally crossing one of those sharp geographical boundaries U.S. cities are known for. A small group of young men aggressively shouted, "honky" at me with some colorful ac-companying words, demanding to know what I was doing there. That was my first day in the U.S., and I wondered whether every day in the U.S. was going to be like this for me. I saw many events much worse than this over my following 10 years in the U.S., but nobody ever called me a honky to my face again.

Finally, and more optimistically...

...one interviewee wrote, "I used to think that students penalize non-native speakers for their accent. I think I was wrong. If you clearly communicate your ideas even with a heavy accent, if you are organized, consistent, fair, and respectful, and interested in the course material yourself, your students will forgive your accent/ethnicity."

3.3.5 Performance

When the students see me in the classroom, my goal is that they think that I love teaching, that I am confident, that I understand the material, that I am well prepared, that I love them, and that there is no place that I would rather be than standing in front of them at that moment. In fact, only some of those things are true.

Even if you had an awful day, you are sick, your family is at home vomiting into buckets because of food poisoning and you know you are next, your irrational penny-pinching micro-managing boss hates you, your workload is impossible, you were just forced to take a pay cut, etc., you have to set it all aside. Conditional upon being in the classroom, you need to put on the facade and do your job.

I put on my suit and tie and my "Professor" title the same way that a soldier puts on a uniform and assumes a rank. Most students expect to see me in suit and like to call me "Professor," the same way that most patients expect to see a doctor in a white coat whom they call, "Doctor," and many Christian parishioners expect their parish priest to wear a clerical collar and be addressed as "Father" or "Reverend," or something similar. Putting on a suit and adopting the professorial demeanor are part of the non-verbal language, or body language, I use in the classroom; they are part of my tradecraft (Navarro, 2019).

Navarro (2019) writes that you are always broadcasting. Your clothing, your body positioning, your hands, your face, etc., are sending a message, whether you are speaking or not. Eison (1990) also emphasizes that active speaking is both verbal and non-verbal. The clothing, the rank, the office (in the "position of authority" sense of the word) are all part of our culture. So, in order to play the part, I literally *play the part*; it is a performance. I act as if there is no place I would rather be. Different disciplines have different expectations about how you play that role, just as different genres of film, theater or music have different expectations. (See also the "Market Street" story in Section 3.3.7.)

Several of my interviewees said that you must be authentic in the classroom. You must not adopt a persona. They said that you must be yourself and that your passion must be genuine. They said that you cannot pretend to like the students and pretend to like teaching them because your young students are perceptive enough to see through any facade.

One interviewee wrote, "Find what presentation style fits you best rather than imitating someone who you are not. In essence, 'work within your own capabilities.' "

Another wrote, "Be yourself. Do not put on a persona as it will eventually break down and students will see through it."

Another wrote, "Most importantly, I am authentic. I never try to be anyone other than myself. I don't try to replicate anyone else's style that just wouldn't work. I am totally myself in the classroom, unafraid to make mistakes or share my world and the passion for my subject."

Emerson says much the same thing:

"Insist on yourself; never imitate. Your own gift you can present every moment with the cumulative force of a whole life's cultivation; but of the adopted talent of another, you have only an extemporaneous, half possession" (Emerson, 1841, para. 43).

I was surprised when interviewee after interviewee mentioned authenticity in the classroom, because I *disagree completely*. It is not because I think my interviewees or Emerson are wrong, but because a "one size fits all" approach fails here. Excellent teachers can differ completely in their approach to authenticity, driven by differences in the clay that they are made out of (e.g., "Clay," 2021).

For example, I have *no choice but to be inauthentic* in the classroom. I cannot be myself in the classroom because I am a typical introverted MIT geek. I *must* act like someone else—or I would just sit in the back row of the lecture theater with my head down hacking code. So, chameleon-like, I am happy to adopt other peoples' styles if I think they will work for me. I do this often with great success. When I refer to "playing the part" or "putting on a performance," I mean literally *exactly that*.

Depending upon your nature, you may have to act in the classroom. Personally, after 30 years of acting in the classroom, I think I deserve an Academy Award for lifetime achievement (pun intended).

3.3.6 Make a Memorable Point

Staging/theatrics matter. You can seemingly go off course with some *non sequitur* only to arrive at a memorable point. For example, I was talking to my students about CVs and cover letters. Then I stopped, opened a thick old book, and used the document camera to project the following first page of a story on screen. I read it out, with my verbal annotation shown here in square brackets.

"When I was twenty-seven years old, I was a mining-broker's clerk in San Francisco, and an expert in all the details of stock traffic [i.e., he was a stock broker's clerk]. I was alone in the world, and had nothing to depend upon but my wits and a clean reputation; but these were setting my feet in the road to eventual fortune, and

I was content with the prospect.

My time was my own after the afternoon board, Saturdays [i.e., when the stock market closed for the week on Saturday], and I was accustomed to put it in on a little sail-boat on the bay. One day I ventured too far, and was carried out to sea. Just at nightfall, when hope was about gone, I was picked up by a small brig [i.e., a sailing ship with two square-rigged masts] which was bound for London. It was a long and stormy voyage, and they made me work my passage without pay, as a common sailor. When I stepped ashore in London my clothes were ragged and shabby, and I had only a dollar in my pocket..."

Then I told the students that these 161 words are most of the first two paragraphs of a short story *The £1,000,000 Bank-Note* by Twain (1893). Then I asked how many had heard of Mark Twain. A surprising number had. Then I explained that "Mark Twain" was an obvious *nom de plume* (which none of them were aware of), and I explained a possible riverboat origin of the name (though other explanations exist), and I mentioned that Twain's real name was Samuel Langhorne Clemens.

Then I asked how many of them thought that these 161 words were well written and concise, and skillfully designed to grab the reader and drag him or her into the story. Most of them thought so. Then I explained that the ideal cover letter to accompany their undergraduate banking CV should be 160 words long, and that if Twain can take a stock broker's clerk from gainful employment in San Francisco, to sailing in San Francisco Bay, to being adrift at sea, to a just-in-time rescue, to working his passage onboard a brig, to stepping ashore in London with only a dollar in his pocket, then they could surely write a concise cover letter to accompany their CV in the same number of words. Surely they, with their short life stories, could tell an employer what they bring to the table, what makes them different from other candidates, and so on, in the same number of words.

This made a particular impression upon my students because so many of them had told me that it was *impossible* to fashion an effective sales pitch in so few words. It was interesting and memorable and made a clear point. I also put a pdf copy online for those who wanted to see what comes next in the story (Twain, 1893), emphasizing that the point of a cover letter is to grab the employer recipient and drag them into wanting to know what comes next (i.e., by granting the student an interview).

3.3.7 Discipline

In Section 3.3.5, I said that I put on my suit and tie as part of the *performance*. Dressing well also helps with discipline in my Discipline. I always wear a dark suit, conservative tie, pressed white shirt, black belt, and black shoes. Failing that, there is business dress casual. It serves purposes beyond performance. It shows that you respect them enough to dress up for the occasion. It creates a model for business behavior (even though formal dress is becoming less popular in business nowadays). It gets their attention, and they are more likely to show respectful behavior in the classroom.

Story (Market Street): I was early for a job interview on Fremont Street in San Francisco. I did not, however, want to arrive too early at the building or bump awkwardly into my interviewers while waiting outside it. So, I chose to stand and wait for 20 minutes at a small public plaza a few blocks away on Market Street (a main thoroughfare). It was nice weather. I was wearing a charcoal-gray pinstripe suit, conservative tie, pressed white shirt, black belt, and black shoes. I had a conservative new haircut and was holding a black leather fo-

lio. I was looking occasionally at my new wrist-
watch, and calmly watching the constant flow
of pedestrians, mostly tourists. There were at
least a dozen other casually-dressed locals waiting nearby in the plaza for various other reasons.

As I waited, a young woman came up to me
to ask directions. "Do you know where Second
Street is?" I smiled and said, "Yes, I do. Take
a couple of steps this way. Look there in the
distance. Can you see that circular sign above
the street, just past the streetcar? It's hard to
read it from here, but it says 'Second Street'."
She said, "Thank you," and set off. Then someone came up to me and asked, "Do you know
where the old San Francisco Mint Building is?"
I said, "Yes I do. The 'Granite Lady' is on Fifth
Street. I don't think it is open to the public
right now, but if you just want to see it, head
on down that way. You will come to First Street
(see the sign there?), then Second Street, and
so on. When you come to Fifth Street turn
left, and it is a couple of blocks up on your
right." Then another person stopped to ask me
for directions, then another, then another, and
so on. Although there were a dozen other people standing around, doing nothing, I was the

only person that these tourists stopped to ask for directions.

I am convinced that my conservative clean-cut appearance made me stand out as an authority figure to this series of complete strangers. This ties in with the non-verbal broadcasting discussed in Navarro (2019). It reinforces my opinion that dressing well matters in how you present in the classroom.

Note, however, that when I was a U.S. college professor visiting Paris for a friend's wedding, and wearing a similar outfit, a young French woman in Hippie clothes mistook me for an evil capitalist and came up to lecture me on the *Metro*. She launched into a venomous diatribe about "cochon capitalistes" (or words to that effect) before she got off at the next stop. Fortunately my French was poor enough that I caught only about 5% of her broadside. My non-verbal broadcasting, like her verbal broadcasting, was lost in translation. Her *non-verbal* broadcasting, however, was 100% clear!

I once calculated the aggregate fees of all the students in my class divided by the number of minutes of class time offered. In my largest classes, the students, in aggregate, were paying $200 per minute to be there and to listen to me. I told them so on the first day. If students were talking out of turn or disrupting a class, I told them to be quiet, and I reminded them that their classmates were paying $200 a minute to see this material, to listen to me, and not to listen to their disruptive chatter.

> One interviewee recommended that you pay attention to the type of noise that your students are generating. Is it two students only, speaking loudly without regard to their notes, or many students suddenly pointing at their notes and consulting each other? The latter can be an indication that you made a mistake, or explained something poorly. Ask them to tell you what is wrong. (Note that rather than interrupt the class and ask for clarification, students from some cultures may prefer to ask those around them.)

Although I never tolerate non-class-related talking in undergraduate lectures, the rules are different with MBA students. Talking to each other, talking in class, etc. is fine because they are old enough and experienced enough to usually have something of value to say.

Do watch out, however, for the students who

have nothing to say, but talk only for the sake of talking (and this has happened to me most often with U.S. MBA students). Their suggestions, questions, and comments are a waste of class time; they are trying to grab the limelight or to stand out. Do not suffer these fools. They make themselves known, through their actions, quite quickly. Talk to them privately and tell them that they are wasting their classmates' time by talking when they have nothing to say. Tell them privately to think more deeply about the topics and about whether their experience allows them to add value in the classroom.

In an informal small-group tutorial, it is fine if my students arrive late, leave early, talk among themselves, etc., but once I have 100+ undergraduates in the room and it is a formal lecture, I do not allow talking out of turn. The students are told that they can leave early or arrive late if they do so with minimum disruption, but talking is not allowed because it is so disruptive.

If students have a question for a neighbor (but not for me), then I tell them to write it in the margin of their notes, and to get their neighbor to write a reply. (If you do not think that students talking out of turn is disruptive to other students, then go and sit in the middle of a big class in progress.)

One of my interviewees, let me call him "Prof. White," told me years ago that he had advised his students to write down questions to each other so as to not disrupt class with their talking. When a student came to his office hours to ask a question, however, he noticed that in the margin of the student's notes was written, "Prof. White is an idiot."

I tell my students that if they have a question for me, they should raise a hand and wait for me to acknowledge them, wait for me to walk a little towards them, and to only then ask their question. I tell them that if I do not notice them, they can cough, or say, "Question," to get my attention.

One reason that I ask students to get my attention before asking a question is that most classrooms are set up for the students to hear the instructor, but not conversely. Also, I have some hearing loss. So, I am often lip reading student questions in addition to listening. This means that I need to identify clearly who is speaking to me before they get to the heart of their question.

An interviewee with profound hearing loss wrote that many situations are a struggle, even with hearing aids: "In lectures, I talk, and I don't accept questions until the end when I invite questioners to step outside the lecture hall where the sound is better. In seminars I always try to have an open-plan set-up so that when someone speaks I can approach them, and get close to them so that I can observe and hear. And I insist only one person speaks at once; a cacophony of speakers is hell for me. Breakouts in the same room are a complete no-no—it's like being in a crowded bar. Thus, my teaching style is determined by my hearing. Most of my colleagues and students don't know; at least I don't think they do. But my students have said that they appreciate my personal attention (taking them to one side to talk, focusing on them)."

The same interviewee stressed "Pay attention— you don't have to be deaf to have a reason to focus on someone."

Another wrote, "I had a hearing-impaired student once who asked that I face the class when speaking so that he could read my lips. I had never thought of that before. I now try to write on the board first and then discuss."

When disruptive students continue to talk after being asked not to more than once, I stop the class, single them out, point at them, and say, "Your talking is disruptive. It is disrespectful to your peers. Do you think you are *more important* than them?" [Pause.] "Do you think that you are somehow *entitled* to disrupt the class that your peers paid to attend?" [Pause.] "Do you think that you are *better* than them? [Pause.] They did not pay good money to come here to listen to *you!*"

If need be, I add, "If you have a question for me, then ask it. If you do not have a question for me, then be quiet and stop disrespecting your classmates. If you *do not* have a question and you *cannot* be quiet, then *get out!* If you want to talk, then do it on the other side of that door." [Pointing at the door.] I have never had a student continue to be disruptive after such a warning.

Note that I focus on the disrespect that the students are showing to their *classmates*, not the disrespect that they are showing to *me*. If you instead tell them that their disruptive behavior is disrespectful to *you*, then you will be less successful. They do not know you or relate to you, or care what you think of them. They do, however, care about what their *classmates* think of them.

In N.Z., in particular, I have found that suggesting that a student's behavior makes him or her look like they think they are better than their class-mates is very effective at stopping them from talk-ing out of turn or being disruptive. Kiwis value *equality* the way that U.S. people value *liberty* or *freedom* (McDonald, 2020; see also my Footnote 3 on p. 188). So, acting as if you are better than someone else invites immediate ridicule from your peers and others. Pointing out such student arro-gance in the classroom exploits this peer pressure, and stops disruptive misbehavior dead in its tracks.

> One interviewee said, "When I was a student I had one outstanding teacher. She was really tough on students and had a fearsome reputa-tion. In the lecture she was super scary, BUT one-on-one in her office, she was the nicest most helpful person. The things that stood out for me were her level of organisation, her technical knowledge and her ability to clearly communi-cate the context of what we were doing. She was somehow able to link ideas together, loop back, and explain how things connected. When I sat in a lecture, I knew that every word that came out of her mouth was deliberate and held meaning."

When teaching big (500+ students) introductory

classes, I get contacted multiple times each semester by student groups wanting to "speak to your class for five minutes at the start of class." Ha! No way! Often they turn up while I am prepping the room, when there are only five minutes until I am to start speaking. First of all, the start of class is when my students are most attentive. So, why would I give them that precious time? If anything, I might give them the *last* five minutes, but why give away the crown jewels? Second of all, as mentioned already, I worked out what my students, in aggretage, pay to be there, and it is about $200 per minute of class time. So, five minutes is worth about $1,000. Why gift that to some special-interest group? At best I will agree to show a slide from them at half time, or at the bottom of the hour. You can tell these folks to "Email me a slide, and I will put it on screen for five minutes at half-time tomorrow, but you are *not* talking to my students." Similarly, if someone gives me an admin announcement, I never put it on screen at the start of class (when students are most attentive). Instead, I put it up at half-time.

Many years ago I co-taught a big first-year course. My colleague went first for six weeks. To size-up the big class, I sneaked into the last couple of his classes before I took over. I sat in the audience pretending to be an adult student. He barely looked at the audience, and did not notice me. Sitting there was truly awful, and an embarrassment to view. The students around me smelled like beer (at 10AM!), were talking constantly, fidgeting a lot in their seats, and obviously not paying attention. They made as much noise as my students typically make five minutes *before* class starts. My colleague had zero respect/authority in the room. The entire experience was a shambles. He was older than I, but had been my student 20 years earlier.

When I started teaching the next week, I told the students that I had sat in on their classes and was appalled at the disrespect they were showing to their classmates by making constant noise and talking out of turn (I did not address the disrespect they showed to my colleague, because, as mentioned in Section 3.3.7, pointing out their disrespect to their peers is much more effective). I told them that I would not have accepted it from the instructor they had just finished with when he was my student 20 years ago, and I would not accept if from them. That got their attention because they could see that I was clearly much younger than he. In stark contrast to what I had seen earlier, the students were as nearly silent as a class could be after I took over.

Many students think of the classroom as *their space* and your little bit at the front as *your space.* With this attitude, they will talk among themselves, make romantic advances to each other, browse social media, not take notes, etc. So, even in a large class of say, 500+ persons, in a giant lecture theater, I make a point of walking up into the classroom and imposing myself upon "their" territory. I make clear that it is *my* space (or *our* space), and not theirs. No individual student is free to do what they please at the expense of a fee-paying peer or at the expense of disrupting my class.

One interviewee identified a memorable teacher "...who in a 120-seat lecture hall went halfway up the aisle, and halfway into the row to stand right beside a student who had thought they were 'safe' and proceeded to cold call and lecture to that student. We all started paying more attention after that."

Conversely, another memorable teacher was "...a French instructor who allowed herself to be coerced into taking the class outside to sit under a big oak tree and sing songs in French as she played her guitar."

One luxury of standing in front of the classroom is

that I get to move around freely. Your students do not have this luxury of movement; they are *pinned down*. Exercising the option to walk about can be entertaining, but also, it subconsciously reminds them who is in charge. Sometimes I stop, and walk right out the door to look at the weather, and then walk back in again to report on the heavy rain or the snow, or whatever it is. After a particularly poor response to a simple question, I once walked out the side door of the lecture theater, beside the blackboard, walked around and came back in through the rear door, continuing the conversation as soon as I appeared behind them. It caught them off-guard and reinforced the correct answer to the question.

Your students are pinned down, but stopping at half time in a two-hour lecture (Section 3.2.2) helps to address this inequity. They know in advance that they will have time to themselves when they can get up and move, eat a sandwich, go to the toilet, etc., and they look forward to that liberty.

3.3.8 Kindness Matters

Kindness matters.

Story (Pencil-Case Man): Part-way through a large class in a tiered classroom, a young man came into the room, walking right in between me and the students. He was ducking his head down and from side to side, looking under chairs, tables and desks, ignoring me and my students. I stopped talking, and we were all just staring at him. *Nobody* walks into the middle of a big class that is in session! So, I asked politely "May I help you, Sir?" He said, "Yes, I lost my pencil case."

Some instructors would have kicked the young man out at that stage, for his rudeness. I got the impression, however, that he was not 100% *compos mentis*. So, without missing a beat, my comeback to "I lost my pencil case" was to say, "What color is it?," which the students laughed gently at. (They were laughing at me, not him.) He said, "Black." I asked him where he had been sitting in a previous class. He pointed. Then I asked the students to all look around and under their seats, and so on, to see if they could see it. They could not find it. I checked in the drawer under the front desk, telling him what I was doing and that lost property is sometimes there. It was not there either. I told him where the University's lost property office was, and he left, looking slightly forlorn.

I said to the students that a little kindness goes a long way. Like me, I think they could tell that he was not 100% mentally sound. I also mentioned that he demonstrated good goal-driven behavior. That is, he lost his pencil case, and what does he do? He goes to look for it, regardless of interrupting 500+ people in a class in session. I/we could have been unkind to the young man, but I think that my simple demonstration of kindness in assisting him set a good example. It also served as a two-minute break to refresh the students' brains.

Epilogue (Pencil-Case Man): Six weeks after meeting pencil-case man, we conducted a paper-based end-of-semester teaching evaluation in the last 10 minutes of class. During this period, etiquette dictates that the instructor has to leave the room so that the students can fill the forms in and so that the class representative can collect them, without any influence from the instructor. Before leaving, however, I put some preselected gentle music on the loud speakers, and I flipped through a photo gallery to find an odd/amusing image (of the kind that I often show during bottom-of-the-hour breaks). I settled on a very close-up colorful picture of a praying mantis that was standing on its rear legs with both front legs in the air, one to the left, and one to the right, with its head facing the camera. As I was leaving, I noticed that the mantis looked like it had lost something and was perplexed. So, I raised my arms and mimicked its pose for a second, and said, "Aaaah... ...where's my pencil case?" which got a roar of laughter. We were not laughing at the young man, *per se*, but rather at the oddness of the entire situation. I think the laughter helped my teaching evaluations.

In answer to my question "Is there anything unusual that you did with your students that other teachers do not do?" one interviewee wrote, "Yes, find a way to make them laugh. In context this often requires something unusual and unexpected. I believe it made my class more entertaining, but I do not believe it made me a better teacher"

I replied to the above interviewee to disagree with him about laughter not making him a better teacher. I often make jokes or tell funny (both funny ha-ha, and funny peculiar) stories in the classroom. I do it because laughter truly does serve as medicine for bored or tired students.

Former FBI hostage negotiator Chris Voss says that if you can put your opponent in a good mood, by smiling or making them think that you like them, then you have a 31% better chance of success (Voss, 2018); I think that making them laugh is even better than that. Voss also discusses the use of upward and downward inflection in the voice. With hindsight, very few of my own instructors used laughter; 95% of them were the "straight man" (or woman) who never smiled, laughed, or did anything other than cover the material. They were a cheerless bunch. Some of them (especially at MIT and Harvard) made up for it by being blindingly brilliant and nice and/or helpful, but if they had also made us laugh, they would have been even better.

Here is an analogy. I have a big old fireproof safe in my house. I keep old photograph albums and rare books in it; things that simply cannot be replaced after a fire. It is at least 100 years old, and the tumbler mechanism was sticking and had become unreliable. I dismantled the inside of the (six-inch thick!) door to get to the tumbler mechanism (which, incidentally, looked absolutely nothing like what I was expecting). I vacuumed out old rust from inside the door and old dirt and old graphite from inside the brass tumbler mechanism, and I puffed micro-fine greaseless graphite powder into the tumblers. I reassembled everything, and now it works like new! I think that making my students laugh is like puffing graphite powder into the tumblers of my safe; everything clicks into place much more smoothly than it otherwise would. Laughter is an intangible catalyst for classroom learning.

A female colleague told me, however, that she never tells jokes or funny stories in the classroom because she fears that as a woman subject to sexism, doing so means that she will not be taken seriously as a professional. That was an eye-opener to me. I wonder if there are minority groups who feel that because of racism they too cannot tell a joke for fear of not being taken seriously. My gut instinct is, however, that if you teach well, then you will earn your students' respect and you can use humor to change the pace in the classroom and to improve the students' ability to learn/comprehend. If in doubt, perhaps you should save your humor for the second half of the semester, after you have already earned your students' respect.

One interviewee wrote, "I work hard to build a good rapport with my class that also establishes clear lines of respect. That means dressing appropriately, speaking well, respecting everyone in my class and demonstrating that respect in tangible ways that all the class can see, role modelling behaviour that I expect my students to also adhere to."

The move to online learning during the COVID-19 lockdown in 2020 presented challenges.

One interviewee wrote, "Online is tricky, I have no idea what I'm doing. I have no training in online teaching (not that I have any in face-to-face teaching either), but I would say that my particular style is really hard to replicate in an online setting. I like creating a relationship with my students, and it's very hard to do that through a computer."

To build rapport during online learning, I gave many individual students personalized attention that was tailored to their respective needs. For example, I created some mentally-stimulating problems for a talented Czech student who stayed in N.Z. during our lockdown, even when his fellow countrymen went home. A dozen students sent me thankful emails at the end of the semester, including the following one from that Czech student.

Story (COVID Lockdown Email): My student wrote "This semester was not easy for me and nor for the other fellow international students. Most of us had been saving money for several years before we came here, and then we watched our dream semester fall apart.

"In the end, I do not regret going to New Zealand and staying here the whole semester, even though the overall experience was different than I expected.

"You and your teaching saved my semester. I am not exaggerating when I say that you are the best educator and mentor I have ever seen. Your teaching style, knowledge and the time you dedicate to students are unprecedented. Your lectures and problem sets made me think hard and aroused my interest and curiosity. I spent countless evenings pondering various investment topics during quarantine, and I enjoyed all of them."

3.3.9 The Loud-Mouth

We have all had that keen student who sits in the front row and asks five times more questions than anyone else. He or she is usually the first to raise a hand when you pose a question. Sometimes the "loud-mouth" student is very intelligent, and adds to the discourse. Sometimes the loud-mouth student is a little dim, but thinks highly of himself or herself. Sometimes the loud-mouth student seems to be only agreeing with the professor, in a somewhat sycophantic/obsequious fashion.

> "Students from a higher 'power distance' culture may see [an invitation to speak up] as an invitation to indicate agreement and praise their lecturers, regardless of what they really think.[3] Students from some cultures may regard others who continually ask questions as being 'greedy' with lecturers' time. Behavior involving students constantly voicing their own opinion without considering others is regarded as rude and disrespectful in some cultures due to its disruptive effect on group harmony. Students from high 'uncertainty avoidance' cultures (see Footnote 2 on p. 133) may feel intimidated and [be]

---

[3]In high power distance cultures, people expect and accept that power is distributed unequally (Beugelsdijk et al., 2015). Beugelsdijk et al. (2013) rank countries on power distance, putting Taiwan, Pakistan, Indonesia, and India towards the high end (i.e., further from equality), Mexico and Japan in the middle, and N.Z., Canada, Australia, Germany, Norway, and Denmark towards the low end (i.e., closer to equality).

reluctant to speak up for fear of their question being perceived as trivial and stupid" (Tharapos, 2018).

The loud-mouth student in the front row is useful if he or she asks questions that other students do not ask (because they are too shy/humble, are worried about being wrong, or they have not yet figured out that they too have the same question). So, it can be good to let the loud-mouth student *ask* as many unsolicited questions as possible.

When you want students to *answer* questions, however, you may benefit from a wider sample of students answering your questions. So, I often say, "This is a question for students who have not talked to me yet today," or "This is a question only for people wearing green shirts," or "This is a question only for people on the south side of the room [pointing]," or something similar.

I had a professor at MIT who warned us that he would sometimes intentionally look right through students who were monopolizing the answering of questions, and he did exactly that to me on several occasions. It felt odd at first, but after a while it was just fine; I knew he wanted to hear from more people, and so did my classmates!

3.4 Method of Instruction/EDIP

Let me finish this chapter with something different. I veered from interviewing *university* instructors to ask how an instructor of *military* personnel teaches combative techniques to military trainees.

Close-quarters battle (CQB), close-quarters combat (CQC), and military self-defense (MSD) all involve fighting at close range. Geoff "Tank" Todd is a Special Operations CQB Master Chief Instructor with over 30 years' experience in teaching CQB/CQC/MSD. His extraordinary lineage in European military close combat learning and instruction has led to structure and clarity in his "Method of Instruction." He uses the following six steps.

1. **State:** State the technique that is going to be instructed. For example, "We are going to execute a leg stamp."

2. **Explain:** Use words to explain what the technique is and why it is important. For example, "The leg stamp is a primary unarmed means of destroying the integrity of the knee joint and destabilizing and incapacitating an enemy opponent. This leg stamp is executed by..."

3. **Demonstrate:** Demonstrate the technique in

full and at full speed, and then also in parts, as necessary.

4. **Q&A:** Call for questions and provide answers as needed.

5. **Brief:** Give a safety brief (e.g., "You will execute the leg stamp at half speed using half power at first."). Discuss roles that will be played by the trainees (e.g., "Work in pairs, alternate being the enemy party, do 10 repetitions each, and then stop.").

6. **Critique:** Direct the trainees to practice the technique, subject to the brief, and critique only major faults at first.

This Method of Instruction is sometimes called an EDIP approach, standing for Explain, Demonstrate, Imitate and Practice (USMC, 2012). It has evolved over decades in high-stakes disciplines where clarity of instruction and mastery of skills are much more important than in most university subjects; Deficiencies in military training can lead to injuries or death in training or on the battlefield.

As university instructors, we follow many of these same steps in our teaching, and in roughly the same order. So, comparing and contrasting these very disciplined military methods with your own methods may help you to add thoughtful structure and discipline to your university teaching; it certainly helped me.

Rejoice, O Young Man, in Thy Youth
(Ecclesiastes Chap. 11, Ver. 9; KJV)

I tell my final-year students that after my undergraduate study, I never again sat in a room with 100+ people who were the same age as I was. I invite the students to "pause, and look around the room; look at faces, look at the group. Appreciate this moment in time, because you will not be here again."

Chapter 4

Outside the Classroom

Let me discuss several topics that relate to your behavior outside the classroom.

4.1 Work-Work Boundaries

Student engagement is an important part of teaching, but sometimes you need student *disengagement* so that you can focus on research, service, or non-student-facing teaching prep. Disengaging is difficult when teaching large classes, because the deluge of student requests can easily swamp you.

I tried putting a do-not-disturb sign on my office door when I needed to work on a *deeply* mathematical research problem. Even if it was the only sign on my door apart from my name, students would still hammer on my door wanting to talk to me (God save you if you have 500+ students!).

Similarly, some secretarial support staff see my do-not-disturb sign and still knock and then immediately use their master key to open my door and enter if I do not open the door within a few seconds; they think they have a special place in the Department (which they do) and that my do-not-disturb sign does not apply to them (but it does). My Head of Department knocks on my door and calls out that it is him (as if he thinks that *increases* the probability I will open it). Senior administrators come knocking, ignoring any sign, because they think that nothing applies to them.

Most students do not even see the do-not-disturb sign because they pay no attention to detail, and if they do see it, they often ignore it because they never switch off their social media and they assume that you too are "always on." Some folks who respect the sign and do not knock, then pick up the phone and call instead. So, I now have to also turn off my office phone.

The net result is that I am unable to establish a boundary that guarantees that I can have time to concentrate undisturbed for even a short window of time in my University office. This is a significant impediment to working on deep research problems.

I have had greater success with a more specific sign that says, "Please do not disturb until 2PM." In this case, people are more likely to wait, because I give them a definite time when they can come back (as long as that time is not more than about an hour away). Even then, however, they almost always knock early, assuming that five or 10 minutes does not matter (but it often does if there is a conference call or other time-sensitive event). I now compensate by writing a time 10 minutes later than the time that I forecast I will be done.

You could try a "Do not disturb: Zoom meeting in progress" sign. That seems to work fairly well. One of my colleagues got a big bright red octagonal stop sign, like the road signs at intersections in the street, saying, "STOP. DO NOT KNOCK ON THIS DOOR."

My University does not allow me to work from home for more than a couple of days at a time. They do not, however, have any control over where I spend my vacation! So, for the last five years, I have

🔍 taken anywhere from a week to a month of vacation and worked full time on research at a vacation house by myself. The upside is that I got some exceptionally deep and creative research done (accompanied by ocean views). The downside is that I come back from vacation needing a vacation. Instead of getting it, however, I have to walk into the classroom and teach. Having no break shortchanges the students to some extent. This is, however, the best solution I have found to getting deep research completed; If you face the same constraints, be aware, however, of the costs of my creative solution.

4.2 I'll Do It!

My Department offered a first-year course that was voted by the students to be the lowest-rated first-year course in the entire University (out of 129 departments!). That's a problem, because students choose their majors based on their first-year courses. Eventually, the course was redesigned, the previous instructor departed, and I became Department Head. I was very busy, but I assigned myself to teach the first few weeks of the course. Doing so was a low-cost way to monitor directly the instruction of our largest class (and source of majors).

4.3 Oh, the Humanity of it!

I won a teaching award for being one of the top 20 teachers at my University (with 20,000 students and 3,000 instructors). It was one of at least a dozen teaching awards I have been nominated for in my career, but this one was different. Yes, I did a good job in the classroom that semester and I had outstanding teaching evaluations, but that was always true. What made this semester different from the others was the *riot* that took place.

Our University was going to host students from another University, several hundred miles away, for the "Undie 500." This event required that cars costing under NZD500 (USD350) be filled with students and driven from their campus to ours for drunken revelry. One year prior, in August 2006, the Undie 500 had brought with it student mayhem on a medium scale: public drunkenness and the setting of fires in the streets, etc. In August 2007, however, I heard from a friend with a relative in the Police Force that the Police were going to take a *very tough* stance this time, and that they would be out in force to avoid a repeat of the previous year's lawbreaking.

So, during the last class before the event, I

told my students during a bottom-of-the-hour break that the Police would have a heavy presence on campus, and they needed to take care of themselves, stay out of trouble, and watch out for their friends. I reminded them that an arrest record could stop them travelling to the U.S. for 10 years.

On Friday August 24, 2007, 1,200 students arrived at our campus in 150 cars and vans that certainly looked like they cost less than $500 (more cars had set off, but, unsurprisingly, some broke down).[1] That evening, drunken students set more than a dozen fires and 32 people were arrested. On the following evening, they upped the ante, setting more than 70 fires in the streets near the campus; one fire threatened a house.

N.Z. Police are usually unarmed. So, sixty Police officers with riot helmets and batons, and not much else, turned up to face the students. Two-thousand drunken students massed and hurled bottles and verbal abuse at Police, setting fire to vehicles. One student threw a computer at Police. Fire fighters and EMTs were unable to get through to extinguish fires or to assist some students who were injured in a drunken assault. Twelve-foot high

---

[1] All statistics are from the *Otago Daily Times* newspaper of Monday August 27, 2007.

flames threatened overhead power lines. The riot Police moved in with batons to clear the scene so that the emergency personnel could do their jobs. Police made an additional 37 arrests.

The front page of the paper on the following Monday morning showed photographs of a student on the ground with a helmeted Police officer ramming a baton into him, a stand-off between Police and hundreds of students around a fire in the street (with flames 10 feet in the air), and a morning-after picture of the debris-strewn aftermath.

I doubt that any other instructor knew about the upcoming Police action, let alone told the students about it. I think that I won a teaching award that semester because I gave my students an advance warning of the heavy Police behavior that they would face.

It was the *human* aspect of my two-minute heart-to-heart warning that won them over, not my 20 years of preparation, my use of classroom technology, or my outstanding teaching. This was a case of "high touch" trumping "high tech."

One interviewee wrote that she wanted students to feel that they mattered to her. She went on to discuss her thoughtful interactions with students. She said that she arrives five to 10 minutes before the start of class and uses that time to have short one-to-one conversations with students, asking about their extra-curricular activities, aspirations for the future, what's bothering them and what may be hindering their study, etc. She tries to be the last person to leave the classroom, because a surprising number of students will "hang back to clarify or discuss an issue or ask a question that they did not feel comfortable doing in class." She tries to remember their names and the details of their conversations and to use these in subsequent conversations, attempting to elevate the human aspect of teaching the mass of students.

Another wrote, "I also ask the students to prepare interesting topics they would like to talk about in the first or last five minutes of each class. If they volunteer, THEY present a topic that is related to class or finance in general. They really want to be heard or to be recognized. Do you understand what I mean? I am not sure that my words mean what I want them to. I am trying to say that they want me to know that they are there."

Another wrote, "I teach at a private university with a number of wealthy students and have had students who are intimidated because of their background or circumstances. I had to become aware of this and make myself more approachable, particularly outside of the classroom. This meant discussing topics in office hours or after a lecture rather than trying to force participation within the class."

Another wrote, "Try to learn as many names as you can. Students appreciate being an individual. I was once told that I was one of only two faculty who tried to learn names during a student's entire degree program... ...and they really appreciated it." See also Section 2.2.3 about learning and using names.

Another wrote, "I had some great enthusiastic teachers, who put you at ease. They were interesting and generally 'people persons' who were knowledgeable and personable. The human frailty of a people person will normally save the day. With a bit of humour."

I mentioned, in Section 1.1.4, that in the last *Survey of Graduate Student Opinions* that I saw, I was mentioned more often and in greater depth than anyone else in my department. I think that one reason for this is the time I spend helping good students to get good jobs; this practical life-changing service helps win hearts and minds.

I have conducted more than 300 job interviews as the interviewer (as both a finance practitioner and a finance academic), and collected feedback from candidates or interviewers from an additional 500+ finance practitioner interviews. I put this experience to good use by frequently asking to see students' CVs and cover letters, giving copious feedback, conducting mock job interviews, etc. Although this has never been part of my formal job description, I think that helping a good student to get a good job is one of the most valuable and rewarding things I can do with my time. So, I regularly act as a middle-man between students and employers, between employers and the University (e.g., when employers are scheduling recruiting visits), between competing students, and between competing employers.

4.4 Language & Courtesy

When sending emails to first-year students, I usually make them very formal. I start with, say, "Dear Mr. Smith," and when signing off, I always use, "Regards, Prof. Crack." I do that even when the student has addressed their email to me as "Dear Tim," or "Hey Tim"—using the diminutive version of my first name. I want them to think about business communication. Similarly, if I see a cover letter that starts with "Hay Bob" (yes, "hay" instead of "hey") instead of "Dear Mr. Jones," I point out that the banker they are writing to is three times their age and that such an informal approach is likely completely inappropriate.

When a student turns up for an on-campus interview with an investment banker but chooses to wear a T-shirt, jeans, and white tennis shoes, I point out that this is not what was expected. The etiquette may be different in different disciplines, but in a business school I think that modeling this behavior matters.

If you teach any sort of course using symbolic notation, undergraduate students will inevitably come to you and ask that you use the same algebraic notation that other instructors use (e.g., π for inflation, R for a simple rate of interest, σ for standard deviation, z for a complex number, etc.). This request is absolutely ridiculous and not to be entertained for one second. Instructors often use the same notation as the textbook they assign. Different books use different notation. It is impossible to co-ordinate each symbol across instructors, across disciplines, and across years and courses. I politely tell the enquiring student that this is impossible, and that they need to be flexible enough to understand the concepts, whatever the notation.

Looking back over three decades, I have had several colleagues who never let anybody finish a sentence and who were immediately condescending towards anything said to them (ironic given that I sat in on some of their classes, and they were truly awful). When asked questions, they often stop the questioner mid-question and shoot off in the wrong direction, answering the wrong question. (When this happens several times during a job interview, we know that this is not the candidate for us.)

Do not be the person who interacts with students or colleagues in this way; it builds an awful reputation. Instead, listen to questions patiently and do not interrupt the speaker except for points of minor clarification. Ask them to repeat a question or rephrase it if it is not clear. Students (and colleagues) like to be heard.

Questions from your students help you to hone your teaching repertoire and may lead directly to research publications. So, respect that gift by hearing them out.

4.5 Textbooks

I have heard people say that you should not use a textbook because anything in a textbook is already stale. My answer to that short-sighted criticism was to write my own textbook, self-publish it, and to update it each year that I teach using it. For example, when teaching in 2020, my book already had citations to academic literature, practitioner literature, and some events from 2020. During the year, I annotate my text with improvements, and then I edit it and republish it.

There have been many times when a student in my advanced class has complained to my boss or my boss's boss that there is a conflict of interest in my class because I wrote the textbook and workbook that are used in my class, and I sell them to my students. This raises several interesting points.

First, when I was a student in the U.S., roughly half of my instructors used their own textbook without complaint. Nevertheless, my University does not allow an instructor to *require* his/her own book in his/her class; it can, however, be *recommended*.

Second, my books are printed overseas and imported. If it costs, say, \$21.65 to land the book on my desk, then I round the price down to the nearest dollar and charge the students $21. So, the books are sold below cost, with the price difference coming out of my pocket (usually $200–$300 per semester). I know from past experience (and from talking to the University Bookshop) that if students had to pay full price to get my book from the Bookshop, only one-third of them would buy it. Selling my books to students just below cost, however, helps to guarantee that almost all my students have the same edition of the book in their hands. This, in turn, makes my job much easier as a teacher!

Third, I tell the students in advance and through different channels (e.g., in class, by email, on BlackBoard) that I am selling the books below cost to address any possible conflict of interest.

Fourth, even though I addressed the conflict of interest issue by losing money on every copy I sell, my University's policy is still that my textbook cannot be required for my course. So, I list the book only as *recommended*, and I tell the students that "I am not allowed to tell you that this book is *required*," which they laugh at.

Finally, in every case where I saw a student complaining of a conflict of interest, it turned out that the student was also a law student; they are always happy to advocate for their fellow students.

4.6 Influencing Attendance

Something unexpected happened when I started using my own textbook in my advanced class. For 10 years I handed out notes that I had written. The notes were formatted using LaTeX and were broken into chapters. My notes were clearly in the process of being turned into a textbook. The difference between my notes at Year 10 and the textbook they became at Year 11 was little more than an updating and the addition of a cover and binding. Nevertheless, as soon as I started using a book instead of notes, my class attendance dropped suddenly.

Using notes only, in a class of size 120, I usually had 125 students in the room, because a few masters and PhD students would sneak in. When my book came out, however, attendance at my class dropped suddenly to about 100 out of 120 students. Having a book in their hands gave 15% of students the confidence to not come to class. So, be aware of this unintended consequence of putting a cover and a binding on your class notes!

I noticed that attendance was dropping in my big 100-level class. I told my 500+ students that "Each class I teach contains material that is in the mid-term exam and in the final exam. If you miss one class, you likely lose about four percentage points in the mid-term exam. If you score below 40% in the mid-term exam, we do not let you sit the final exam, and you have to pay again to repeat the course. Also, each class I teach contains material that we build upon in other classes later in the semester. So, if you miss a class now, it makes later classes more difficult to understand and it makes it all the more difficult for you to catch up." Class attendance increased immediately, and the effect lasted quite some time.

After teaching a few weeks of another large class, the attendance was so low that I sent out an email saying something like "Class attendance was worrying low today. I discussed this with a colleague. He asked me how long it took me to prepare for today's class. I told him that it took me 25 years to prepare for today's class. I am building upon my experience as a practitioner in the financial markets, my experience as a small business owner, my experience as a trader in the international financial markets, my experience in publishing research in the best journals in my field, and my experience teaching this material for 20+ years. All of this experience appears in the classes I teach. You can work your way through the textbook by yourself, but it is much easier to simply come and sit in my class and have me guide you and your classmates through it." Class attendance jumped dramatically, and then only slowly declined again.

4.7 "Prof. Is that a Mistake?"

"Out of the mouth of babes and sucklings..." (Psalms Chap. 8, Ver. 2; KJV).

I mentioned, in Section 3.2.1, that relatively untalented students sometimes surprise me with exceptional questions, but they are not always interested in the answer when they find out how complex it is. For me, however, these questions are gems.

It is equally valuable when a student tells me that I made a mistake. I investigate such cases thoroughly, because at least one of us has something to learn. If the matter is complex, I may have to tell the student that I need to think about it further, and then get back to the student (and the class) at the next meeting, if possible.

One of my students pointed out an error he thought I had made with a complex topic. After some research, I declared him correct, apologized for my error, included his correction in the next revision of my textbook, and acknowledged him at the front of the book. Soon after publishing the revised edition, however, I realized with a jolt that my original statement was correct after all. So, I revised the book again before using it in class. I left his name in the acknowledgements, even though he was wrong, because I ended up learning the material very deeply as a result of his intervention. The moral of the story is that student criticisms of complex material need to be investigated thoroughly.

Story (Back of the Envelope): I included a question on an assignment that required the students to do some analytical algebra to decide how much, and when, one group of investors needed to invest in order to achieve the same wealth as another group of investors following a slightly different strategy. After a week, two of my best students came to me at half-time in class and told me that the problem could not be solved analytically (some types of problem cannot be, but I had not thought this was one of those). They asked whether they could instead solve it numerically (i.e., getting the computer to walk through the algebra until it found the solution); this was something I had told them explicitly *not* to do. I took the students' word for it that it could not be solved analytically, because they were among my best students. So, when class resumed in five minutes, I apologized and announced that everyone could instead use numerical techniques. I went back to my office after class, however, grabbed a scrap envelope and did the algebra on the back of it in two minutes. The next day, I went back to class, waved the envelope at them and said that the two students who told me it could not be done need a kick up the backside, but that because I had already announced that they could use numerical techniques, I would not reverse my announcement. In Section 8.1, I reiterate that you should always confirm that your assignment/exam questions can be completed before handing them out, which I failed to do in this case (I too deserved a kick up the backside).

4.8 Changing Demography

From 1940 to 2020, the proportion of the adult (aged 25+) U.S. population that has completed four or more years of college increased by a factor of 6.7 for men (from 5.5% to 36.7%) and by a factor of 10.0 for women (from 3.8% to 38.3%) (Statista, 2021).

In the 40 years since I entered university, these U.S. participation statistics have increased by 50% for men, and by 150% for women. U.K. statistics show similar rates of growth in university participation (Bolton, 2012).

These aggressive changes have led to higher academic hurdles for entry to employment and higher expectations by families of participation in university study (and dramatic and worrying increases in the aggregate value of U.S. student debt!).

One side effect of these trends is that I now see a proportion of students of low academic ability who would never have even considered attending university 20 years ago, but who now feel pressured by their families to attend. This familial pressure causes stress. On top of that, some of these students, especially ones from low socio-economic backgrounds, carry debt burdens that compound their stress. Some of these stressed students are dramatically unsuited to being at university and need to be counselled on study habits etc.

One interviewee wrote, "One of the greatest inequalities is comparing my singing performance to that of a trained vocalist, or my differential calculus exam scores to that of a math genius. Encourage students to swim in their own lane at a pace that is beneficial. If they are drowning, help them choose a better major."

Unfortunately, some students need to be counselled out of the university entirely, and directed towards trades, farming, the military, nursing, etc. Some, however, will stick stubbornly to their dream (or their parents' dream) that they complete university, whatever the financial or emotional cost. As such, you will almost certainly find yourself providing counselling well beyond the academic sphere. You are acting *in loco parentis* (Section 3.1.6). So, be sure that you know at least a little about your university's pastoral care policies and resources (student mental health, chaplaincy, etc.), because you will need to direct students to these or similar services beyond your area of expertise.

From a completely different angle, I listen often to the YouTube recordings made by Dave Ramsey (Ramsey, 2021). He has outstanding advice for getting out of debt. He often talks about communicating with your spouse or family member about financial issues (income, expenses, debt, investing, etc.). One piece of advice he has is "To be unclear is to be unkind." This applies equally well to the student-teacher counselling relationship, and for many of the same reasons.

4.9 Any Crazy in the Family?

Every family has some crazy in it. If you go to a big family gathering and look around the table and don't see any crazy, then it must be *you*! The same is true in any class (or, indeed, in any academic department) of more than about 10 persons.

If you are a new teacher, you may be surprised to find that some of your students do not view you as entirely human. They slot you into a category in their head (e.g., this is the person who stands in front of my "102" class). So, they will do a double take if they see you in the supermarket buying breakfast cereal ("Oh, that's so cute!" I heard one student say). They will look surprised if they see you with a child in the office ("Where did you get this child? Should we call the police?") or if they see you with your spouse ("What! He has a wife?")

Your students do not think that you have a life, that you go on vacation, that you can operate power tools, that you can teach three of the other classes they took already that were taught by someone else when they took them, etc. So, when they say crazy stuff to you, like "Oh, I don't suppose you watch television," just go with it. Say, "No, but I saw it in a department store window once," or something like that. Have fun with it; Keep them guessing!

Story (Argentum Vulpes): When I was young and single and had not been a university teacher for long, I was delivering a lecture to a small group. I was looking around, making eye contact with people, and trying to read the room. There was an attractive young woman sitting in the front row whom I had spoken to several times outside of class. She made eye contact, smiled at me, and very clearly mouthed the words "I love you."

She knew that I knew what she had said. I was surprised, but I did not react in any way. I kept on teaching. Out of class later, she came to my office and complained, somewhat teasingly, that I did not pay attention to her comments in class, to which I could only smile very slightly.

In the next class, she made a point of mentioning loudly "When I was in your office yesterday..." when she asked a question. I think she had told her friends what she did and was joking with them at my expense, suggesting loosely that something inappropriate had happened between us in my office.

Fast forward 25 years, and a female student who

told me as I walked by her in the corridor that the other female students thought I was a "silver fox" got a laugh, but no comment. I kept on walking. If in doubt, ignore it and get on with the job. There is no room for any form of flirtatious behavior between teacher and student. (Note also that I never allow a student to close my office door during office hours. If they have something private to discuss, I tell them to do it quietly, but the door stays open!)

4.10   Work-Life Boundaries

Some instructors discuss their personal lives in the classroom, while others never reveal an iota of personal information to their students. Pick a level of disclosure that suits your personality or the course content.

I often disclose my professional background, because I teach in the same area, and it brings credibility to the classroom. For example, when discussing hedge funds and long-short investing, I give the example of having worked with hedge fund managers sitting beside me in my old job, and of subsequently setting up a small long-short hedge fund position in my own brokerage account. On another occasion, we discussed a newly-legislated increase to 10% in the maximum employee contribution rate to the N.Z.-Government-backed retirement savings scheme. I told my students that I had put the sign-up form in front of my son (who was then their age) and I told him "You are signing this!" to increase his contribution rate to 10%. They found it funny, but it served a purpose, beyond making them laugh, because I had taught them that they should contribute at least 10% (and preferably 15%) of pre-tax income each month to their retirement savings scheme in order to build wealth (Crack, 2020a).

You should be cautious about disclosing religious or political beliefs, or where you stand on the liberal–conservative spectrum, lest you be judged harshly in "the thousand-eyed present" (Emerson, 1841, para. 13).

Some instructors give out their home phone number or their mobile/cell phone number. Personally, I would never do this, because I view that as stepping over the boundary between work life and home life. I think these boundaries are important if you wish to establish and maintain a sensible work-life balance, and if you wish to establish and maintain discipline and mutual respect in the classroom.

One interviewee wrote, "I feel that I have to compete with the students' cell phones. I have to be more interesting than Facebook and Instagram in order to get their attention. I give a show. Each lesson. I tell them stories about relevant financial news. I laugh about myself mainly. I also mention my family members. That works for me. I do not try to be their friend and I am really OK with them not loving or liking me. I know that they appreciate me. (My family loves me. It is more than enough for me.)"

Chapter 5

Efficiencies

I discuss teaching efficiencies in many places in this book, especially in the Assignments and Exams chapters (i.e., Chapters 7 and 8, respectively). Let me mention a few other efficiencies here.

5.1 Teach, Conference, Prize, & Publish

I use an unusual analogy to teach my 500+ first-year students about the ease and danger of accumulating credit card debt. The analogy is between excess weight and excess debt, and how easy they are to attain, how difficult they are to lose, and how they tend to come back again later unless you exhibit discipline. A colleague using my teaching slides queried my analogy, because I had left only limited notes about it. I explained the details of the analogy, and we saw an opportunity.

We wrote a short pedagogical working paper about using the analogy in the classroom. It included supportive survey evidence from students before and after their exposure to the analogy. I saw a conference coming up that invited pedagogical papers, and I could see that there were few pedagogical papers on the agenda. So, I thought that we would have a good chance of getting a best pedagogical paper award and the $1,000 tax-free prize that went with it. We submitted it and won, splitting the $1,000 prize! We also published the paper in an ABDC B-rated journal (Crack and Roberts, 2015a). (Our journals are ranked as A*, A, B, C, etc. by the Australian Business Deans Council [ABDC]). After some discussion, we came up with a deeper theoretical follow-up question and wrote a paper that we got published in an ABDC-A rated journal (Crack and Roberts, 2015b).

So, I turned a good teaching idea into a half-dozen lines on my CV (and that is not even counting the excellent teaching evaluations, nominations for teaching awards, and winning of teaching awards for that course). Now I am using it again as an example in this book! The Head Instructor at my gym talks about "economy of movement." This example is an academic-career-oriented equivalent notion.

5.2 You as the TA

I taught an introductory class of 500+ students. I was the sole professor, but I was supported by a team of eight teaching assistants (TAs) who taught about 25 small-group tutorials where the students worked through weekly assignment problems. It was my job to pick the TAs, meet with them weekly, and manage their workloads, etc. I wanted to stay in touch with student understanding of the weekly assignment problems, so, I assigned myself as a tutor in one of the weekly tutorials. This was a foolish and inefficient beginner's mistake.

The problem was that on an almost weekly basis, one of my many TAs would call in sick or have a job interview, etc. Then I would have to scout around to find another TA to replace him or her. It was an inefficient waste of time and effort. I learned from my mistake, and I achieved the same goal (to stay in touch with student understanding of the weekly assignments) much more efficiently in the following semester: Instead of assigning myself as a tutor, I assigned myself to be the person who steps in when a TA was going to be absent. That way, I saw a different group of students each week, I got the same exposure to student understanding of the assignment problems, and I saved myself the trouble of running around trying to find replacement TAs when one called in sick. There was never a scheduling conflict, because tutorials never overlapped with each other or with lectures.

5.3   RAs Galore

Your time is valuable. If the university gives you 100+ advanced undergraduate students, then use them as research assistants (RAs)! If you have some interest in a particular topic, and you want to add a page or two to your notes or to a textbook about this topic, or you are thinking about a research project along those lines, then set some part of it as an assignment question. Send the 100+ students off to dig out information and references, or to answer some basic question. This is a much more efficient use of your time than *you* doing that digging work. What they lack in training, they make up for in sheer numbers. Be aware, however, that sometimes every student misses a vital citation or gets the answer to your question wrong. If that happens, consider asking them to do it again!

See, however, a contrary story in Section 11.7, where Prof. Plum took this way too far when exploiting a graduate student!

5.4 TAs Galore

I never hand out suggested solutions to a complex assignment until after all my grading is complete. There are two reasons for this. First, I do not want to include a bad answer in my solutions that I do not discover to be bad until I grade my best students' assignments. Second, it is because I use the students' solutions to help write my own solutions! It is a tremendous efficiency.

As I am grading, I have a solutions document open on my PC. It starts as a nearly-empty shell with a few simple solutions in it. As I grade, however, I add anything to my solutions that the students say that is particularly noteworthy (either good or bad). My solution document grows as I grade, and by the time I am done grading, it contains most of the material I need to give out alongside the graded assignments. I note down exactly where I awarded points, and I make pointed comments to address common misunderstandings I saw. Again, it is a numbers game: In a class of 100+ students, there are usually one or two students who make exceptional comments that I can borrow. I disclose to the class that I have borrowed some of the best student answers that I saw.

5.5 Simplified ID Numbers

My students have University ID numbers that are usually seven digits long. If they put these numbers on their assignments/exams, and then I have to scan my spreadsheet for that number to enter their grade, it is woefully inefficient. My brain is not programmed for picking out the correct seven-digit number from a list of similar looking seven-digit numbers. You can rank the class list in the spreadsheet, sorting on student ID number, but you are still searching among seven-digit numbers. Sorting on names is better, but still problematic, because names are often presented in different forms, and many names are the same or similar to each other.

My solution is to wait until all the students are signed into the course, and to then assign numbers from 1 to 200 (or whatever the count of students is). Then, I put a box on the front of their assignments or exams that has room for their "FINC302 Student Number," in addition to a space for their official student ID number. Then, when I am entering grades, it is three times faster, and much less of a strain, to find students' names in the spreadsheet based on the low numbers I assigned.

I am saving both time and critical thinking efforts, each of which are better spent on research projects. Also, because I am assigning the numbers, I can make the order of them the same as the native ordering of their names in the system (usually alphabetical by surname), unlike the official student ID numbers, which are not related to names.

I also use the mathematics of *order statistics* with these numbers, to assign computer terminal time for group work. For example, in groups of five students, in a class of 150, I say something like this: "To manage demand for the Bloomberg Terminal, please note the *lowest* 'FINC302 Student Number' in your group. If it is in the range 1–20, then do this assignment question during the first week that it is in your hands; if it is in the range 21–150, then do it in the second week." Given how order statistics work, that odd-looking split usually works out fine.

5.6 Email from Students

In my academic Discipline, the first-year classes might be 1,100 students (half per semester), the second-year classes might be 200 students, the third-year classes might be 120 students, and the fourth-year (postgraduate in N.Z.) classes might be only 25 students. (Your discipline may experience a scaling up or down of these numbers, but retain roughly the same relative sizes.)

An endogeneity problem with teaching the largest classes is that it is these very students who are the greenest about email etiquette. So, you must *train* these students, or their "perfect storm" of numbers and ignorance will swamp your inbox with poorly-conceived emails.

Let me give several pieces of advice to improve the efficiency with which you handle student emails, to improve the "answerability" of student emails, and to reduce the likelihood that you are overrun by hordes to students wanting unnecessary face-to-face meetings. Each of these pieces of email-related advice is something whose contagion will help your colleagues who face the same students. See also Section 4.4 regarding email etiquette.

First, students like to email me questions before

an exam. In a class of 500+ students this can mean a steady flow of emails arriving for a solid week. Replying *quickly* to these emails in the days leading up to an exam can help to prevent the build up of a backlog of unanswered emails. To achieve this end, I like to push the students toward sending me emails that I can reply to quickly and efficiently in the small windows of time between other jobs.

Unfortunately, some students are in the habit of noting down questions as they are studying, and they send me an email only when they get to the end of their study material, by which time they have accumulated a large count of questions. By that time, however, the exam is near, and I am busy grading their last assignment, talking to other students in extra office hours, or attending the extra meetings scheduled by the admin boffins (who foolishly assume that because classes are over, this is a good time to suddenly squeeze in lots of meetings and seminars).

So, I tell my students clearly that if I see two emails from students waiting for a reply, and Matthew's email has a list of 10 questions, but Mark's email has only one question, then I will reply to Mark first, because I can do that in the two minutes I have spare between meetings or between other tasks. It may, however, be some time before I can squeeze in a reply to Matthew's 10 questions. If a new email pops up from Luke with only one question, then I will take a minute to reply to Luke, but now I am out of time again and off to another meeting. If I get back from the meeting and I see an email from John with only one question, then I will reply to John, and Matthew still has to wait because now I have a queue of people for office hours.

I tell the students that if they all wait and accumulate long lists of questions just before the exam, then this creates a possibly unanswerable logjam of emails, and anyone with many questions may have to wait until *after* the exam to get a reply! That gets their attention, and leads to a more manageable workflow. They can understand the logic of this example, and they adapt to it and send me shorter emails. (Another benefit of this approach is that if your PC/email crashes, losing the email you are typing, it is better that this happens on a two-minute typed response than a 30-minute typed response.) See also Section 10.5.

Second, I tell the students the following story, before translating it to their direct circumstances. When I started work at my new job, I got a calm voicemail from my boss saying, "I need to speak to you urgently. My phone number is..." I tried telephoning her immediately, without success. I did not leave a message, because what message could I leave? (There was no point leaving her my phone number, because she already had that to call me in the first place, and I did not know what else she needed from me.) I tried sending an email, with no response. I tried telephoning again. I spent two hours, non-stop, trying to contact my boss to find out what the emergency was. Eventually I got hold of her and she said calmly, "Oh, I just want to know if you and your wife can come over for dinner on Saturday?" *Well, how the hell should I know?!* Then I had to call my busy wife, several times, to find out whether she was free or not. She was not. I called my boss back and left a polite "No, thank you."

After telling my students this story, I told them what should have happened. My boss was focused only on herself and not thinking at all about the *recipient* of her message. My boss should have left me a message saying what her question was. If her voicemail had said, "Can you and your wife come over for dinner on Saturday?," then I would have known it was not a dire emergency, and I could have left a voicemail for my wife to respond to. Then I could have left a voicemail message for my boss, politely declining. That would have taken less than five minutes' effort. Instead, I wasted more than two hours of my life because of the self-centered, thoughtless and un-businesslike message from my boss.

I tell my students that I get similarly thoughtless and un-businesslike emails from students all the time; it is ignorance for the most part. For example, they send an email to ask, "Can I ask you a question?" *What do they think my job is?!* Of course they can ask me a question! That's why my email address is in the syllabus and online and why I invite email questions in class. I tell them that they must not behave this way in the workplace once they graduate. They need to think one step ahead and anticipate what options the recipient of the message faces. If the recipient can answer the question, which is likely, then by not including the question, you force them to ask you what the question is, and then you have to reply with the question, and then they have to reply with the answer. What a circus!

I tell them that "Time is money, and who are you to be forcing your boss to get information from you that you should have supplied in the first place? That creates an awful impression." They risk getting a response that says, "If you had included your question in your email, then I would be responding to it right now. I have a long meeting starting in five minutes, and I cannot now respond until after the weekend." Instead, I tell the students to always include their question in their email message so that the recipient can better judge the urgency of the question (as part of the constant *triage* process that any academic or business person takes part in). The recipient can then better manage their time so as to squeeze in a reply as quickly as possible between other jobs.

Third, for the big first-year classes, no matter what you tell your students in the syllabus or on Day 1, many of the green students think that to ask a question, they must make an appointment to see you face to face. Unfortunately, my green first year students sit in a class with 500+ peers! If they all get face-to-face meetings, I will never get any research done. Nevertheless, I often get emails from students saying, "Can I come to see you outside of office hours to ask a question?" The sad simple truth is that you must never say, "Yes" immediately. The reason is that nine times out of 10, when a first-year student thinks that they need an appointment to see you in person, they simply don't know that their one-line question can be handled effectively by email (and efficiently by you, in a two-minute gap between other jobs). If my student's question needs a hand-drawn diagram of explanation, that's fine. I can draw it, hand the drawing to my secretary, and ask him to scan it to pdf and email it to the student, while I walk off to yet another meeting.

Again, the moral of the story is that in large classes you must train your students to always include their question in their email. If not, and you automatically answer, "Yes" to these meeting requests, then you risk being overrun by unnecessary short meetings with students. It takes time to schedule each of those meetings, and when they are sprinkled throughout each and every day, they disrupt your ability to get any sizable stretch of uninterrupted time to do research. As the character of "Sgt. Barnes" says in the movie *Platoon*, "I got no fight with any man who does what he's told, but when he don't, the machine breaks down. And when the machine breaks down, we break down." In other words, if your position is overrun by hordes of students, it's time to fly the flag upside down, because you can no longer do your job.

Fourth, and less importantly, I often used to get emails from students saying, "Can I come to see you during your office hours?" A simple "Yes," is fine, but you can head off most of these requests by announcing clearly on Day 1 that "You do not need to send me an email or telephone me to ask whether you can attend office hours. Please just turn up and come on in!" See also Chapter 10 about office hours.

Finally, give the foregoing advice to your students repeatedly, not just during their first week.

5.7 Anticipate Your Book

The first time you teach a course, you may use the textbook that the previous instructor used. As you get deeper into the topic, however, you begin to notice that book's deficiencies. So, you start collecting your own resource material, writing your own notes, exercises, and examples, etc., to augment that book. After a few years, your notes start to look like a book. Pretty soon they are a book!

I turned my class notes into a book in three different courses. If you do not do so, then you are failing to exploit an opportunity. Without a book, once you leave that course behind, what do you have to show for it, apart from a record of high teaching evaluations? If you turn it into a book, however, and revise it every two or three years, then you have a permanent record of the efforts you put in, and you are also diversifying your streams of income.

So, when you start creating additional material, use software (like LaTeX) that allows you to make your notes look like sections and chapters of a book. Start with that goal, or at least allowing for that goal. Then the process of transforming your material into a book is made much easier.

I talked about passion in Section 3.3.1. After teaching the same class 10 times, the balance between the two meanings of the word passion (i.e., *that which must be endured* and *consuming emotion*, respectively) can tilt away from the latter and toward the former. Creating a book, however, gives you something to polish and republish. It can rekindle your emotive curiosity about the topic because each new class of students asks questions that lead you to expand or polish some section of your book. At the same time, changes in the world force you to revise your book. Creating a book is therefore kind of like having grandchildren to play with after your children grow up. I love using class experiences to annotate my textbook, knowing that when the semester is over, I get to revise and republish an improved edition.

Note, however, that my University (a State

school) places little or no value on the books I write (including this one!). In terms of writing, they care only about research papers published in peer-reviewed journals, because these bring research funding from the government. It does not matter that only 1,000 people might read one of my research papers, whereas 10,000 or 50,000+ people might read one of my books.

Nevertheless, I view my books as one more outlet for my teaching efforts. If I spend 10 years in the classroom and write my own notes, then it takes little effort to turn those notes into a book. Of course, care must be taken from Day 1 that I am not breaching someone else's copyright. That is, you need to be aware as you go along that if you use material from somewhere else, then it must be fair usage under copyright law (and correctly referenced/disclosed as such), or you must seek copyright permission (which sometimes requires a fee, and sometimes does not).

Finally, after several years of publishing eBooks on `www.Amazon.com`, I wrote Crack (2020b) to help make the steps much easier for self-publishing authors. I now consult this book each time I publish an eBook; you may find it similarly useful when you publish your first eBook.

Chapter 6

Admin Boffins

A "boffin" is a person engaged in research or scientific investigations in some egg-headed arcane area. An "admin boffin" is an administrator at the university who is intent on poking their stuck-up, stickybeak, toffee-nose into teaching matters, and collecting teaching-related data. There is an old saying: "He who can, does. He who cannot, teaches" (Shaw, 1903), with the follow-up, usually attributed to H.L. Mencken, "Those who cannot teach, administrate; and, those who cannot administrate go into politics." Because they are one step removed from your teaching, admin boffins often have a narrow, laserlike, value-destroying focus.

You may be blessed with the perfect boss, but academic bosses change often. You may soon face a meddling micro-manager who knows less about your area of expertise and how to teach it than you do. The longer you are an academic, the more of these value-destroying bosses you will see. They typically do not last long, and may soon be replaced by someone who is similarly bad, just along a different dimension.

If you are doing an excellent job but your boss changes what you do, then this may destroy value for your students, your career, your department, and your university. If, however, you have built up a long record of excellent teaching evaluations and have a string of teaching awards under your belt, then this history should act as something of a buffer or defense against irrational requests from admin boffins. Some stories follow.

6.1 Student Complaints

Paraphrasing Abbadie (1684), you can please some of the people all the time, and all of the people some of the time, but you cannot please all of the people all of the time. Even if you are doing an unambiguously excellent job in the classroom, there will always be a small group, maybe 2% of students, who complain about something you are doing. They are often the less-skilled, lazy, or entitled students (or all three!). The other 98% of students may be perfectly happy, but these 2% will raise a stink with your department chair/head. However, you must never confuse a student-centered approach (Section 1.1.4) with thinking that you need to change what you do in response to every student complaint or criticism! Your boss will come to you and say, "What are you going to do about this?!" You have to have the guts to calmly say, "Nothing whatsoever," and to then argue calmly why doing nothing is the right thing to do. (See, for example, the Excel-based example given in Section 3.2.8.)

Inexperienced department chairs/heads, especially lower-ranked ones lacking in self-confidence, think that *something* has to be done when students complain, but they are often wrong. (The same thing happens in the financial markets: If you are a long-term investor, often the best thing to do in the face of volatile news is *nothing*.) Older more experienced chairs/heads will deflect the student and not even bring the complaint to you. If, however, you have a new boss who lacks confidence and is trying to impress his/her boss, then they may engage in destructive micromanagement.

Managing your boss has always been important (e.g., Gabarro and Kotter, 1980), but managing a micromanaging boss is particularly troublesome (e.g., Financial Samurai, 2020). The older and more entrenched you are, the more likely it is that you can stand your ground against a micromanaging boss.

Let me give a few example complaints plus typical responses for my boss (in square brackets).

- "I hate Prof. Crack's course because I have to come to class to find out what is in the course." [I add value in the classroom. Students come to class to see explanations and emphasis. If other instructors are not adding value in the classroom, then they are not doing their jobs.]

- "This material is too difficult." [I taught this course exactly the same way with great success for 15 years; This student has not been coming to class, refuses to come to office hours, and never emails me any questions.]

- "I enjoyed the first part of the course, but now that we are discussing calculus, I am not enjoying it any more." [It's a university, not a seaside resort; The students are not meant to enjoy all of it; Some of it is *hard work*, including this part.

The student should come to my office hours or email questions to me.]

- "I cannot understand this numerical optimization. The professor needs to find a YouTube video on the topic." [There are no YouTube videos on this; It is a proprietary investment practitioner technique that nobody is teaching online; See the step-by-step instructions I gave; if the student is stuck on one step, then they should ask me about it in class, during office hours, or via email.]

- "He expected us to memorize numerical facts; A course should not be about memorization, but about understanding." [A few numerical facts are so important that they *do* have to be memorized. For example, you need to know the typical range of dividend yields or P/E ratios for stocks and the likelihood that the broad stock market rises on any random day. These are key building blocks in the foundation for understanding how markets behave and how investors should behave in those markets.]

I am faced with constant calls from students to dumb down my course material. I have resisted the pressure for the most part, but a reduction in difficulty has been necessary because of declining average skills in the pool of incoming students; see also Section 4.8. I would, however, rather teach it better than reduce the level of difficulty. There is nothing wrong with having challenging material in your class, and getting student complaints because of it, as long as you understand it well, can teach it clearly, and you offer appropriate support.

You do, however, have to be realistic about the depth of what you make examinable in your class. If I were teaching a physics class, I doubt that any students would complain about the mathematical difficulty of my material and I doubt that my head of department would entertain these complaints.

Many business students are, however, woefully innumerate. So, they need good physical examples, illustrative spreadsheets that they can play with, and simple intuition, etc. The students gain a sense of satisfaction and achievement (and they feel that they got value for money) if you set them a mountain to scale, but you offer them the right equipment and advice, and guide them on the path to success.

Finally, note that mismatches in preferred sensory learning style (Section 1.1.6) and method of instruction can lead to misplaced/inappropriate complaints from students (Willingham, Hughes, and Dobolyi, 2015, p. 268, col. 2).

6.2 Senseless Boffinry

A former student of mine was enrolled in a final-year class taught by one of my colleagues. The student came to speak to me a week before her final exam. It was the easiest class we offered at that level, but she was having personal issues that were confounding her study. In my 30 years of teaching up to that point, I had never seen a student so nervous/distraught.

Unlike when I was a student and a professor in the U.S., the final exams at my N.Z. University are administered centrally by the University boffins. So, instructors have no presence in or control over the final examination room at all. Given the student's unusual distress, I took the unusual step of contacting the central administrators and asking them to put the student in a separate room by herself for her final exam.

Assigning a separate exam room is something done regularly for students with disabilities and for those who are adversely affected by the presence of other people. I told the admin boffins that in 30 years of teaching, I had never seen a student this distraught, and that I had never before asked for such special consideration for a student. I told them that I feared that she would have a health event that would disrupt the entire exam room if she was in a room with the other 100+ students in her class. The administrators refused my request. I appealed, and they refused again.

On the afternoon of her final exam, I heard rumors that there had been some sort of disruptive event in that final exam. I guessed immediately that it was my former student. It took several hours before reliable news came back to me, from another of my former students. My distraught former student had vomited, passed out, hit the floor and stayed down. Students around her came to her aid. The entire room was disrupted and distracted. Emergency services personnel were called, etc. Cleaners must have come too. The students who came to her aid appealed for special consideration, both because of the time they spent aiding her, and the distress they felt because of witnessing her health crisis.

The majority of these problems could have been avoided if the administration of the exam had not been centralized, or if the administrators had had more trust in the frontline teachers. The basic problem is that once administrators insinuate themselves into the teaching process, they break the informed bond/rapport between instructors and students (that we spend so much time cultivating!). The moral of the story is that, wherever possible, you should resist any moves to put admin boffins 🔑 between you and your students.

Epilogue (Whiteboards): I mentioned, in Section 3.2.5, that my University does not supply wide-tipped marker pens for the whiteboards in the biggest auditorium on campus, and that I had to import them at my own expense in order to exploit the wonderful resource of a full wall of whiteboards at the front of this biggest classroom. The whiteboards proved so unpopular in the big auditorium, however, that the University removed all but one of the eight or so whiteboards that I had used so successfully. This was driven, I think, by the admin boffins who refused to supply the correct pens for them. A remaining board now sits over to one side; you have to slide it into place on rails if you need it. Given that it makes sense to write only in large font with wide-tipped pens in this room, however, having only one board is almost useless, because you run out of space so quickly.

The students now face an industrial-looking bare wall at the front of the largest room, where once they saw a wall of whiteboards. I complained that the boffins could at least have left the boards there for instructors who *do* use them, but to no avail. In this regard, Swift famously wrote, "Reasoning will never make a man correct an ill opinion, which by reasoning he never acquired" (Swift, 1721, p. 27). Let me paraphrase this as "It is pointless to attempt to use logic and reason to change a man's mind when he made up his mind already *without* the use of logic or reason."

My University introduced new "core" courses that all students in the Business School have to include in their degree. I was responsible for 99% of the new finance course, while professors in other departments built courses for accounting, economics, management, marketing, information systems, etc.

Over three or four semesters, the admin boffins collected data on the new core courses. They gave a presentation to each department with bar charts showing pass rates over the multiple semesters. In every course except mine, the bar charts showed pass rates trending strongly up or strongly down over subsequent semesters as the courses got "bedded in." For my course, however, the bar chart was absolutely dead level, showing no change in pass rates over successive semesters. That was because I took the Deming approach (Section 1.1.1), and I built quality into the course from Day 1. The difference in the bar charts was really striking!

The admin boffins complained about the significant trends in pass rates and how bad/inconsistent that was, but they said not one word about the consistent pass rates in the class I had created. They never sought me out to ask how I had created what they said that they wanted.[1] This is a poorly implemented case of "management by exception." The bottom line is that there was no focus on creating or delivering a quality product. Instead, the boffins were trying to *inspect quality into the product.*

As mentioned, in Section 1.1.3, a prerequisite for a teacher to be outstanding is that they act differently from other teachers. When I taught our big first-year class, I knew that many of my students were green first-years, so I added information throughout the course syllabus to help the inexperienced students who were new to the University. Many of these additions were to the part of the syllabus that dealt with administration and study

---

[1]This reminds me of the WWII allied bomber pilots returning to England, their airplanes riddled with bullet holes and flak damage. The military boffins collected data on the areas of most damage and suggested that *these* areas needed to be reinforced on other airplanes (Wallis, 1980). I hope that you can see why this is the wrong conclusion!

success, rather than with course content, *per se.*

One day, an admin boffin declared, however, that although I could keep the part of my syllabus that described course content, they wanted a single document common to all core courses (required of all business majors) to cover all *administrative* content. The only reason given was that they thought it would be nice for the students if that part of the course syllabi "looked the same" for each course.

I argued that making things the same was not a good reason, or indeed a reason at all, and that I added value by including helpful comments that they planned to remove. They purposely did not distribute an agenda before the meeting where this was discussed. So, although I attended the meeting and I argued that I added value with comments in that part of my syllabus, I had not brought it with me to show them because no agenda had been circulated to suggest that I needed to. I left the meeting to walk to my office to get my course syllabus, but by the time I got back, five minutes later, the meeting was over, the last person was walking out of the door, the change was implemented, and more value was destroyed by senseless boffinry.

To make things look the same is rarely a good reason for anything. Would we declare that we will hire only white men aged in their 50s because we think it would be nice for the students if their instructors all look the same? Of course not! Doing this with the course syllabi was a "foolish consistency" (to quote Emerson [1841, para. 14], again). So, the next time you are invited to an agenda-less meeting of any size, insist on an agenda, and the next time someone suggests a foolish consistency that destroys value, quote Emerson.

I mentioned, in Section 2.2.3, that you should take care scheduling big assignments or exams near weekends and semester ends. In similar vein, be sure to tell your admin boffins not to schedule research seminars on the Friday before a new semester starts or during the first week of classes. It is too disruptive to your last-minute teaching prep.

6.3 Value-Destroying Policy

Admin boffins are often out of touch with those at the tip of the spear. So, they unintentionally create value-destroying policy. Let me give an example concerning anti-cheating policy.

Most academics are expected to create and publish original research. Good research gets you promoted much more quickly than good teaching does, and it also makes you more mobile.

> One interviewee wrote, "As teachers are re-
> warded for academic research and not teaching,
> a focus on teaching will undoubtedly come a sad
> second. That is a teaching reality. You have to
> love teaching to do a great job of it."

At one time, however, the admin boffins in my Department adopted a Policy that old exam or assignment questions could not be re-used within three
years of being used previously, and if they were re-
used subsequently, they must have new numbers in
them. The idea was that this Policy would reduce
cheating by students. In fact, this Policy was disrespectful of faculty and destroyed value for each
academic, for the Department as a whole, for the
Business School, and for the University.

If academics had unlimited time, this Policy
would be fine, but our time is heavily constrained,
and these constraints are binding. For example, many faculty members already work such long
hours that they miss children's birthday parties,
children's sporting events, family dinners, parent-
teacher meetings, etc. If you demand that faculty
spend more time creating *original assessment*, when
time constraints are binding, then something else

has to give. It may be less time spent creating *original research*. It may be a reduction in sleep for already sleep-deprived faculty, or even less time spent with families. Each of these outcomes destroys morale and ultimately destroys value. It is a case of not seeing the forest for the trees.

Instead, an anti-cheating Policy should use *intelligent design* to address cheating. The academics should sit down and collect intelligent anti-cheating assessment-design ideas from all instructors, and then deploy those techniques, rather than blindly taxing the time of every academic and destroying value. The Policy described was akin to a drunk who loses his keys when crossing a farmer's field but searches for them under a lamppost in the street, because that is where the light is. That is, the Policy targeted something misleadingly obvious, rather than getting to the heart of the matter.

Let me give one example of intelligent anti-cheating assessment design (see also Section 8.7 regarding online exams). My final exams are "embargoed." That is, the exam is printed on colored paper to make it stand out to the invigilators (recall that I am not allowed to attend my own final exam), and no student may leave the exam room with it. (They may view it in my office later if they wish.) Then, the following year, I re-use those final exam questions in my mid-term exam, with only a low, say 10%, weight in the overall assessment. This minimizes the impact of any possible information leakage. (Section 8.3 explains why a selection of these mid-term questions also get re-used in that year's final exam.) The year after that, I take those mid-term exam questions, now firmly in the public domain because my mid-term exams are not embargoed, and I put them into a workbook that my students can buy below cost from me. It is also for sale on www.Amazon.com as a test bank for other instructors (Crack, 2021a). So, one exam question gets used three or four times at the University and once outside the University, over a three-year period. This intelligent and efficient use (and re-use) of original assessment creates more time for original research, while reducing opportunities to cheat.

Let me give a further example of the value destruction associated with this type of Policy. I give assignments to my students using the *Bloomberg Professional Service* (a licensed computer terminal used by investment professionals to get instant real-time access to data from every financial market in the world, analytics, news, etc.).

One *Bloomberg* task I set uses exactly the same

assignment questions every year. I ask the students to use stock market investing rules based on Graham (2006 [1949, 1973]), a book that billionaire Warren Buffett describes as "By far the best book on investing ever written" (Graham, 2006 [1949, 1973], front cover). This exercise whittles the list of 75,000+ stocks available globally to a shortlist of about 10 "value stocks." The students must then pick one of the shortlisted stocks and give a sales pitch for it based on the screening techniques from Graham (2006 [1949, 1973]).

This exercise is very valuable because, not only do the students learn about the techniques in Graham (2006 [1949, 1973]), but the implementation using the *Bloomberg Professional Service* can easily be tweaked to implement *competing* investment criteria (e.g., growth investing; environment, social and governance [ESG] investing; and, etc.).

The *Bloomberg Professional Service* uses a native programming language typed into the terminal, and not easily copied by any means. At the end of each semester, I delete all student code from the *Bloomberg Professional Service*. So, code from one semester's students cannot easily be passed to students in another semester. Also, with the ever-changing financial markets, even if students use exactly the same code from one year to the next (and they do not), the shortlist of stocks and the associated stock pitch typically changes. So, this exercise uses intelligent design to thwart cheats. Nevertheless, it breached our Policy and I stopped using it the year that the Policy was enacted. This action destroyed value for our students because they lost both hands-on exposure to a great trading strategy and education in the use of an applied practitioner tool. A complaint from a postgraduate instructor that students coming out of my course did not have data handling skills prompted me to starting using it again, contrary to the Policy.

The last I heard was that this ill-thought-out Policy was followed for a short period of time, given lip service after that, and then routinely ignored. So, when establishing policy in your own department, be on the lookout for value-destroying ideas.

Chapter 7

Assignments

One interviewee wrote, "The design of assessments is important for giving students an idea of what you find important. Assignments should be practice for exams. If an important professional skill (e.g., Excel or the *Bloomberg Professional Service*) is in an assignment, but not on the final exam, let them know why."

7.1 Survey Instruments

The assignments we create for our students are really just *survey instruments*. Like any survey, our assignments must be designed carefully, so that we collect information that allows us to meaningfully assess and distinguish between our students' abilities. Careful design, however, takes time and effort, and mistakes are easy to make.

Careful design of assignments is not just concerned with academic content. We are also required to manage the collection of the grade data and the production of suggested solutions, etc. So, careful design should anticipate these needs. As such, my advice here is mostly mechanical, based on intelligent design that produces meaningful assessments, clear rankings, student satisfaction, efficiencies where possible, and good data handling protocols.

7.2 Creation

Part of your job is to create assessments that separate the pack. You need to raise enough hurdles to distinguish between student achievement levels, rank students and assign grades.

When I give assignments in my final-year class, I find it very effective to include an easy question, a medium-difficulty question, and a very difficult question (each of which typically contain multiple sub-questions). This approach almost invariably produces a nice separation between students' grades and a bell-shaped distribution with clearly exceptional students, a bunch in the middle, and then the clearly untalented/lazy students. I usually put the questions in the assignment in order of difficulty, so that students are eased into the work.

With my difficult assignment questions, I purposely push the students beyond the point where they can do the assignments without my help. (Partly to prepare them for the same experience in the workforce.) However, I always stand ready to assist with all problems that arise. If I did not stand ready to assist, my classes would be a train wreck with many complaints. Standing ready to help with difficult applied problems means, however, that the students are able to complete very challenging problems, gaining a real sense of satisfaction. This boosts their confidence in themselves and often gives them an extra line to put on their CV, describing the skills they gained.

Sometimes I make up an assignment that is simply too long. I want, however, to expose the students to all the material and I want all the content to be examinable. So, I leave all the questions there, but I give the students a *choice*. For example, I say, "You have a CHOICE between Q1A or Q1B,"

and "You have a CHOICE between Q2A or Q2B."
Then the students feel happy both because they see
a long-looking assignment that turns out to not be
so long in practice, and because they get to choose
which questions to answer. They really like having
that element of self-determination/empowerment in
their question selection.

Story (Invest Early and Invest Often):
In a heavily quantitative course, I subjected the
students to so much quantitative material that
they needed a change of gears. So, I asked
them to create some advertising copy to sell a
government-backed retirement savings scheme
to people their age. They had to create a single-
page (A4 or $8\frac{1}{2} \times 11$) black-and-white poster
that grabbed the eye and gave brief, but sound,
financial motivations to invest in the scheme.

The students welcomed the change of gears
and did an outstanding job. The half-dozen
best posters were copied onto colored paper
and posted around campus, with the authors'
names appearing in small font in one corner.
The work was artistically creative and it may
have helped some young investors. Distributing
the best work gave the students well-deserved
public recognition of their efforts.

Story (*plus ça change, plus c'est la même chose*[1]): Fischer S. Black and Robert C. Merton are famous in my Discipline for work in the late 1960s and early 1970s that subsequently enabled Merton (and Black's co-author Myron S. Scholes) to win the Nobel Prize. (Years later, my shared office as a PhD student at MIT was still referred to as "Fischer Black's old office," such was his lasting fame.)

I was told that when Black and Merton were instructors at MIT in the mid- to late-1970s, Black would ask his students the same questions each year, but the answers were always different. Merton, however, would ask his students different questions each year, but the answers were always the same!

That is, their science was advancing so quickly at that time that Black's fundamental questions had new and better answers each year, whereas Merton's approach, applying fundamental principles, did not change from year to year. You can think of these as two competing approaches to setting assignment/exam questions.

---

[1] An aphorism/epigram that is often translated from French as "The more things change, the more they stay the same," from Karr (1849).

7.3 Roll the Die!

I wanted to instill in my students a mistrust of the database system they were using to download financial data for an assignment. They needed to know that systems go down, that the data they see today might not be there tomorrow, and that it matters if you are working to a deadline. They needed to acquire a sense of urgency in data acquisition!

So, I showed them a big yellow die with one of "yes," "no" and "maybe" appearing on each of the six faces. I told them that every day the assignment was in their hands, if the database was up, I would ask myself the question "Should I call IT and ask them to pull the plug on the database?" and I would roll the die to find the answer. I wanted them to understand that a system crash was in the hands of the Gods (not in my hands, I was only rolling the die, not choosing the *outcome*). On days when the database was down, I would ask myself "Should I call IT and ask them to plug the database back in?" and roll the die again.

So, it could easily happen that 72 hours before their work was due, the plug would be pulled on the database, never to be reconnected. Welcome to working with data and systems in the real world! I did call IT several times, and it did inconvenience some students, but none complained; it was a creative opportunity for lifelong learning.

7.4 Coversheets

During the last 10 years of my teaching, I have always used a standardized coversheet for assignments. Students have to enter their names, their class ID number (this is not their student ID number; see discussion in Section 5.5), and a contact email address for their chosen "group leader." There is designated space to one side for me to enter a column of scores and a total score. (This coversheet is available at `www.KelleySchool.com`.)

My coversheet has multiple benefits. First, and most importantly, when it is time for me to transfer their grades from their coversheet to my spreadsheet, the student names, student numbers, and grades are always to be found in *exactly the same place* on the first page of every assignment. This simplifies and significantly reduces the searching done by my tired eyes late at night. Second, I often need to regrade a question on all assignments before they are handed back to the students. This is usually a case of me being more generous after having graded most of the assignments. So, this requires that I find and regrade every assignment that got, say, less than 10 on Question 3. Having an identical layout on every coversheet dramatically saves my search time. Third, my required coversheet stops students from creating their own coversheet. In my experience, half of my students spend time creating fancy coversheets. This is a waste of their time, and given that every one is different from every other one, it is a pain in the neck trying to harvest information from them to enter into my spreadsheet. Avoiding this time-wasting exercise means that they can get straight to work. Fourth, a structured coversheet means that students are much less likely to leave information out. Fifth, I need only photocopy the front page of each assignment to capture all information. This means that when time is tight (and it often is), I have the flexibility to hand back the assignments before I enter the grades in the spreadsheet. I need only subsequently view my single-page photocopy for each assignment to enter the grades. Sixth, I staple the pile of copied coversheets together and I bring it to class. Then, if a student approaches me in class, graded assignment in hand, and says, "We think we deserve five extra points on Question 3," I can quickly view their assignment, and I can write the extra five points on it and on my copied coversheet, and turn the corner over on my copy to make it stand out in the pile of copied cover sheets. This gives me a structured written record of their changed grade, and this in turn saves me taking their regraded assignment away with me to record the new grade. Doing so would require time and effort to return it at some later date. Seventh, if I want to check how students did on one question, it is easy to find the grades for that specific question in the same place on the front page of each assignment (or on my retained copy). Eighth, on almost every assignment I give, at least one group fails to supply an answer to a question, fails to email me a required spreadsheet, or emails me the wrong spreadsheet. Then I can quickly pull the group leader's contact email off the front of their coversheet and ask for the missing information.

7.5 Some Grading Advice

I warn my students in advance that I give copious feedback on assignments. On a single page they might find 10 comments. If they did poorly, my comments aim to lift them to a passing grade. If they did very well, my comments lift them even higher, with deeper questions about existing course content or comments beyond course content.

During the COVID-19 lockdown, my students handed in their written assignments by emailing Microsoft Word files to me. I asked specifically for Word documents that I could edit, and not for pdf documents, because I wanted to be able to type my comments into their documents. In this case, the Word document for my standardized coversheet became the first page of their answers.

With hardcopy assignments, I usually write comments in red ink. With Word documents during online teaching, I typed in red font to make it show up. One efficiency with typed comments is that when I give a lengthy comment with graphs, advice and examples, it is easier to copy and paste the same comment into other students' assignments that it is with hand-written annotations on hardcopy assignments.

I always number the physical assignments or physical exams that students hand in. These control numbers are useful for keeping track of how many assignments were handed in. If I got 147 exams, then the first one will say, "1/147" in the top right corner, the second one "2," then "3," up to "147." That way, I can be sure I did not lose one.

When handing them back, I tell the students that the number in the top right is just a control number, not a grade (or the first student wants to know why he or she got only 1 out of 147!)

When grading, be on the lookout for variation in answers that identifies a question as poorly worded. In this case, you may have to admit multiple answers. If you use the question again, be careful to fix the wording.

I give my students a grading scheme for any work that they do. It gives enough detail that for the most part they can grade their own work to see if their grade matches mine. My full disclosure means that I almost never get students coming back to me to ask for something to be regraded.

When I was a young academic, however, I worked as a TA for a new professor who took a completely different approach. To avoid students questioning grades on long-answer questions, we were instructed to write nothing on the students' work except for the total grade for each question. Any partial credit calculation had to be done on a separate paper that the students did not see, and no grading scheme was to be distributed. It was the complete opposite of full disclosure. I thought it was terribly unfair on multiple levels (e.g., the students could not see clearly where their errors were, the students could not spot errors in grading, and it was condescending to treat the students with such a lack of respect). The students complained, and no wonder.

When grading complex Excel-spreadsheet-based assignments, my students often send me answers that are quite different from what I am expecting. I make a point of reconciling their answer with mine. So, I edit their spreadsheet, one step at a time, until their answer matches my answer, writing each step required in a bullet-point list on their assignment. Then I deduct marks based on the errors, and I record each error in my answer key and the grade deducted, so that students can grade their own work to confirm that the grades are allocated correctly (and to make sure that I am consistent in my grading across assignments). Again, students rarely question their grades, which saves my time.

When discussing job interviews, I tell my students that the interview is not over when you walk out of the door. If you get back to your hotel room and realize that you said something wrong, or that you gave an answer that was insufficient, then you should send an email to the interviewer to add more detail. The same applies to grading assignments and exams. Tell your students that even though they handed it in, and you graded it, the process is not over. In most cases, their grade won't change, but they should be encouraged to come back to you to discuss your comments. Doing so can help them to master the material.

Note that if you give assignments that require the writing of code or the creating of Excel spreadsheets, you should never give out explicit worked solutions. That is, never give out model code or model worked spreadsheets. As soon as you do so, they enter the public domain and will be circulated to all future generations of students. You can manually (or online) write on students' assignments where their errors were, but do not distribute your model answers in worked form.

Even if you grade assignments quickly, some impatient students will ask whether you graded their assignment yet, and what their grade is. You should *never* give out preliminary or indicative grades on assignments to impatient students. Similarly, you should not upload assignment grades to the Internet until you have finished grading *all* of the assignments. The reason is that as you grade, you are collecting information on relative performance. So, you may get three-quarters of the way through your grading when you find a student answer that is unusually good or unusually bad, that causes you to change your grading scheme. Then, you have to go back and regrade the assignments from the beginning again, but usually just on one question. If you already reported a grade to someone whose assignment you had "finished" grading, however, then you may have to revise that grade, possibly making the student unhappy. It is all about managing expectations; students hate unpleasant surprises!

If you have, say, 12 assignments, tell the students that only the best 10 count. It is an efficiency because you do not have to expend admin effort on special cases when students miss one or two assignments. It is also simple to code in Excel (e.g., using the =SUM command and several =SMALL commands).

When grading assignments, if a student (or a group) gets 99%, then I write that down, but I cross it out, and I write, "100%" beside it instead, adding "If you can earn 99%, then you deserve 100%!" The numerical impact is virtually nil (it's not like these are marginal students!). The psychological impact, however, is enough for them to notice. The hard-working student who gets 99% is annoyed at himself or herself or at me. The 1% gift means much more to them than it does to me.

7.6 Final Checklist

I always include a checklist at the end of any assignment in my advanced class. The checklist includes directions telling the students where to hand in their work and it also includes a series of check boxes. These boxes are beside the names of the spreadsheets that my students should have emailed to me, beside a reminder to remove external links in spreadsheets, and beside a reminder to remove "hard coding" or "non-dynamic" cells, etc.[2]

I tell the group leaders that it is their responsibility to check the checklist. This significantly reduces the time and effort that I have to spend chasing students because of missing or corrupt work.

You might argue that I am wasting my time chasing students, and that I should just give them zero for work that was due and not properly handed in. The problem, however, is that if the students do the work but fail to hand it in because of a lack of communication/co-ordination in their group, then

---

[2]Hard-coded cells in Excel are cell calculations where numbers are entered as digits instead of as cell references. Non-dynamic cells are cells that do not update when raw data are revised. Either of these issues interferes with a spreadsheet user's ability to audit (or in my case, to grade) a spreadsheet.

they are very unhappy when they get zero for that part. This can lead to significant time wasting with appeals to me, to the head of my department, and to the Dean. It is simply not worth the time and effort involved; it takes less time and effort to give the students a checklist and to then chase the few stragglers who ignore it. The stragglers appreciate your efforts on their behalf, and your actions add to the intangible learning environment. You are adding a personal touch, by recognizing, and making allowances for, human error.

Chapter 8

Exams

Exams, like assignments (see Chapter 7), are survey instruments that must be designed with care. Unlike assignments, however, most exams are in students' hands for only a brief window of time, and they usually carry more marks than assignments. Students therefore feel more time pressure and more pressure to perform in an exam than on an assignment. So, any error you make in creating an exam carries more weight than an error in an assignment, and the Deming approach (to build quality in from Day 1; see Section 1.1.1) is all the more important.

One interviewee wrote, "Exams should test what you want them to learn when you set up the course. You should weight the exam in proportion to the amount of time spent on the topic. (To the contrary, I once co-taught a course with someone who put 10% weight on a 10-minute topic.)"

8.1 Creation

I tell my students that after class I go back to my office. I put a do-not-disturb sign on my office door, I review what we did in class and I make up three or four exam questions based on what we did in class that day.[1] I tell them that the questions I create usually focus on whatever we emphasized most or whatever was most important.

I tell the students that if they want to do well in my exams, then they should be doing exactly what I am doing! That is, after class, they should sit down and ask themselves "What was emphasized?" and "What was most important?" I tell them to talk to their classmates or to me to make sure that they understand the material. I tell them that doing this

---

[1]In the last few weeks of the semester, however, I have to stop doing this because administrative deadlines mean that I have to have created my exam already, else the exam won't be ready in time. The students do not need to know this detail.

when it is fresh in their mind is much better than waiting until the end of the semester.

On an intangible level, publicizing this approach also serves to reassure the students that their exam is being prepared carefully and actually covers their course content. (See the counter example "Exam Surprise!" story a couple of pages ahead.) Publicizing and discussing my approach provides an opportunity to encourage the students to revise my material in real time as they go through the semester, keeping up with the content and reinforcing key ideas in a timely fashion.

Note also the inbuilt efficiency in the previous paragraphs! If you create an exam question the same day that you taught the material, the creation process flows naturally and quickly; Both the material and the emphasis you placed on it are fresh in your mind. So, your exam will line up with student expectations. If, however, you wait until the end of the semester to create your final exam, then you are shooting yourself in the foot. You have to rush to complete the exam when the content is not fresh in mind. It takes more time and effort (and some stress) to create your exam at the end of the semester, and your emphasis in the exam might not match your original emphasis in the classroom.

By the time I put my final exam together, I have a collection of questions ready that I have been accumulating all semester. Some questions are easy, some are difficult, some are very difficult, and some are nearly impossible. This range of difficulties means that there is something for everyone. As such, it produces a clear spread of grades.

I know that my students are nervous when they start my exam, so I pull the easier questions to the front end of the exam and I shunt the impossible ones to the end. I put a diamond ◇ or a double diamond ◇◇ beside questions that are very difficult or nearly impossible, respectively. I tell my students, in advance of the exam, that the symbols are there to warn them. Otherwise, if they stumble upon a nearly impossible question without warning, it can be surprising and upsetting; I am managing student expectations.

With multiple-choice questions, each of my exam questions is worth the same number of points. I do not bother giving more points for more difficult questions. I tell the students not to get hung up on a diamond or double-diamond question, because it is worth the same as the simplest question. It makes the exam easy to understand, and I never have any difficulty getting a clear separation in grades between students of different skill levels.

To counter in-room cheating with multiple-choice questions, I have sometimes created two versions of an exam (often just the same multiple-choice questions, but in a different order). Then I hand them out to alternate seats, so that no person is sitting next to someone with the same exam.

Sometimes I include many options in multiple-choice exams, to reduce the value of guessing. Even with only five options per question, however, my exam questions are usually so carefully constructed that even *semi*-educated guessing destroys value.

When grading multiple-choice questions, I always give either 1 or 0 for each answer (and very rarely a half-point, as mentioned in Section 8.8). My questions are typically so difficult that subtracting a fraction of a point for a wrong answer (as some people do) is pointlessly complicated and just confuses matters; I prefer simplicity of form.

After creating an exam or assignment, I always print out my instruction sheets and then attempt it as if I were the student. Only then do I see whether there are creation problems or not.

Story (Exam Surprise!): I was a student in a postgraduate course in statistics more than 30 years ago. It was a "topics" course. That is, the content was focused on a handful of high-level topics, and the topics changed from year to year. This was back in the days when a course lasted all year (not just a semester), and the grade for the course depended 100% on the final exam (not upon some weighted average of the grades from assignments and exams). Two weeks before the last class, the instructor had a family emergency and had to leave the country suddenly. A new instructor taught us for the final two weeks. When it came time to sit the three-hour final exam, it contained five long questions, each taking up a page of the examination script. In those days, every three-hour exam started with a 10-minute reading period during which you could annotate the examination script with notes, but you could not write anything in your blue answer booklets.

I opened my exam to find, with some surprise, that Question 1 examined us on content that had not been in the course. I flipped the page. Question 2 also examined us on content that had not been in the course. I flipped the page again. Question 3 similarly examined us on content that had not been in the course. My heart was now pounding 💜. I flipped the page again.

About half of Question 4 examined us on content from the course. Thankfully, all of Question 5 examined us on content from the course. So, in summary, only 30% of my postgraduate statistics final exam covered topics that had also been covered in the year-long course, and my final grade depended 100% upon the exam.

Obviously, the original instructor had left without creating more than one question for the final exam. The new guy had created the exam based on what he thought was in the course, without being able to confirm the content.

I looked across at my buddy, Ian, sitting at the next table. Over the preceding year, he and I had often discussed the high-level course content that we were now *not* facing. He looked at me with a face like that of a deer in the headlights. I looked at him, he looked at me, I looked at him, and he looked at me. Then the exam invigilator started looking at both of us, wondering what was going on. (We could not be cheating yet, because we had not yet finished the 10-minute reading period, neither of us had picked up a pen yet, and we were not talking.)

I closed the exam script and sat back in my

chair. I put my feet up on a little foot rest those old tables had. I looked out the window at the trees blowing in the wind. I closed my eyes and rested, waiting for my heart rate to slow. After a few minutes, I opened my eyes to find the invigilator looking at me, wondering again what was going on. (Why was I neither reading nor annotating my exam script? Why was I sitting calmly with my eyes closed?)

I rested for about 10–15 minutes. I figured that this delay would not make *any difference* to the outcome of the exam. Then I dove into the exam and used every ounce of my intuition and experience to attempt the questions that covered content not in the course that I had just taken and studied for so carefully. Some of the notation was completely new to me (which is a challenge in a postgraduate statistics class). I had to guess what it meant, and write down that I was guessing that it meant this or that.

My memory is that I earned 68% on the exam (a "B-"), which was the lowest grade of my student career. No student complained; students did not complain in those days. A senior academic did, however, take me aside weeks later to ask me why I had done so badly. When I started to explain, however, he interrupted me aggressively and told me that it was my fault and that he did not want to hear excuses.

It is stressful enough when you have to sit an exam in the first place, doubly stressful when it is for a year-long course and your grade depends 100% upon your performance, and triply stressful when the majority of the exam content was not in the course that you studied so hard for. I guess I cannot think of a more fitting end to the story than to have someone senior tell me that it was all my fault. *How wonderful. Not.*

Let me repeat the advice that I gave at the beginning of this section. At the end of every class, or after every assignment, you should go back to your office and create examination content based on what you did. This strategy hedges the risks that led to the problems I described with my postgraduate statistics exam, and more besides. For example, if you have to leave suddenly, just before the end of the semester, then this strategy means that you will have 90% of the final exam created already. In the more usual case, where you are present at the end of the semester, this approach guarantees that your questions cover content that was actually in the course, and in proportion to its presentation.

8.2 Grade Distribution

As a junior academic in N.Z., I noticed that when U.S. academics visited to teach a class, they handed out "A" grades like they were cheap candy. The N.Z. students were surprised, amazed, and confused by this because the N.Z. academics teaching their other classes were handing out very few "A" grades. The visiting U.S. academics were creating much easier and less challenging questions for our students than was the N.Z. norm.

One reason for this is that the last year of high school in N.Z. is kind of like the first year of university in the U.S., and, commensurate with this, N.Z. undergraduate degrees last only three years while a standard U.S. undergraduate degree lasts four years. So, the U.S. academics were in the habit of "babying" the students, not realizing that they were a full year ahead of what they might expect from a U.S. student of the same age. When told this, one of our American visitors said, "An A is an A is an A," but she was giving "A" grades to students earning a "B" or "C" in other classes. (She also told me that if the milk was left out of the fridge for more than a minute or two, she would not drink it because it would go bad—not realizing that you can leave it out of the fridge overnight in many Kiwi kitchens and it will still be refrigerator-cold come the morning!)

The moral of the story is that different countries have different norms for grade distributions. So, as a new teacher in a new country, you need to be sure that you understand what is expected of you.

Aside: Two other examples of differing norms relating to grade distributions come to mind. First, when I applied for admission to the Graduate School at MIT, the admissions committee had to find a Kiwi to interpret my grade transcript. They worried that my many "A+" grades were evidence of a foreign university's generous grading policy. In fact, the opposite was true, which worked in my favor. Second, when foreign students apply for graduate study at my N.Z. University, we have to consult a long document that allows us to translate any foreign grade into a domestic one before we can determine whether they meet our hurdle for entry.

One interviewee wrote, "Grade to a standard, not a distribution. If they demonstrate what you want them to know, pass them. Remember every time you teach a course that you face a random sample from the population. Some samples will be good; others not so good. In

> larger classes you will be more likely to have
> reasonably good samples and the distribution
> will fit. Not so with smaller classes."

Finally, be careful where you get examination questions from! We hired a guy who decided to source his entire final exam from an online test bank. Somehow the identity of the online source got out to the students. There were over 100 students in the class, and all but one (an adult student who was out of the loop) got an "A" or an "A+" on the final exam. There was no sensible separation between students' grades. The whole thing was a fiasco.

8.3   Mechanical Advice

I give my students examples of my past exams, so that they can see the depth, difficulty, and style of my questions. When I teach a new course for the first time, however, I have no past exams. So, I make up sample exam questions to distribute before my exams. It removes a significant element of uncertainty from the students' minds. I am not suggesting that you repeat exam questions, just that you show students the "shape" of the questions you will ask, so as to manage their expectations.

As mentioned, in Section 1.1.8, I like to structure the grading for my courses so that if a student does better on the final exam than they did on the mid-term exam, then the mid-term exam grade is erased and replaced by the final exam grade in the weighted-average calculation (i.e., awarding a "plussage" form of extra credit).

You might not have noticed the built-in efficiency in this plussage approach. This calculation means that if a student misses your mid-term examination because of illness, you do not need to do anything about it. You do not need to ask for a medical certificate or meet with the student to discuss the issue. You do not need to make special arrangements for the student. Instead, you just point at the course syllabus and remind the student that the mid-term examination was not compulsory in the first place, and that their zero grade for missing it will be replaced by their final exam grade.

Similarly, if a student tells you that he or she is rowing in the Olympics and will miss your mid-term exam, the same applies. You do not need to spend any of your valuable time communicating with them to figure out a solution; just point at the syllabus. It is a wonderful built-in time/effort-saving efficiency.

After a mid-term exam, I always review student

performance on my examination questions. I pick out the 10% of questions on the mid-term exam that the students found the most difficult, and I put them in the final exam. Students who revise their errors are doubly rewarded for their efforts (because of plussage), but those who ignore their errors are doubly punished.

I used to give long-answer exam questions where, for example, the answers from parts (a), (b), (c), and (d) feed as an input into the analysis in part (e), and then the answer to (e) is combined with analysis in parts (f) and (g) to produce a final answer and a decision in part (h), or something like that. With several questions like this on the final exam, and a class size of 500+ students, it took two weeks of hard work to grade the exam. It then took another two weeks to mentally recover enough to be in any shape to do any research; and, this course ran twice a year, plus in Summer School.

One year, however, we tried an experiment. We gave basically the same exam, but we broke each question down into a self-contained multiple-choice question. The content being examined was identical; it was only the form that changed. It took 10 minutes to carry the multiple-choice forms over to IT to process. It took none of our time (or mental energy) to grade it. IT emailed us the scores, which we uploaded to our spreadsheet.

Our large class sizes yielded very good samples for conducting statistical tests. We found no difference at all in the performance of the students on long-answer versus multiple-choice questions. None whatsoever! We categorized the sample using every characteristic we had (sex, race, major, domestic versus foreign students, etc.), and we still got good subsample sizes, and found no differences whatsoever in performance. We never went back to long-answer questions in that course. The effort to create the exams was essentially the same, but the multiple-choice questions gave back many weeks of our lives we had previously been losing each year!

There is an added benefit to multiple-choice questions that might not be immediately obvious. I said at the beginning of this chapter that you making an error on an exam question typically carries more weight than does you making an error on an assignment question. That is because of the extra time pressure and grade pressure the students feel in an exam, but it is also because of the short window of time available to you to fix an exam error. In the long-answer exams just described, an error by you in an early part of the exam filters through to the later parts, and may make some later parts unsolvable. Even if the exam questions are perfect, an error by a student still causes a "domino effect" that makes grading very difficult without a spreadsheet. Both of these issues are fixed in the multiple-choice version of such an exam because an error in one question need not propagate.

I taught a class where students had to get 40% on the mid-term exam to be able to continue in the course; getting less than 40% was an immediate fail. I knew from past experience that many students thought that all they had to do was to study and ace the previous semester's mid-term exam in order to pass. I told them, however, that every year students came to me and said, "I studied and aced last semester's mid-term exam. I got 80% on it, but I got less than 40% on your mid-term. It is your fault!" To set their expectations, I drew a diagram, like a Venn diagram, where a big rectangle was the examinable course content, and a circle inside it was last semester's mid-term exam, and another overlapping circle was this year's mid-term exam, still under construction. I told them to look at the picture and I asked, "If you get 80% of last semester's mid-term exam correct, what grade should you expect on this semester's mid-term exam?" With a little bit of shading on the diagram, the answer looked like about 40%. I told them that "This is why you need to come to class, do your homework, talk to your tutor, and come to office hours, not just study last year's mid-term exam!"

Before handing back my students' graded midterm exams, I photocopy their answer page. I tell the students that I have retained a copy of their answers. So, if a student has a query about their exam performance, a simple email exchange can solve it because I can see what answers they gave, without having to schedule a face-to-face meeting or physically handle their exam again. This efficiency is true of any multiple-choice exam where grades are entered on one or two sheets. It is not true of long-answer exams, where it would be prohibitively costly (in time and money) to copy all the student answers.

Another benefit of keeping a copy of student answers, and telling them that I have done so, is that they are unlikely to then manually alter their answers and ask for more points. Note that with long-answer exams in large classes, I do sometimes photocopy entire answer booklets, but only in the case of a few students who already have a reputation for dishonesty (or whose honesty I doubt).

8.4 Helpful Spreadsheets

Grading is time consuming and takes mental energy better saved for research. Let me discuss three spreadsheets I use to improve my efficiency.

8.4.1 Weighted-Average Grades

My courses almost always contain multiple types of assessments. A significant number of innumerate first-year business students cannot, however, understand that their overall grade for my class is based on a weighted-average of the grades for component parts according to the proportional weighting described in the course syllabus (e.g., 10% quizzes, 35% mid-term exam, and 55% final exam). The concept of a weighted average is completely unfamiliar to them, and they simply cannot grasp it. (God save us when they are in charge in government and business!)

To address this innumeracy, I built a simple colorful Excel spreadsheet into which they can enter their assignment grades and their mid-term grade, and out of which comes a clear indication of what percentage grade they need on the final exam in order to pass the course. (This sheet is available at www.KelleySchool.com.) It also tells them what their overall course grade will be (numerically, pass or fail, and a letter grade) as a function of any final exam grade they care to enter.

My spreadsheet was a hit and was used for many semesters thereafter by me and by instructors who came after me. The bottom line is that you cannot assume that everyone understands even the simplest weighting scheme, and that using a simple sheet like this saves you the time and effort of having to explain the basic weighting of grades to innumerate students. Your time is much better spent on your research! A CYA by-product of this Excel tool is that no student can come to your office after the exam grades are released to complain that it is unfair that they failed because they did not understand how the weighting scheme worked.

Story (Playing the Odds): Our Economics Department used to have a multiple-choice midterm exam for the big first-year class (there were 938 students in the class when I took it!). There were five options and you had to get a 20% score in order to continue in the course. One classmate knew that the economists distributed the answers evenly (i.e., they always had the same number of (a), (b), (c), (d), and (e), answers). So, he sat down, answered, "(a)" to every question and walked out after two minutes, to everyone's surprise. He got exactly 20% and then studied harder for the final exam.

8.4.2 Question Creation

Why spend time and mental energy creating original assessment when you can instead spend that time and effort creating original research?!

For numerical exam problems, I created an Excel spreadsheet into which I can put different inputs, and out of which comes a ready-to-use examination question. (This sheet is available at www.KelleySchool.com.) For example, to generate multiple-choice questions, the spreadsheet uses dynamic text, as a function of inputs, so that the wording of the question and the wording of the possible answers change when you change the inputs. The generated questions can then just be copied and pasted into an exam.

Several of my colleagues have sought this dynamic question-generating Excel spreadsheet from me for their courses. It has two extra features that might not be immediately obvious. First, when you are creating multiple-choice questions, you can use the sheet to create, say, four *wrong* answers, based on the inputs and common bad logic, to accompany the one correct answer. (This gives students the same opportunity to give a wrong answer that they have in a long-answer exam.) Then, when you change the inputs, you immediately get a new version of the question with another set of common wrong answers using the same bad logic. Second, for long-answer questions, the spreadsheet can be helpful for assigning partial credit because you can use it as a tool to reconcile the Excel formulae with incorrect student answers.

8.4.3 Peer Override

When students work in groups, I find that about one group out of every 150 groups has a significant issue with students not contributing equally to the group effort. (I am talking only about problems that are significant enough to push the students to come to me; many other smaller problems surely exist.)

So, I include a note in my course syllabus stating that "If any student feels that an equal allocation of grades in their group work is not fair for any assignment, then I will, upon request, use an Excel-based standard peer assessment form to change the grade. For example, maybe you worked really hard and your team mates did not, or maybe everyone thinks that one student was not pulling their weight. Send me an e-mail to inform me. I will keep your identify anonymous, I will e-mail a form to each member of your group to fill in, and half the grades on your problem set will be reassigned using the University's standard peer assessment form. Each person scores each member of the group on a half-dozen types of group contribution, and each person's total is than ranked relative to the group average. The calculation will not allow the highest-ranked person to get over 100% or the lowest-ranked person to get below half of the original group score. A worked example appears in a spreadsheet on BlackBoard. If I have not heard back from all group members after 14 days, then I will use the information I have by that date to assign grades."

This peer-override spreadsheet, coupled with the advertisement of it in your syllabus, saves you time and effort that can be better spent on developing your research agenda. It's existence also serves as a small deterrent to potential free riders. You can find an example of this assessment spreadsheet online at www.KelleySchool.com.

The 14-day time limit is important, because of an endogeneity problem you might not have noticed. You are likely dealing with one or two lazy, entitled, unethical or untalented students. These are, however, exactly the sorts of students who will *not* return an email/spreadsheet from you! So, when sending out this peer override spreadsheet to your students, be sure to point at the course syllabus (to cover yourself if questioned by your boss) and to tell them clearly about the 14-day time limit for them to return it to you.

If the non-performing students do not respond after seven days, then send them a reminder. If they still have not responded after 14 days, then send a second reminder (the third request you have sent to them), with a 24-hour extension. Then go with whatever data you have after that 24-hour extension runs out. Without the time limit, however, you face a possibly never-ending wait for the spreadsheets to be returned to you.

After the fact, you can recommend that the students discuss their issues between themselves. You can advise the better students to change their group membership if the issues are not resolved, even if this breaches previously-announced required minimum or maximum group sizes. A lazy student may get ejected from their group, and have to flounder around a bit, but it kills the free-rider problem you had, and, arguably, that student deserves it.

8.5   Errors in Questions

I mentioned, in Section 5.3 and Section 5.4, that I press undergraduate students into service as unofficial RAs and TAs, respectively, because their sheer numbers create efficiencies. After an exam, I similarly exploit my students, but it is not a numbers game this time.

After any exam, I pick out the half-dozen top-scoring students and I check to see which questions they got wrong. Then I double-check their incorrect answers to make sure that *I* did not make a mistake. This is important for the exam in question, but also because many of my exam questions get recycled. Endogenously, there are not many of these questions to check, because these are the top-scoring students. I have, rarely, found that I made a mistake and then I have to go back and regrade that question (sometimes allowing more than one multiple-choice answer to be accepted). This second opinion is available for free and it takes only a few minutes to exploit. It is better that you use this approach to discover an error while the exams are still in your hands, than it is to hand the exams back and get student complaints.

Suppose that you discover, after the fact, that

you had a single technically-correct-but-poorly-worded question on your exam. The most talented students likely read between the lines and answered correctly, but the less talented students may have missed your intent, and lost a point because of it. In a very small class (say, 20 or fewer), you can speak individually to each student who got this question wrong to judge whether he or she would have earned the point had your question been better worded. In a large class, however, this approach is an inefficient waste of time that you could be spending on research. So, just award students the maximum of the following two grades: the percentage grade based on the exam including the poorly-worded question, and the percentage grade for the exam if the poorly-worded question is plucked from the exam; it is not perfect, but it has worked for me.

8.6 Race Against the Clock

When I was a student, I wrote more quickly than anyone else I knew. Nevertheless, one of my senior university teachers consistently gave exams I could never finish, even though I knew all of the material nearly perfectly. I could finish maybe 85% of his exams. So, in a class of 40 students, I would get roughly 85% (i.e., the proportion of his exam that I could complete in his time limit), the next best student would get maybe 75%, and then the grades would fall off down to failing territory. We all told him that his exams were simply a race against the clock, and not a test of knowledge, *per se*, but he never changed his behavior. I thought it was inappropriate, partly because I had an unfair physical advantage not related to knowledge of the material.

Similarly, we had to hire a teacher to fill in for a semester after a brutal culling of half the Department by the admin boffins. The visitor came from a foreign country. I was his direct supervisor. When he created an exam for his 250+ students, it was twice as long as could sensibly be completed in the allotted time. He refused to change it, saying that this was how exams were set in his country. So, I had to *order* him to do so as his direct supervisor. I think it was only the threat of non-payment that got him to alter it.

One interviewee wrote, "Always, always, always do your assignments and exams before handing them out, as they are rarely correct on the first draft. Take the assessment from the students' perspective, using any formula sheets or other material allowed/given. Ensure all information

> "required is there. Look for and consider other possible answers; if they exist, then you need to either accept them or rewrite the question. Consider having someone else go over your assessments if you think there could be an issue."

After creating an exam, I sit it myself. Then I edit the questions to improve them, and sit it again. Then I edit it again, and sit it again, and so on. When I have run out of edits to make, I sit the near-final version of my exam as quickly as I possibly can. However long it takes me, I give the students *six times* that amount of time (your ratio may differ). If this is more time than is allocated in the exam, then I cut out or simplify some material; if this is less time than is allocated, I do the opposite. I tell the students that I am doing this and have done it for many years. I announce, "It took me 30 minutes to complete your three-hour exam." Knowing that I am aware of timing issues removes doubt in their mind and avoids a race against the clock.

As an aside, I wrote so quickly as a student, and had such enormous capacity for retention, that in final exams I consumed the blue answer booklets more quickly than anyone else. Unfortunately, the first couple of times this happened to me, the exam invigilators were elderly people who took so long to get to me with my raised hand that I ended up sitting there wasting time with nothing to write my answers on. After that experience, I raised my hand in the exam room to ask for extra answer books as soon as I sat down. After I did that a few times, the invigilators began to recognize me and would bring me extra answer books as soon as I entered the room, not even waiting for me to raise a hand. So, nowadays, when I run an exam, I make sure that my students have more answer books than they need, and I watch them like a hawk for any raised hands so that I can respond quickly. In some cases, I also tell them that there is a pile of extra blue books on the table at the front, and they are welcome to come and get some if they need them (self-serve, instead of waiting in line; another efficiency).

8.7 Online Exams

The BlackBoard software I use has a "Student Preview" mode that, in theory, enables instructors to view the Blackboard course and exams, etc., as a student sees them. After seeing screenshots from students, however, I realized that the Student Preview mode does not show me exactly what the students see. Also, I cannot see in advance what an instructor sees when a student is sitting an exam.

To remedy this, I ask our IT people to create a fake student in my class and to give me the login credentials for that student. Then, I am able to log into the system as a student, and simultaneously log into the system as an instructor, and run all sorts of tests. Doing so is much more informative than is the Student Preview mode. I can see what happens to me as a student if I am sitting an online exam and my internet service cuts out. I can see what happens to me as a student if I try to get back into the exam after that outage. I can see what an instructor sees when a student is part-way through an exam. I can crash the system as a student and reset it as an instructor, and see what the effect is on the student. I can experiment with exceptional start and end times for a student's exam, and then see how that looks to the instructor versus to the student, etc.

My hacking meant that I could correct misinformation that was being spread by admin boffins, and it led to changes in University-wide advice for online exam implementation. It makes no sense for me to include detailed advice here, because successive software implementations/upgrades could render my advice null and void. Instead, let me suggest only that you get your IT folks to add you as a fake student in your own course, so that you can see exactly what your online exam interface looks like. I found that for some things I needed two computers (one where I logged in as a student, and one where I logged in as the instructor).

When giving online exams during the COVID-19 lockdown, my students were required to download their exams using the BlackBoard software. After many tests, however, I found that sometimes an exam did not download fully; maybe one or two questions would fail to appear. So, I told the students in advance to make sure that their exam had downloaded fully, and if after a minute it had not, then they should exit and download it again. Otherwise, if they discovered partway through their exam that questions were missing, and they exited the exam after already entering some answers, their previous answers would be lost.

Of course, some students completely ignored my advice, and emailed me partway through the exam to say that they were missing Question 22, or something like that. I anticipated these requests and had pdf copies of each individual question ready in advance. (See further discussion following.) Then I emailed them the pdf file of the missing question within one minute of their request, without them having to exit their exam and lose their answers.

Before we started using online exams, I usually created all my exams using the LaTeX document preparation system. The online exam interface offered by BlackBoard has its own equation editor, which is poor by comparison. Also, as discussed in Section 6.3, I wanted to re-use my final exam questions in the following year's mid-term exam and the year after that in a workbook to accompany the course. The workbook for the course and all of the old practice exams available to the students use LaTeX. So, for consistency with the past and for anticipated future use, I wanted to be able to use LaTeX, instead of BlackBoard's awful equation editor. (BlackBoard promised a future version that uses LaTeX commands, but I have not seen it yet.)

So, my solution was to use LaTeX to create my exam document as usual, but to then cut and paste the questions from the pdf version of the document, save them as .png files, and upload them one at a time as images to my BlackBoard-based exam. The .png format gives higher-resolution images and smaller file sizes than any other format I have tried.

I created small test versions of my exams (using questions from old exams) and I got student volunteers with different computer systems, and sitting in different countries, to test them for ease of use. In practice, the only change in exam format that came about because of this consultation was that I changed the setting for multiple-choice answers from vertical (the default) to horizontal, because a student pointed out that he could not simultaneously see the question and all the possible answers if I used a vertical layout of possible answers. Note that in this case, the LaTeX version of the question includes full answers (i.e., letter choices plus written answers), and BlackBoard supplies only a matching row of letter choices to click on.

The online exams produced using this approach looked great, and looked just like the LaTeX versions that the students had practiced with. The small file sizes were particularly important for successful exam downloads. The implementation works almost flawlessly.

There were two by-product benefits of this approach. First, I want to create a LaTeX version of my exam anyway, for the reasons given above. Being able to cut and paste the questions from my pdf file means that I avoid the risk of transcription errors that could arise if I have to translate my questions into BlackBoard's equation editor. Second, cutting and pasting individual questions from my exam gives me a pdf copy of each individual exam question. As mentioned already, I can email these mid-exam to students for whom that question does not download properly. My students seem very happy with this approach.

When giving online exams using a multiple-choice format, I told the students in advance that there was a chance that their PC would crash mid-exam, losing all the answers that they had given. So, I printed up a single page with the numbers of the exam questions and I asked the students to print that out at home and to enter their letter answers by hand on that page as they went along, so that they could transcribe their answers quickly in the event of an internet outage or PC crash. Sure enough, it saved some students from disaster. Those that it did not save from disaster also benefitted because they had less to worry about— knowing that they had some insurance against a surprise computer outage.

When giving quizzes using BlackBoard, you can hide a student's score from them at the end of the quiz. This stops students knowing directly that they scored 100% and passing photos of the questions and their (now known to be correct) answers to other students who did not yet sit the quiz. (It does not need to be 100%, of course; many cheating students would be more than happy with a low pass.) This approach does not, however, completely solve the problem, because a student's hidden quiz score can still be reverse engineered from his or her gradebook total. If it is a multiple-choice quiz, an excellent subterfuge is for you to incorrectly tell BlackBoard that every question has answer, "(a)," and to tell the students that you did this to reduce cheating. Once the quiz is over, you can tell Black-Board the correct answers, and have BlackBoard regrade the quiz. A similar tactic can be used for other online exam answers.

8.8 An Efficient Hybrid

In some classes I taught, I used long-answer midterm and final exams, whereas in other classes I used only multiple-choice exams. Some students favor one type of exam. For example, some students like to express themselves and they feel constrained by multiple-choice answers, whereas other students, especially quants and those for whom English is a second language, often prefer multiple-choice answers.

During the last 10 years of my teaching, I created and adopted a new type of hybrid examination, which has slowly started to spread in my Department. I create multiple-choice examination questions, with, say, five answers, and a multiple-choice answer sheet to go with it, but I tell the students that they are welcome to give long-answer justifications to their multiple-choice responses. So, my answer sheet has one page for the multiple-choice responses, and then several more pages for longer answers. (See example 50-answer and 75-answer answer sheets at www.KelleySchool.com.)

After more than ten years of using this hybrid exam, I have found that over 90% of students treat the exam as a strictly multiple-choice exam and leave the extra pages blank, 5% of students write one or two justifications, usually short sentences and possibly a diagram, and fewer than 5% of students go completely nuts, and fill up the pages. (I tell the students these statistics in class well before the exam to set expectations.)

There are several interesting observations to make about my hybrid exams. First, in practice, I can ignore almost all the justifications given, because they almost all justify a multiple-choice answer that is already correct. Second, very rarely, a student chooses a correct multiple-choice answer, but proceeds to give a justification that shows that they do not understand. In this case, I mark them wrong and take away the point. Third, rarely (and typically only for a student at the pass-fail boundary in a final exam), a student's answer indicates partial understanding, and I give a half point, even though the multiple-choice answer is incorrect.

For my hybrid exam, I bring to my exam room a plastic overhead transparency sheet onto which I have photocopied an answer sheet with the correct answers circled, but using larger circles than any sane student would use. Then at about half-way through a two-hour exam, the first students start to leave, I stop walking around the room, and I sit down at a desk at the front. I have a specially marked cardboard box over to one side that students put their answers sheets into, and another for their question sheets. (I show these boxes to the students in class, well before the exam.)

At half time, I pick up the first few completed answer sheets. I check to see if any justifications exist. Suppose the student correctly justifies an incorrect letter choice. For example, they correctly tell me why the answer is \$1,256.27, but they incorrectly chose answer, "(a)" instead of answer, "(b)"

I always ask the same question: "Does the student understand?" That's all I care about. In this case, I will put a big red check/tick mark through the incorrect letter answer on the answer sheet, so that it shows up as correct at the next step. I also cross out each justification after I read it, as a deliberate indication to the student that I read what the student wrote. Then I lay my plastic sheet master answer key over the top of the student's answer sheet and I manually count up the correct answers. I already cut the corner out of the plastic master key, so that I can write the total in the corner of the student's answer sheet. Then I move to the next student's answer sheet. When I have graded the first handful, I go get another handful, and so on. It can take as little as 15 seconds to manually grade an exam if the student gives no justifications.

By the time I get to the two-hour mark, there are usually five students left in the exam room, and I am just waiting for them to bring me their answers. The last student usually gives up within 15 minutes, then I grade his exam (yes, it has always been a male; your experience may differ). Then two minutes after the last student leaves, I walk out of the exam room, having finished my grading. I return to my office and enter the grades into my spreadsheet, run a few checks, and then upload them for the students to see. In a class of 125, say, I have the grades online one hour after the last student leaves the exam room. Most students appreciate the speed with which their grades are released.

My hybrid exams have an endogenous nature about them that students like because each student's preference (for multiple-choice or long-answer, or somewhere in-between) determines the nature of their exam.

Students appreciate the option/opportunity to *express* themselves in my hybrid exams. Even though 90% of them do not exercise this option, it gives them a feeling of confidence going into the exam (giving them a visible demonstration that you took their preferences into account).

My technique of manually grading the exams cannot be done via computer. I had one colleague, however, who had a very large first-year class (i.e., 500+) and needed to grade the multiple-choice answers by computer. Nevertheless, she allowed students to give justifications to *any five* answers only. This limitation meant that the implementation was still feasible, even in her large class. She likely also had fewer than 10% justifications in her low-level class.

8.9 Exam Etiquette

Never make jokes in the classroom about upcoming exams. Students find it to be almost the least funny topic that you can discuss. You can, however, make jokes about exams that have passed. For example, I gave a multiple-choice exam with 50 questions in an advanced class. Each question had five options to choose from, but the lowest grade in the class was 8/50, which is less than would have been expected by random guessing and chance alone. The students in that quantitative class found that statistic amusing.

As a student, I never walked out of an exam early, even if I had already finished with an hour to spare. I figured that there was always option value in staying. Why throw that away? For example, I often heard other students say that they left the exam room early, walked out into the fresh air, and then suddenly realized that they could have given a better answer (or even *an* answer) to a question, but now it was too late. So, I formed a simple "patience hypothesis" about my students: The longer a student stays in the exam room, the higher should be his or her grade, on average.

One semester, I ran an experiment to test my

patience hypothesis. I was careful to keep track of the order in which my 120 students handed in their mid-term exam. In my two-hour exam, students trickled out steadily from about the 55-minute mark until about the 130-minute mark. I plotted a picture of grades versus the order in which the students handed in their exam. I put a trend line on the plot and there was a clear upward trend: The longer my students sat in the exam room, the higher was their grade, on average. My patience hypothesis looked good! I put a moving average on the picture when I showed it to the students so as to not breach privacy by revealing the grades of the (very visibly) first and last students to leave.

On average, each person leaving the room earned one-tenth of one percent more than the previous person. With 120 people in the class, the difference in grades between the first and last persons to leave was 12%. This difference is more than two notches in letter grades (e.g., from a 68% "B-" to an 80% "A-"), and could easily be the difference between a pass and a fail.

Could this effect be, however, due entirely to an endogeneity issue, driven by the more talented students staying longer? If so, then no useful strategy could be recommended for other students. I downloaded my students' other grades, and sure enough, better students did stay longer. Even after controlling for this fact, however, half the effect remained, which was still enough to matter.

So, there is a benefit to staying in the exam room. I show the empirics to my students and I argue that they throw away option value by walking out early. If they stay, however, they have time to check things over, re-read questions, re-read answers, relax a little and maybe solve a difficult problem they previously set aside, etc. I recommend that you tell your students this story and that you also describe the interesting endogeneity issue.

If you do allow your students to leave their exam room early, be sure to tell them clearly in advance that they are not to talk until they step outside the building. Otherwise, a growing hum of conversation develops in the hallway right outside your exam room door(s), and it disturbs the remaining students.

I have run other experiments to see how students behave in a two-hour exam. For example, I tried sitting up front for the entire exam, and getting up to walk about only when a student raised a hand to ask a question. Alternatively, I tried walking around the room every five minutes during the first hour, and then sitting up front grading (see Section 8.8) during the second hour. I discovered that four times as many people ask me questions if I walk around during the first hour of the exam than if I remain seated.

I think what is going on is that if I purposely walk about every few minutes, then students who are a little shy, or too polite (or who are simply reluctant to force me to get to my feet and walk over), will not ask a marginal question. If I walk about, however, and I am passing nearby, the hurdle to ask me a question is lower. Nowadays, I always walk about during the first hour of my exam; I feel that I am better serving my students. A side benefit is that when I am walking about, the students think that I am watching them for cheating, and are less likely to engage in it. I also often pick up a pen, pencil, eraser, or calculator that a student has dropped and I hand it back, which is appreciated.

I often ask a graduate student to sit anonymously in my exam room, near the back, just to watch for things I cannot see (acting like a covert sky marshal). My assistant can communicate with me using hand signals. Although I have only one assistant, I tell the students that there are two of them, to reduce the likelihood of in-room cheating.

Note that my exams are short enough that the students have usually read all the questions by half time. So, that's why I can sit down and start grading in the second half of the exam. If you have the sort of exam where students are still reading new material after the first hour, however, then maybe you need to walk about for longer than I do.

When I walk around an exam room, I always have a copy of the exam and a pen with me. Then, if a student points at a difficult question and asks for clarification, I can stand back and look at *my* copy of the exam questions, without having to take the exam question paper out of the student's hands (which might force them to halt their work). I tell my students in advance that if I discover that a question requires clarification, then I will write it up on the board. I don't announce amendments verbally because my movements in the quiet room are so obvious, and everyone is facing me.

I never ask students to stop writing or to put down their pens at the end of an exam. If it is a two-hour exam, I book the room for three or four hours. I need 45 minutes to set the room up (less if I have multiple assistants). After two hours of exam time, there are usually only five students left, out of 120. I wait for them to finish. Eventually there is one student left (yes *that* student again; I knew it would be him). He is usually done within 15 more minutes; he has run out of things to write.

You must be available to answer student questions during your exam. If not, you are being grossly unprofessional. For the students who end up not needing your help, knowing that you are there is part of the intangible environment. It provides reassurance, the same way that your house, car, or life insurance provides you with peace of mind. For the students who *do* need your help, your availability can be essential.

I mentioned, in Section 6.2, that instructors have no presence in, or control over, the final examination room at my N.Z. University. Students, however, often have questions during their final exam. So, my University requires that all examiners remain available by telephone while their examination is in progress. If a student has a question, he or she raises a hand and tells an invigilator. The invigilator then telephones the central University boffins, and they, in turn, telephone the examiner, usually in his or her office.

This protocol does not always work. For example, we hired a visiting instructor to cover a class after a culling of half our Department. He decided, however, that the students had no right to ask questions (yes, this is the same guy I mentioned on p. 296, whose exam was going to be twice as long as was feasible). So, he left his office and was nowhere to be found during his exam. He reported to me, and so I got the call from the central admin boffins, and I had to answer his students' questions as best as possible on his behalf.

Let me also give an example from my PhD student days. My instructor left the exam room, writing his office phone number on the board in case of questions. This was before cell phones, but there was a phone on the wall just outside the door of the exam room. His exam was only one big question. Unfortunately, he used a phrase that I had never seen before (his asked about a "tender offer;" a common phrase in the U.S. at that time, but completely unknown to me, fresh off the boat). So, I was stuck. I stepped outside to phone him, with no response. I tried again a few minutes later, and then maybe 10 minutes after that, still with no success. I left the room and walked to his office in the next building. He was not there. I was stumped. (Goodness knows what my classmates thought I was doing leaving the room so much.)

After the exam, I explained to him that I could

not answer his exam question because I did not know what a "tender offer" was, and he was not at the phone number he gave or in his office. (He had gone out for a long lunch!) He said I must have missed a class where this was mentioned, which was not true, and I told him so; I had never missed a class. (This was the same professor, now at Harvard, whose slang caused issues for me as mentioned in Section 3.3.4.) As soon as he defined a tender offer, I was able to write the 15-page answer out for him. I was, however, given an "incomplete" on the exam, and I had to do some other work later to make it up, through no fault of my own. I am still annoyed, 30 years later! The bottom line is that you must make yourself easily available to your students during your exams. (Note that my hybrid exam format, discussed in Section 8.8, allows students to make and state assumptions if they need to, and the multiple-choice format minimizes the fallout from any single ill-posed question.)

When giving an exam, you never know in advance how many students will attend. So, you will often be contacted by some panicked student after the exam asking for the chance to sit the exam late. To keep your options open, do the following: Do not allow students to bring paper into the exam;

require that they write their answers on the exam script; and, state on the exam that no part of the examination script may be taken from the examination room and no blue booklets (with or without any workings) can be taken from the examination room. Tell your students that they are "not to discuss the exam with anyone because some students will be sitting it later," even though you will not yet know if this is the case.

Be sure to walk around the room 10 minutes into the exam and to pick up any blank exam scripts you laid out that no student used (so that no student picks one up on the way out). Then, when some student emails you after the exam and says, "I thought it was tomorrow," you can reasonably allow that student to sit the exam first thing the next day. If their classmates took home all the questions, however, then it is in the public domain already, and you cannot reasonably allow a late student to sit the exam.

In most cases, the late student is not a cheat, and did not talk to other students about the exam. You can tell the student that you will reserve your right to not include their grade for the late exam if anything seems out of order. You can compare the student's performance with his or her performance in other classes or other parts of your course to see if the late student's grade is unusually good, without good reason.

Story (Take-Home Final): I was a PhD student in a heavily quantitative course taught by Prof. Chi-fu Huang at MIT. In the second week of the semester, he handed out our take-home final exam. The questions appeared relatively short. He said nothing else about it. I was puzzled as to why it was handed out so early in the semester.

After a couple of weeks, I started working on the exam. I recorded a tally mark for each hour I spent on it: ||||, etc. I remember sitting outside the Business School at 2AM talking to my buddy Olivier about the extraordinary time it was taking (but not about content, obviously).

Ultimately, it took me 125 hours to complete his take-home final exam! That's why he handed it out so early! I certainly felt a great sense of accomplishment when I finished it. I like to give my students a similar sense of accomplishment, but I have never set an assignment or project (and certainly never an exam) that required more than about 30 hours of work.

Chapter 9

Teaching Evaluations

I argue in Section 1.1.1 (the Deming approach) that teaching evaluations cannot be used to "inspect quality into" a product (i.e., your teaching). Evaluations do, however, serve the purpose of establishing a record of your performance. Other things being equal, this record can help to get you retained and/or promoted, and can protect you, at least to some extent, from the meddling interference of bad bosses and other admin boffins in your teaching. So, you should actively take actions to make your teaching evaluations look as good as possible.

Story (Dr. Jekyll and Prof. Hyde 🗒):
I pinned up two completed paper-based teaching evaluation forms on the noticeboard outside my office door. Their juxtaposition became a regular talking point in the corridor.

These two forms were from two students in the same class in the same semester. One was overwhelmingly positive, with the best scores possible given for each question, and hand-written comments extolling the virtues of my teaching: very organized, following the textbook, clear explanations, etc. The other was overwhelmingly negative, with the worst scores possible given for each question, and hand-written comments damning my awful teaching: very disorganized, not following the textbook at all, unclear explanations, etc.

I deduced that the overwhelmingly negative evaluation was from some lackadaisical student who had rarely come to class. So, I now make a point of showing this pair of forms to students in large first-year classes. I tell them that if they do not attend my class on a regular basis, then it is unethical for them to comment on what I do in the classroom, and they should recuse themselves from my evaluation.

9.1   The Kiss of Death

The first time I was given responsibility to teach my own class, over 30 years ago, I got very good teaching evaluations.[1] On the basis of those, I was nominated for the inaugural "Commerce Division Teaching Award" at my University. I have several observations about this award.

First, I was inexperienced, and I did not win this newly established award. The teacher who won the award was in another department and had an office next door to me. (He used to smoke like a chimney in his office, and the smoke would creep into my office via the cheap drop ceilings.)

Second, I was told later that the winner was terminated soon afterwards because he did not do enough research! So, for many years afterward, I viewed teaching awards as "the kiss of death." I have softened my view to a more balanced one since then: Outstanding teaching is a good thing, as long as you are delivering on the other criteria for promotion: research; service; and, engagement.

---

[1]You can find my teaching evaluations and many comments from students, going back 30 years, at www.KelleySchool.com. Some years are missing because I lost the forms or because I was not evaluated, but there are at least a dozen years of evaluations from at least 10 different courses.

Third, that teaching award was subsequently eliminated. My University now sponsors no teaching awards that you can win based solely on your teaching evaluations. There are a few University-sponsored teaching awards, but to apply for them you have to submit a dossier where you wax lyrical about your teaching ethos; few people have time for that. In addition, the students, through their Students' Association, have established their own teaching awards, with an independent student-led nomination process.

Finally, although my University abandoned teaching awards based on student evaluations, they use those very same evaluations to assess teachers' careers. Huh? The moral of the story is that although many universities say that teaching is as important as research, good teaching is typically less valued and less rewarded than good research. (See also the "Fake Hurdle" story in Section 11.10.)

9.2   Response Rates

In the old days, every teaching evaluation was conducted in class on paper forms, often during the last week of class, when attendance is usually very good. So, response rates were as close to 100% as was humanly possible. My University moved to *online* teaching evaluations in about 2015, however, and I heard reports of poor response rates (close to 30%). So, when it was my turn to do my first online teaching evaluation in 2016, I took several actions that led to an 86% response rate.

First, I told my students about the online evaluation in each class leading up to the date it went live. Second, I sent them a reminder email when it went live (the University sent me an email to tell me it had gone live). Third, I showed the online evaluation form in class by logging into the University's Web site, and I demonstrated that it would take only one minute to fill the online form, including adding comments. I told the students that "If I can spend 64 hours in front of you this semester, then you can spend one minute filling this form for me." Fourth, I showed them online that I could see how many of them had completed the evaluation, and I promised that if the response rate was at or above 85% in the last class, then I would give away a prize of a lottery ticket worth potentially $1 million. I told them that I had an alternate prize for anyone who did not want the lottery ticket (a bag of chocolate fish; a Kiwi delicacy). My evaluation went live one week before my last class. Two days before my last class, I had a 61% response rate, and I reminded them of my promise.

The response rate ticked over the 85% hurdle three-quarters of the way through my last class (most of that happened during our half-time break). So, at the bottom of the second hour, I loaded the class list into an Excel file projected on screen, and I had a student flip a coin: heads meant the first half of the list was deleted, and tails meant the second half was deleted. Each successive deletion of names was accompanied by a Hollywood-overacted groan from the students whose names were cut and were out of the running. Eventually, I had three students' names left, all present in class. I asked the three remaining students to call "heads" or "tails" and then we had two students left. Then a final toss gave me a winner. The winner wanted the lottery ticket; the chocolate fish went to the runner up.

The evaluation still had 10 days to run after my last class, but no additional persons completed it (even though the University sent targeted emails to the non-responders asking them to do so).[2] So, I

---

[2]You can view my first online evaluation at this link: http://www.KelleySchool.com/Teaching_Evaluations_2016.pdf.

think my prize-giving helped very much to produce the high response rate, and after that, nobody cared enough to complete it.

I advertised my successful approach within my Department, and the University picked up on it and subsequently included my words in an email distribution to all faculty on campus.[3]

The effort required to get a high response rate is no more than the effort I used to put into creating and distributing the traditional paper forms. Also, the act of doing it provides engagement and entertainment, at a cost of less than $10 in prizes.

Aside: I like to release my teaching evaluations publically as soon as I get them. For example, in the teaching evaluation mentioned above, the first question ranks me out of 5 on how organized I am. Out of 102 respondents, 89 gave me a 1, 10 gave me a 2, and one each gave me a 3, 4, or 5. By releasing that information publically, the one student who gave me the 5 can see that he or she is the outlier, not me. It is also entertaining for the students to see the outliers. You can also read the outlier complaints from students, many of which are silly.

---

[3]Some schools do not release grades immediately unless the student has completed evaluations in all their courses (e.g., NYU, 2021).

Epilogue (Response Rates): As an experiment, the next semester I did nothing at all to encourage participation, and I got a 39% response rate, but with similarly high evaluation scores. As a statistician, however, high scores and a high response rate are more convincing than high scores and a low response rate, especially in a large class.

9.3 Timing Your Evaluation

You often have control over the date(s) that your evaluation is to be conducted, and you should choose that timing carefully.

Some teachers choose to run their evaluation mid-way through the semester, so as to get feedback that they can act on in real time. I spend enough time preparing my classes, however, that I rarely get any actionable feedback. So, I schedule my evaluations at the end of the semester.

Once you choose which part of the semester to conduct your teaching evaluations, I cannot stress highly enough the importance of choosing the day carefully. Under no circumstances should you have the evaluation within one day of your students sitting a test, an exam, or handing in a big assignment of yours. In fact, try to avoid timing the evaluation to coincide with *any* stressful event in their lives.

Do not simply eliminate the negative; Try to accentuate the positive! Apart from prizes to encourage *participation*, I never give students a bribe (e.g., cookies) on the day of the evaluation. I do, however, often purposely schedule some of our most interesting discussions or material for the day of (or the week leading up to) the evaluation. Sometimes this is a natural time for a summing up of and a bringing together of different concepts discussed, or a revelation about something we studied earlier.

In my experience, the last class you give in a semester is often the last time that many students see you before they fill in their teaching evaluations. So, finish strongly, *with a bang not a whimper!*

For example, one semester I finished by showing my finance major students some video interviews with financial practitioners who were purposely misleading investors with statements that, while only just true, could easily be misunderstood by investors and lead to bad outcomes for them. We had an excellent interactive discussion about the ethics of financial practitioners and the requirement for a healthy dose of skepticism on the part of investors. It built upon all that we had done that semester and left them with strong impressions and opinions. Then they completed my evaluation.

Another semester, I finished by walking through a dozen concrete actions they could take that would lead to a healthy and wealthy retirement (Crack, 2020a, pp. 340–344). I finished with the exhortation that they, as finance majors in a business school, were likely to become wealthy if they followed these steps, and that it was their duty in that event to then give generously to support those who were less fortunate. After a semester focused on making money in the financial markets, summarizing how they could do that successfully and then exhorting them to *give it away* got their attention. They walked away with those thought-provoking ideas in their heads, and they carried their thoughtfulness over to their teaching evaluations. (Recall also the praying mantis story in Section 3.3.8!)

Finally, invite your students to make comments. Tell them that "It is nice if you say something positive, but please also add something constructively critical. What could I do better? Conversely, if you are going to criticize, look around for something that you did like and that you would like to see more of, and point that out." This request produces many more comments than if I stay silent.

9.4 Mother Knows Best

Teaching evaluations can come from unexpected directions. I sometimes get a student's angry or concerned mother contacting me by telephone without giving her name (it has never been a father). They think they are anonymous, but I have always been able to deduce immediately whose parent it is, though I do not let on that I know.

Story (Mothers Calling): The phone call usually starts with "My child is a good student." (I am thinking "Really? Have you seen John's grade transcript? Do you know that John has been skipping classes?"); Then "My child is fearful of failing and worries that the pass rate in your course will be very low." I tell her that the pass rate in my advanced class was 97% last year, as announced in class repeatedly, and which her child would know if he had attended my class regularly; Finally, "My child is depressed, is seeking counselling, and is taking prescription medication to deal with the depression about your class." I tell her I am sorry to hear it. I advise her to tell him to come to class, come to my office hours, email me with questions, work on the assignments and hand them in, because that worked for 97% of people in the course the previous year. In every case, after some further discussion, the mother recognizes within a few minutes that I am a caring and experienced teacher, doing a good job and having successful outcomes, and that I am not at fault.

I had a mother call me up once and angrily demand to know the pass rate in the big first-year class whose grades I had just released. She quoted the "Freedom of Information Act." (I have no idea whether it even applies to me.) I told her that the pass rate was 75% that semester. I told her *softly-softly* that she did not need to quote a legal Act to get the information, and that we had advertised the expected pass rates widely from Day 1, to set student expectations. We were hollering it from the rooftops, not keeping it secret! I told her that the pass rate was the same as it was in each of the previous four semesters, and as announced in the first week of class, and as mentioned in the syllabus which she could download from the Web. Her response was "Oh." After a few minutes of gentle conversation, she went away to light a fire under her child's backside.

Chapter 10

Office Hours

Most universities require you to hold office hours. First-year students do not always understand what these are, so be sure to explain to them that they are welcome to come to your office at these times without an appointment.

10.1 Scheduling

Most of my students are doing other obviously-related classes at the same level. So, I avoid those class meeting times when setting my office hours. For a two-hour slot, I spread it across class periods, for example, 2:30PM–4:30PM (touching the

2PM–3PM, 3PM–4PM, and 4PM–5PM class periods).
This gives students three one-hour time slots that
overlap with my office hours, in case of conflicts.
If choosing one-hour slots, I choose, say, 1:30PM–
2:30PM and 3:30PM–4:30PM, then my office hours
overlap with four class periods instead of two.

Students love to have extra office hours the day
before an exam or on the due date of a big assignment. It is not necessarily because they left their
work to the last minute (although many do!); Sometimes, it is just that they accumulate questions as
they are studying, and they do not take any action
until just before the exam. (See also Section 5.6 and
Section 10.5.) Surprise your students a few days before the event by announcing extra office hours to
help them with any final concerns. Even if they
do not attend, they will feel less stressed knowing
that you are available *if* they need you; it's a free-to-
them insurance policy, and your visible action helps
to cultivate the intangible learning environment.

10.2 Rules

When holding office hours, I tell my students in
advance that I have six chairs in my office. "So,
if you see someone in there, do not wait outside

for them to finish; they may be there for an hour. Come on in and I will take turns taking questions from different students. That way, you benefit from hearing other students' questions and my answers."

Story (Prof. Psychic): I had a student sit outside my office for 45 minutes one time when I was talking to a single student. The student who was waiting was out of my line of sight, and I did not know he was there. He ran out of time and left, and then sent me a scathing email telling me that I was wasting his time, etc. I replied politely to say that I am not a psychic, that I had no idea he was there, that there were five empty chairs in my office he could have sat upon, and that I had previously announced to the class that they should not do what he did.

Nowadays, I often get up from my chair and peek outside to see if any students are sitting outside instead of coming in. Alternatively, if I think I hear someone sitting outside my office door, I ask a student I am talking to to get up and see if anyone is sitting on the seats outside my door, and to invite them in if they are there.

When I have two or more students sitting in front of me in my office and one of them asks a question, I often ask another student to answer it. Doing so serves multiple purposes. First, if the student you ask does actually understand the concept, then explaining it to someone else helps reinforce it for the student doing the explaining. (Claiming to understand something and being able to explain it to someone else are two different things; see Section 1.3.) Second, if the student I call upon to answer the question has a less than perfect understanding, then I can correct him or her (gently) during the discussion (thus helping two students at the same time). Third, sometimes the student doing the explaining has a different way of looking at things that I did not think of; this adds value.

One interviewee gave the quote, "The first thing that we do in my house is we say 'Do you want empathy or do you want a solution?'" (Lisa Feldman Barrett, 2020). He went on to say, "Students who need both should take precedence in the allocation of office hours; Students who only need a solution should rely on their peers." Although this may be true in a first-year course, my experience has been that in an advanced final-year course, my students often cannot rely upon their peers.

Finally, as mentioned already in Section 4.9, for my protection, I never allow a student to close my office door during office hours. If they have something private to discuss, I ask them to speak quietly.

10.3 Crocodile Tears

A side effect of teaching large classes is that the large number of students under my care means that there are high odds that I will have students in tears in my office multiple times per semester. The students have typically failed their mid-term exam (and are therefore not allowed to proceed to the final exam) or have failed their final exam (and are therefore not allowed to proceed to higher-level study in the field, or are not allowed to graduate).

In my experience, I see twice as many males in tears as I do females, even in classes that have more balanced proportions of males and females than that. The largest proportion, by far, are young male first-year students who always say *exactly* the same thing: "Please, can't you give me *just one more chance*?" (How on Earth do they co-ordinate this identical response among themselves?!)

About half of these young men drop to their knees while saying this, with their hands clasped together. (No female student has ever done this; why is that?) See also Section 11.3 for a story about a final-year business student from a different major who underestimated my required first-year class.

Given these experiences, I now make a point of emphasizing in multiple classes and in multiple emails leading up to exams, that "*This* is your chance. Attend lectures, ask questions in class, do the homework, attend tutorials, ask questions in tutorials, come to office hours, and send me emails. If you fail this exam, do not come to me asking me for '*just one more chance.*' *This* is your chance!" This announcement reduces, but does not stop, the count of crying male students in my office, but at least I can now point students (and my boss) to the many warnings made in class and sent by email.

I hate seeing my students in tears, but I can think of only one example in over 30 years where it was not the student's own fault. (She was being harassed by a male student in a shared house; I went to considerable lengths to help her out.)

The bottom line is that you must set clear expectations for your students and give them every opportunity to succeed, but you must not be surprised or influenced by tearful students whose reckless abandon has led them to academic ruin.

10.4 Level Playing Field

I want students to have a level playing field. I think it is *grossly* unfair if one group of students talks to me in my office hours (or engages in emailed Q&A with me) and gets assistance on a live assignment, but other students do not hear or see my words.

So, I tell my students that I will use BlackBoard (or some other online system), to record all the Q&A that takes place in my office or online, and that they should review that resource often, and certainly before their assignment is due.

I keep a pad of paper on my desk, and I use it to note down the advice given in face-to-face office hours. Then I type it into BlackBoard for all to see as soon as possible. (This was somewhat easier to do during the COVID-related lockdown because much of the Q&A advice I gave out was already typed out in emails in the first place. So, I could just copy and paste it to BlackBoard immediately.)

Sometimes while sitting face to face with students in my office, I turn side-on to type the Q&A directly into BlackBoard in real time while talking to the students, basically taking self-dictation. This saves time (so I do not have to do it later) and also demonstrates explicitly to the students concerned that I am doing what I said I would do (i.e., creating a level playing field). As I have mentioned before, being *seen* to be doing what I said I would do is more valuable for the intangible learning environment (and for my teaching evaluations) than simply *doing* what I said I would do; I recommend this visible approach to fairness.

I always include the date at the beginning of these Q&A transcripts so that students can see when I typed additions into the list of comments. Then I type, "QUESTION:" and I repeat the question, and then, "ANSWER:" and I repeat the answer. I add my comments in reverse date order, with the newest at the top of the list, so that students can quickly see the latest additions.

This level-playing-field approach has an added efficiency built into it that you might not immediately notice: Students often have the *same* questions! So, if I type Q&A about an assignment or exam into the online system for all students to see, then this reduces the likelihood that I will have to repeat that reply to another student's identical question, either online or face to face. This reduces the strain on my office hours and on my time, and leaves me with more time for research. Also, if another student emails me the same question, I can simply cut and paste my response from BlackBoard into an email reply, or I can direct them to the BlackBoard Q&A.

There is one other rare benefit of this level-playing-field approach. Sometimes I get an email from a student, and I reply to it, and then I cut and paste the student's question and my response into BlackBoard, only to find out the next day that the email system choked, and the email never went out. Then I resend the email, only to be told by the student that it is OK, because he or she already saw my response on BlackBoard. So, my transcribed Q&A also acts as a backup system, protecting me from email glitches.

10.5   A Two-Tailed Beast

I usually see three grades of students in my office hours. They are from the left-hand tail, the middle, and the right-hand tail of the distribution of student academic performance, respectively.

The few left-hand tail dwellers are often stuck fast. Either they come to office hours every week, and just manage to dig themselves out of the hole they are in, or they come too infrequently, and get buried. The middle-distribution dwellers turn up regularly for a gentle reminder of things they basically already know. The right-hand tail dwellers can get an "A" without doing any further study, but will study enough (with or without me) to get an "A+." When they come to see me during office hours, it is often to ask about peripheral material that appeared in the course, but which was not core material. It is subject matter that they can safely ignore and still get an "A+," but they *need* to know it regardless; see also the following story.

Story (Will-O'-The-Wisp): Thirty years ago, "Geraldine" was a first-year student who came to my office hours with nothing but questions about the peripheral material. She would ask, "Can you answer this question?" and I would say, "Yes," and proceed to do so. She seemed bright and well organized. She never asked a single question about the core material that was emphasized in class and which appeared in all the prior years' practice exams (available to all students in the course).

Geraldine's visits were so frequent, and so interesting, that I arranged a convenient extra office hour each week just for her to come and ask me questions. Week after week, she would come to ask me about the peripheral material, even coming to see me on the morning of her final exam with some last-minute questions.

I assumed that Geraldine was a right-tail student, heading for at least an "A." After her grades came out, however, I realized with a jolt that she was actually a green first-year left-tail student who had absolutely no idea how to study! She had noticed the material at the periphery of the course that was never emphasized and she mistakenly figured that she should spend all her efforts on that, because it seemed less clear than everything else (presumably because little or no class time was spent on it).

The moral of the story is two-fold. First, when presenting material in class, state clearly "This is non-examinable" if there is zero chance of it appearing in an exam. Tell the students that the emphasis placed on material in class corresponds to the appearance of the material in their exams. Second, when talking to students about peripheral material during office hours, say, "You do understand, don't you, that this material is very unlikely to appear in the exam?" This confirms that they are not following some *will-o'-the-wisp* to their doom.

Many students (often from the middle and left tail of the distribution) accumulate questions as they study, leading to a logjam of emails (Section 5.6). They can also create a *physical* logjam of bodies outside your office during office hours. If you get 20 students herding outside your office, typically just before an exam, there are several remedies.

You can decamp immediately to a seminar room and run an impromptu tutorial, leaving a note on your door redirecting other students. (This is very efficient because many students will have the same questions, and you can address them simultaneously.) Less efficiently, you can put a sign-up sheet on your office door, and have groups of five students come back to see you in extra office hours, through the rest of the day. (Time is at a premium during the exam period, and your students will appreciate having a firm appointment, rather than cooling their heels outside your door for some indefinite period.) The worst thing you can do, however, is to try to whittle away at the long line one student at a time; they will hate you for it, and it may impact your evaluations.

Chapter 11

Keep Calm and Carry On

Greene (1592) says, "forewarned, forearmed: burnt children dread the fire." Greene's pamphlet contains many humorous cautionary tales of "conny-catching" so that "gentlemen, marchants, citizens, apprentices, yeomen, and plaine countrey farmers" may protect themselves.[1] Let me now move from advice for run-of-the-mill situations to forewarning you of unpleasant situations you may face.

---

[1] A "conny" is a tame rabbit, and thus easily caught. "Conny-catching" is 16th Century slang for theft through deception (i.e., a confidence trick that preys upon easy marks).

11.1 Civility Costs Nothing

Let me begin with an issue that is no more than a tiresome irritation. Over the last 30 years, I have noticed a steady reduction in the general level of civility, manners, and etiquette in my students.

I mentioned, in Section 4.3, that I have collected experiences from 800+ job interviews. I have read thousands of CVs and written three books about interviewing for jobs. Students who know about my background send me CVs and cover letters to critique, often at the prompting of another faculty member who is aware of my background.

I usually reply by email with 20–30 constructive criticisms, pointing out spelling mistakes, poor word choice, grammatical errors, important points that are missing, wrong item ordering, inconsistencies, etc. Nowadays, however, only one in three of the students that I help by email takes the time to reply to say, "thank you."

I think that this lack of manners connotes entitled behavior. I often also see arrogant and entitled behavior in the students who speak to me in my office. I do not like it, but I do nothing about it, figuring that the offending student will get their comeuppance further downstream in the recruitment process. You might instead take a corrective approach, pointing out that these attitudes are unprofessional and unpopular in the workplace.

I mentioned, in Section 4.4, that some undergraduates call me "Tim." It seems ridiculous to me that when I am three times their age, gray haired, and the author of their 700-page textbook, they discard the titles "Professor," "Prof," "Dr.," "Sir," "Mr.," or even "Timothy," and shorten it all the way down to the diminutive "Tim." What's next in this progression?

The moral of these stories is simply that you should not be surprised to observe low levels of, and a further decline in, common civility. You get to choose whether to educate your students about it (probably the best thing to do) or ignore it and let them pay the price downstream (as I have done).

On a positive note, I have many times announced to my class that "If you are Chinese, please just call me 'Crack'." The Chinese students appreciate this and respond well to it. It both puts them at ease, and solves a problem I know that they have (namely, what should they call me). When I make this invitation, my Chinese students make a point of seeking me out to ask me questions, whereas otherwise, I suspect that they would keep their counsel.

11.2 Keep Your Mouth Shut?

Sometimes it pays to keep your mouth shut; sometimes not. Let me give some parables that vary from unusual to truly awful.

> **Story (Misplaced Affinity):** When I was about 45 years old, I taught an adult woman student who was about my age. Her hair was turning gray. She was out of shape: She looked like she had spent years focused on taking care of her children at the expense of not taking care of herself.
>
> I figured her children were now out of the house or independent enough for her to return to university (or to attend university for the first time); this is not unusual timing for adult students.
>
> When she worked with other students on group work, they told me that she was motherly towards them, and bossed them around like they were her own kids, who were, I assumed, about the same age.
>
> As an instructor, you tend to feel something of an affinity with adult students the same age as you. Unlike the youngest students, you share

history with the adult students. You experienced the same music, the same wars, the same economic ups and downs, the same politicians, etc. It's like the old Simon and Garfunkel lyric "Old friends/Memory brushes the same years/Silently sharing the same fears."

One day she asked me if I could act as a job reference for her. I said yes immediately, partly because adult students often have difficulty competing with their younger peers in the job market, and I have a lot of experience helping good students to get good jobs.

I knew she was a good student in my class, but I did not know how she had performed in other classes. So, I looked up her grades in our computer system. In the top right-hand corner of the grade transcript is the student's birth date. I did a double-take! Was I misreading it? Could that be correct? I even got out my calculator to check. *God's Holy Trousers!* She was only 21 years old!! I had been completely fooled. I would have been less surprised to find that she was 51. Thank goodness I kept my mouth shut about my personal thoughts, because I might have caused considerable offence if I had asked about her adult children.

Story (Mr. Freeze): A colleague turned up to teach class on a hot summer day to find a student sitting there with a big winter jacket and big fluffy earmuffs. He thought the student was playing a prank. He also thought that the student was rude to be wearing big earmuffs because he would not be able to hear what was said in class. He was annoyed, but I do not think he said anything.

In fact, the student had just arrived from a very hot foreign country and our "hot" N.Z. summer day was relatively cold to him. So, he put on all his winter clothing. He was not trying to play a prank or to be rude; he was just freezing and trying to take care of himself. Sometimes keeping your mouth shut in the face of seemingly crazy student behavior is a good idea.

On the other hand, keeping your mouth shut is not *always* a good idea.

Story (Awful Asymmetry): A student came to buy a textbook from me in my office just before the semester started. I noticed immediately that he was dressed very unusually, and with no good reason that I could possibly imagine (then or now).

I spent my youth in that same city, and I came from a very low socio-economic background. I grew up on the wrong side of the railway tracks, and I knew very well the attitudes of many people with the same background who were less fortunate than I. So, my initial reaction to his odd appearance was to think to myself "If this idiot kid goes downtown on a Friday or Saturday night dressed like this, he is going to get his f@#$ing head kicked in."

I had, however, been *conditioned* to keep my mouth shut. Commenting on a student's inappropriate appearance is itself considered inappropriate in this day and age. Quite frankly, I was fearful of being reprimanded by the admin boffins if I said anything and the student complained. So, I said nothing to the student. I did wonder, in my defense, whether he might just have been dressed up for a beginning-of-semester student fancy dress party, but, no, he came to my classes dressed that way.

A few weeks into the semester I got one of those awful emails that the admin folks send out telling me that one of my students was not going to attend class for a little while, and not to penalize his grades if work was due that he did not complete on time. They gave the student's name and ID number, neither of which I recognized in my 150-student class. A few days later I got an email saying that this same student was in the intensive care unit at the hospital, and his parents were coming down from a city in the North Island of N.Z. (about 1,000km from my University). So, I looked up his name and ID number in the University system, and sure enough, it was the oddly-dressed student.

A couple of days after that I got an email saying that he was out of intensive care, his parents would be taking him home to care for him, and not to expect him back. It gave further details. Apparently, he had gone downtown on a Saturday night and someone had beaten him up and kicked him in the head. His head injuries stopped his studies in their tracks and could have cost him his life. To the best of my knowledge, he never returned to campus.

I regretted not saying something to the student. There is an awful asymmetry here in that I will not be reprimanded if I say nothing and my student gets maimed or killed, but I can easily be reprimanded if I open my mouth and try to protect a student, who then complains.

On a selfish level, I take some consolation in thinking that perhaps if I had said something, he would have ignored me anyway, and the outcome would have been the same.

I think it is a sorry state of affairs when political correctness creates a fear of speaking out, for fear of being reprimanded or losing my job, and this fear then stops me from acting *in loco parentis* and saying something that might change the course of a young person's life. I do not know what the solution is, but whatever it is, our advancing climate of political correctness is moving us further from it.

My takeaway lesson was that in future I should just say what I am thinking (albeit tactfully) and take the consequences. I would rather be repremanded than have some student's life shattered or lost because I kept my mouth shut. What would you do?

Story (Repeat Offender): "Dr. Dill" made drunken phone calls to anonymous interviewee "Prof. Sage's" house in the evenings, emailed objectionable photographic images to everyone in their Department, often made inappropriate comments about women (even in Departmental meetings), and accused an administrator of not liking him because she was a racist. (...but she disliked him for more obvious reasons).

Dr. Dill asked for Prof. Sage's opinion on a research paper. Dr. Dill was, however, visibly furious (shaking and red-faced, with clenched fists) when Prof. Sage politely queried a fatal flaw. He sent Prof. Sage emails saying that his problem was, "and always has been, a lack of honesty" (What?) and that accusing Dr. Dill of making an error here was "like saying that women don't menstruate" (Huh? What?).

Dr. Dill ignored Prof. Sage's criticism of his paper and immediately submitted it to a top-tier journal. The single referee pointed only at the same fatal flaw that Prof. Sage had pointed at, rejecting the paper in very few words. Then Dr. Dill sent a sarcastic email to Prof. Sage saying how happy he must be "for being so smart."

Prof. Sage showed the emails to the Dean and HR. He described, but did not show, the objectionable images (which could not be *unseen*). The woman from HR was embarrassed and uncomfortable. He mentioned the drunken phone calls and the comments about women, etc. After some discussion, however, Prof. Sage decided that because he was forced to work with Dr. Dill on a daily basis, he would keep the peace and not lay a formal complaint. No written record was kept by the Dean or HR.

Unfortunately, Dr. Dill subsequently declared to his young female graduate student TA that his wife did not love him, and asked her to come away with him. He asked her for a hug (she felt pressured) and then he kissed her. When the student made a formal complaint, he accused her of leading him on. Dr. Dill's lack of a record meant, however, that he kept his job. In a surprise move, Dr. Dill was later promoted to full professor. In a sickening follow-up, newer faculty sang his praises, unaware of his long history of bad behavior. Dr. Dill retired not long afterwards, thank goodness.

The moral of the story is that with hindsight, Prof. Sage dearly wished that he had registered a formal complaint against Dr. Dill. Perhaps Dr. Dill might have been more reluctant to behave badly again, for fear of losing his job, or, if he still chose to reoffend, then perhaps he would not have been retained or promoted, and a public example would have been made of him.

Prof. Sage regretted that his failure to act contributed to a disgusting outcome for this student, and that he failed in his duty *in loco parentis* to this student. Do not make the same mistake (and have the same regrets)![2]

11.3 Overruled!

A final-year student in a different discipline waited until her last semester to sit my required first-year course. She was so advanced in her own *qualitative* discipline that she did not take my *quantitative* first-year course seriously enough. She got a 48 "Fail D" grade in my course, and she earned it.

She came to my office and turned on the water works. I ignored her tears and I told her that she had a clear fail. (Recall Section 10.3.) I told her when and how she could repeat the course. She had, however, received a job offer from a company whose

---

[2]I have a parallel story from a prior employer of mine. A repeat offender, who had made offensive comments to me, came to class drunk, and then also subsequently propositioned a female student in his office. She told her father, who complained to the Dean. The offender was told that one more event would lead to his dismissal. Years later, after moving on to a new university, he asked me if he could visit my N.Z. university; his email did not merit a response.

leader sat on the Advisory Board for our School of Business. I assume that her job offer was conditional upon her completing her degree.

I was perfectly comfortable with failing her because of the "Truth will out" argument given in Section 1.1.8. That is, she completed multiple assignments, a mid-term examination and a final examination, and everything pointed at her earning a fail. She had plenty of warning, and plenty of experience, but she did nothing about the impending train wreck. She could have come to her tutor or to me to get remedial attention, but no, the first time I laid eyes upon her was when she was in tears in my office after her failing grade was released.

I told her that she could write a letter to the Dean to appeal on compassionate grounds. She did so, and I saw the letter, which was littered with spelling mistakes and grammatical errors akin to those of child in high school; it was an awful embarrassment. The Dean overruled me and directed that her grade be lifted to the lowest possible pass. I felt that this was unfair to the other marginal students in my class who had failed, many of whom were green first-year students. She, however, had no inexperience to use as an excuse.

The moral of the story is that although it is your

job, as the discipline expert, to assess students as passing or failing, you need to accept that in some cases, some admin boffin who is not a discipline expert can step in and overrule your decision. (This is not the first time that some boffin has overruled my grade on grounds other than performance.)

11.4   Extra Time Disclosure?

My University allows extra time in exams for students with disabilities (many of which are invisible to an interviewer). The University does not, however, give any indication of this extra time allowance on official grade transcripts.

Is it fair that a potential employer may see two job candidates with identical grade transcripts, where one candidate required 15% more time in an exam than the other in order to achieve the same grade? As a former practitioner and recruiter, I would want to know if my candidate required this extra time. It might not change my decision, but at least I would be fully informed.

Perhaps it makes sense to disclose an "ET" (for extra time) beside the grades of such students. I understand the University's motivation, but I worry not only that employers are being misled, but that the University may face a legal challenge for failing to disclose this information if a student they recruit from us underperforms their expectations.

11.5 Call the National Guard?

For many years, my N.Z. University has offered extra tutorials for students belonging to minority racial groups that have historically been disadvantaged (with decades of worse health outcomes, lower educational achievement, and lower wealth achievement, when compared with majority racial groups).

In the U.S. in 1963, however, the Kennedy brothers sent the National Guard into the University of Alabama to help to enforce racial *de*-segregation in education. This forced desegregation was a watershed moment, lauded globally. So, why are segregated tutorials still offered in N.Z.?

The socio-cultural environment for these students in N.Z. has been described as "unique," with culturally-sensitive teaching efforts yielding notable improvements in outcomes (Wilson *et al.*, 2011). For example, Reid (2006, Section 7.1) argues that minority students open up and speak more freely in segregated tutorials than in mixed-race ones, and that attendance improves test scores.

Students are, however, disadvantaged for many reasons unrelated to race. So, I find it worrying that we offer students extra help based only upon the association of their *ethnicity* with disadvantage.

High achievers of these ethnicities exist who do *not* need extra help, and low achievers, not of these ethnicities, exist who *do* need extra help. Why not invite *all* students to these tutorials, based only upon *academic* need? Why not address learning inhibitions *directly*, rather than reverting to *racial segregation*? Segregation may improve academic outcomes, but how can it model success for students who must succeed in an *integrated* society?

If you define racism only as a *negative* act towards people of an ethnicity that has historically been disadvantaged, then arguably, racially segregated classes are not racist. If, however, you define racism as treating people differently based upon their ethnicity, then this offering is racist.

11.6   A Professional Dis-Courtesy

A student handed in a mathematics master's thesis for which anonymous interviewee "Prof. Scarlett" was to be an examiner.

Story (A Study in Scarlett): The research goals in the thesis were novel and aspirational. After some detective work, however, Prof. Scarlett concluded that the math in the thesis was not sound. A key assertion was clearly false, and the complicated proofs of all four main propositions were also false. The mathematical notation used had been condensed to the point where its meaning was no longer immediately clear, and, upon close examination, its application was obviously inappropriate.

There were only two possibilities in Prof. Scarlett's mind: the student knew of the errors and was too lazy to fix them (and likely had also unethically condensed the notation to hide the errors, assuming that the examiners would not find them); or, the student was too dim to know that she had made any errors in the first place, and had used notation so poor that she confused even herself. Prof. Scarlett knew the student's supervisor and told him that "as a professional courtesy" she was letting him know in advance that his student's thesis was unsound, before she did any paperwork assessing the thesis.

Prof. Scarlett was surprised to almost immediately get an email from the *student* pleading for a passing grade in order to use the grade to enter a PhD program before an offer with a tight deadline expired. Prof. Scarlett had not expected the supervisor to inform the student (she thought she was just being courteous to an esteemed colleague in the discipline, who would then be discreet; this was her first mistake).

Then Prof. Scarlett got a stream of begging/pleading emails from the student (which is against that university's policy; a student is not allowed to communicate with an examiner after work is submitted and before a grade is released). Prof. Scarlett should have reported the situation and immediately recused herself as an examiner; this was her second mistake.

After many emails from the student and supervisor, Prof. Scarlett agreed to bend the rules and to award a low passing grade *before* the thesis was fixed, but only if the student and the supervisor put in writing that they promised to fix the thesis after the paperwork was processed and before a final copy of the thesis was submitted. The student and the supervisor both gave Prof. Scarlett written assurances that the thesis would be fixed, and Prof. Scarlett trusted them; this was her third mistake.

After about two months, the student sent Prof. Scarlett an email saying that the thesis would not (or could not) be fixed. Again, Prof. Scarlett asked herself if this was a lazy/unethical-student problem or a dim-student problem ("a LOFE problem or a LOFT problem," in her words). She strongly suspected the student to be both lazy and unethical.

A second examiner independently gave a low passing grade, because of the novel/aspirational nature of the work, but he signaled that he thought the thesis had significant issues. Basically, he was holding his nose and saying that a sufficient amount of work had been done for an award of the lowest possible passing grade.

In sum, a thesis that was at best marginal got a low pass and the student went to a PhD program on the basis of it (which apparently she did not complete). It was the only mistake Prof. Scarlett ever made in awarding a grade.

The morals of the story are: Never inform a supervisor of the progress of a thesis (or any) examination that is in progress, no matter how talented or discreet you think the supervisor is; if you find yourself in any way compromised in your role as an examiner, then you must immediately recuse yourself, regardless of the cost to the student; and, never bend the rules to award a grade on a thesis (or anything) if the work has not been properly completed on time and in full, to the letter of the regulations.

11.7 Getting The Boot

I was co-supervising a PhD student (let's call him "Mr. Green") with two seasoned academics, "Prof. Mustard" and "Prof. Plum." Unfortunately, Prof. Plum took the advice in Section 5.3 ("RAs Galore") a few steps too far.

Although we like our PhD students to have some published work outside their thesis when they go on the job market (because it makes them stand out), we have to be careful in managing each student's workload.

Prof. Plum, however, pointed young Mr. Green at a difficult research project of his own and insisted that Mr. Green labor on it to the exclusion of his thesis for weeks on end. Mr. Green went to Prof. Mustard, in tears, and explained that he was being worked so hard that he was making no progress on his thesis. There was a second ethical problem: Prof. Plum was *related* to Mr. Green.

Prof. Plum was exploiting poor Mr. Green, who felt compelled to do the work for familial obligation reasons; it was a perfect storm.

Prof. Mustard took the case one step higher in the university hierarchy, pointed to the two unethical behaviors (supervising a relative and working him like a slave), and Prof. Plum was immediately booted off the supervisory committee for good.

The story has two morals: Do not accept graduate students who are related to supervisors; and, do not exploit graduate students as RAs to the point where their thesis completion is undermined.[3]

11.8   Success or Failure?

I taught an introductory course that had more mathematical content (and a commensurately lower pass rate) than companion courses taught at the same level. Each semester a steady 75% of students passed. Compared with less-mathematical classes taught by competing departments, this class was a constant source of criticism from the admin boffins.

---

[3]When teaching *undergraduates*, however, you sometimes cannot avoid teaching a relative. Check your university's policy. You likely must disclose the relationship, and have all grading for that student assigned to another faculty member.

They could not understand that more mathematical content led naturally to a lower pass rate among their less numerate students.

After some years, the course was passed to a junior instructor without a PhD and some of the most difficult content was removed. This content was replaced with nothing, thus achieving three outcomes in one fell swoop (Shakespeare, 1606): Some difficult content that needed to be covered as a prerequisite for higher-level courses was no longer being taught, interfering with student comprehension in subsequent higher-level classes; the course had less content at a lower average level of difficulty than previously; and, not surprisingly, the pass rate went up. The admin boffins, in their infinite wisdom, ignored the first two results and applauded the third!

11.9   Failure to Launch

Academia seems to attract a higher proportion of unpleasant people than other skilled professions I have worked in or had exposure to. Perhaps it is because these unpleasant people ended up in academia after a "failure to launch." For example, perhaps they did not have the people skills to get a proper job, so they stayed in school. Do that for long enough, and before you know it you have a PhD! You might not, however, know how to "play well with others." This is a day-to-day issue in your life as an academic because you will have to co-teach a course, or sit on a committee, or supervise a student, with one of these people.

You have probably heard of the "Peter principle," which says that people get promoted until they reach a level of responsibility where they are incompetent, and then they get promoted no further (Peter and Hull, 1969).[4] Combine the Peter principle with a failure to launch, and Mother Nature might produce your most recent, current, or next boss. Good luck with that! To protect yourself and your teaching (and your students) from these evils, see Gabarro and Kotter (1980) and Financial Samurai (2020) for brief, but pointed, advice.

After collecting job interview questions from job candidates for 30 years, I have noticed that the "What is your greatest strength?" question is very common. After 30 years of working in academia, I can claim two greatest strengths. My first strength

---

[4]See also Lazear (2004) for a regression-to-the-mean statistical explanation based on permanent and transitory components. Lazear also claims that firms inflate their promotion criteria in order to offset this statistical effect.

is quantitative pattern recognition (good for computer programming, algebraic derivations, and logical arguments). I am sorry to say that my second strength is the ability to get the most out of a few colleagues I do not like, do not trust, and do not respect (especially when I was Department Head).

Although most of my colleagues have been a joy to work with, a small proportion of my academic colleagues have been disorganized, bigoted, arrogant, absent any social skills, or just plain evil. So, you need to be thick skinned to succeed long term in your role as an academic.

11.10 Fake Hurdle

A former boss had to produce an annual review of my performance to go on my permanent record. I had won a University-level teaching award (from the Students' Association) and had consistently excellent teaching evaluations. Nevertheless, he wrote on my performance review that other teachers in the large required first-year courses were consistently scoring above 90% on an overview question on the teaching evaluation form, and that my relative performance was insufficient. (Scoring above 90% approval would have been especially difficult because my big required class was relatively quantitative; I was scoring only above 80%.) What could I do about the negative comments on my annual review?

After this negative review, I asked the admin boffins in the Dean's Office to send me a spreadsheet with the teaching evaluation numbers for the instructors in *all* the large first-year courses. (Any first-year instructor had access to these data; they only had to ask.) I wanted to find out who it was who was *consistently* scoring so *highly* relative to me, so that I could ask them for tips.

When the spreadsheet arrived, I entered formulae to measure the *level* of all the teaching evaluation scores and their *consistency* over time. There were two surprises: *Nobody* teaching in the first-year courses was scoring 90% or more on the overview question my boss had pointed at; and, no matter how I coded the spreadsheet formulae for level and consistency, the first-year instructor who was consistently scoring the highest in their teaching evaluations was *me*! My boss had also written the same false comments on the performance review of a colleague; my colleague said of our boss that "yes, he destroyed a lot of value."

Deming (Section 1.1.1) argues that you cannot "inspect quality into a product." So, a boffin who collects teaching evaluations and uses them in the decision making process is focusing on the *wrong* end of the production line. To go one step further, and to replace *collected* evaluation numbers with *fabricated* numbers, in such a fantastically baroque fashion, is a double-descent into bedlam.

The moral of the story is that you likely know your own teaching evaluations very well, but if anyone compares your evaluation scores to those of your peers, then you need to make 100% sure that the comparison is being done correctly. Some admin boffins may take a dislike to you and simply fabricate data to make you look bad, even when you are doing an excellent job.

Your boss may be a bigoted/prejudiced person, or a bully who has risen to the top through unethical/immoral behavior. Your boss may hold the position because of the Peter principle (see Section 11.9) or he or she may have been assigned the role because no qualified person would take it.

Be 100% professional in your response, don't raise your voice or use provocative language. Instead, calmly insist on seeing the data and analyzing it for yourself. You can use the pretense of wishing to improve your teaching to get access to the data. You may be in for a surprise, or two!

11.11 Impossible vs Unpleasant

When you are asked to do the *impossible*, it is your duty to say, "No." When you are, however, asked to do what is merely *unpleasant*, you have little choice but to comply.

My boss came to see me just before a new semester started. I was working over 80 hours a week, supervising multiple graduate students, had a full teaching load assigned, and was overseeing a time-consuming graduate program. He told me, however, that I had to teach an additional course that semester (i.e., in 2–3 weeks). It was to be an advanced course in an area I did not know, and in which I had never even taken a class as a student.

Given my workload, it was not in the students' best interests, or in the interests of the Department, or the University, for me to teach a hastily prepared advanced-level course completely outside my area of expertise at such short notice.

A better idea would have been to cancel the course and waive program requirements so that the students could substitute an out-of-area course instead (in my area, that could have been a course from accounting, economics, statistics, mathematics, physics, psychology, or information science).

In this case, however, my boss came back to me every day for 4–5 days in a row, insisting, "You *must* teach it!" and "There is *nobody* else!" It would have been a different story if I were not teaching in that semester and had been given more notice, but this was an *impossible ask*. My boss, however, ignorantly viewed it only as an *unpleasant task*.

The pressure from my boss was relentless, and was affecting my ability to do my *actual* job. With the new semester about to overrun my position, I felt that I had no choice but to re-state my argument, and to then go home to work remotely, without permission, not answering my phone or my email—an extraordinary action for me. Within a week, he found some other poor fool who agreed to teach the course to the unsuspecting students.

Staffing constraints mean that most of us will, at some time, have to accept teaching assignments outside our areas of interest. One reason that the university *pays* you is so that your boss can force you to take on these *unpleasant* jobs! As long as the assignment is feasible (unlike mine), then you must accept it, no matter how unpleasant.

Unfortunately, teaching outside your research area can waste valuable research time as you spend your efforts getting up to speed on topics you will never research. At the same time, you will be less skilled in this area than in your area of interest/expertise, and so your students will suffer (along with your teaching evaluations!).

> One interviewee listed "Being interested in the material I teach" as one of the most important drivers of good teaching.

Shaw, however, wrote, "No man can be a pure specialist without being in the strict sense an idiot" (Shaw, 1903). So, I once purposely asked to teach in a new area, because I was curious about it and I thought it would be interesting—even though it was outside my area of expertise. I ended up with three journal articles and a book in that area.

Teaching faculty can also fail to distinguish between impossible asks and unpleasant tasks. For example, a new hire complained to me that he was assigned to the wrong class. In retaliation, he canceled classes, telling students that they should know it already, which was false and disruptive.

> When asked what I had failed to ask, one candidate said, "How do you teach in less than ideal circumstances? Accept the limitations set before you and work on a solution, which will

sometimes fail. It will make you a better teacher even when circumstances improve."

The bottom line is that it is important for you (and your boss) to distinguish between *impossible asks* that you *cannot* comply with and *unpleasant tasks* that you *must* comply with.

11.12 You Want a Revolution?

Some great teachers with limited publishing success circulate futile emails complaining about journal editors, journal ranking, and the peer review system. Do not be that naysayer; your complaints are destructive, not constructive; they lower morale and make you look like a hapless dissident.

Some of my recent research has not found favor with journal editors, but that is my fault, and nobody else's. Late in my career, I knowingly chose to work on research topics that had interested me for more than a decade and which I knew to be out of favor. I used unusual techniques to solve very interesting problems, and I learned some amazing and deeply satisfying things. Some of my research revolutionized how I teach those topics in the classroom. I knew, however, that this research would be a tough sell to journal editors and referees.

If you are a good teacher, but having difficulty publishing, consider redirecting your energies to the more pedagogically-oriented journals, and making your mark there. Then use those journals as a stepping stone to the more research-oriented outlets; see the step-by-step example in Section 5.1.

11.13   Last-Period Parasites

How will your career end? If you are recognized as a consistently outstanding teacher, will you be able to retire gracefully? "No, not necessarily," says one anonymous interviewee in this mini case study.

Story (Ruffled Feathers!): "Dr. Peacock" retired after 20 years of award-winning teaching at her university. She also had an excellent record of research, service, and engagement with the wider community.

Nevertheless, when she gave notice of her retirement, this act triggered six months of hardball tactics from the admin boffins. They tried repeatedly to force her to exit her contract early or to accept a severe cut in salary, either one of which would also reduce her retirement benefit package; no other option was offered.

The hardball tactics used by the boffins included every strategy that Mnookin, Peppet, and Tulumello (2004) warn about. (A handy summary list appears in PON [2020].) These tactics are unethical; they also ignore the possibility of mutually beneficial agreements (PON, 2020). A pettifogging extra tactic was that the boffins did not reply to her emails for weeks at a time. (A colleague of hers, who went through a similar experience with the same boffins, told her that this delaying tactic was used purposefully in the hope that she would give up hope in the interim and capitulate, on their demeaning terms.)

I have a hypothesis for why a good employee was mistreated this way. McKenzie and Lee (2010) say that the "last-period (or end period) problem refers to the costs that can be expected to be incurred from opportunistic behavior when the end of a working relationship approaches."

In the context of retirement, for example, a pre-retiree may be tempted to evade work during the last few months of their contract, because the employer's bargaining power is weakened by this stage. Thus the employer has an incentive to protect themselves by strategically terminating the retiree's contract early. It is like "gardening leave" in the U.K., but without pay.

...but why did the university stoop so low as to use a dozen *unethical hard-bargaining tactics*, instead of behaving better? I have a hypothesis about that too; let me break it down into parts.

Dr. Peacock's employer has the best *research reputation* of any university within a 750-mile radius of their campus (i.e., they are a regional monopolist). Hand in hand with this, they invest heavily in research facilities and reward research publications, using their reputation to attract eager new faculty looking to build research agendas. They are, however, misers when it comes to building their *employee-morale reputation*. Hand in hand with *that*, Dr. Peacock noted that her university had locked up the best employment lawyers in the region.[5]

Macey (2010) argues that if substitute drivers of behavior exist, reputation can cease to be priced in the market and bad actors (he calls them

---

[5]This particular employer is no stranger to strategic behavior. They are known for inflating their promotion criteria relative to that of their rivals, potentially to offset the regression-to-the-mean statistical explanation for the Peter principle (Peter and Hull, 1969), as mentioned in Lazear (2004). (See also Section 11.9.)

"last-period parasites") can emerge.[6]   Something akin to this may have happened here.

Departing employees could not hire better employment lawyers than those owned by the university. So, the university, as a last-period parasite, felt free to use hardball tactics to force early exits to protect themselves from potentially work-averse last-period pre-retirees (while also saving money on benefits packages).   In contrast, they had only a weak incentive to invest time, effort, or money into developing or maintaining employee morale, because their research facilities/reputation brought in eager replacements of departees.

Other employees at the same university (not interviewees for this book) said that hardball tactics were being used widely, and that morale

---

[6]Macey (2010) argues that in heavily-regulated countries, financial market participants are unwilling to pay more to deal with firms that have built up high reputational capital because law and regulation, rather than reputation, are (perhaps mistakenly) assumed to protect market participants from fraud and other abuse. Thus financial firms are prepared to monetize their reputations via one-off frauds, and have weak incentives to invest in controls that would develop and maintain their reputations. He describes this as a move from a "reputational paradigm" to a "parasitic paradigm."

was low everywhere. I have a hypothesis for this wide use of hard-bargaining tactics.

The research reputation of this university makes its employees attractive to other universities (as evidenced by the unusual number of their employees who jump ship or are "poached"). At the same time, the university's research reputation continually attracts replacement faculty. So, given high employee mobility, the admin boffins now treat *every* employee contract as if it poses a potential last-period problem, and they feel free to behave unprofessionally and unethically more widely, while relatively insulated from legal recourse.[7] For example, good teachers were labeled openly as being "a dime a dozen" because the university's research reputation could always replace them with (more valuable) new faculty wishing to build their *research* agendas. High employee turnover also saves on retirement benefit payments generally.

---

[7]Note that the afore-mentioned strategic promotion-criteria inflation, when combined with heavy investment into research reputation, compounds the last-period problem, because it gives employees an additional incentive to "jump ship" at any time for a competitor, who may give them an instant promotion in rank and salary.

> The bottom line is that the income generated by research supremacy combined with the expenses saved by not investing in morale-building exercises/controls (and reinforced by non-vesting retirement benefits) has overwhelmed the costs associated with continual recruitment. This vicious employment equilibrium relegates good teaching to a distant second, behind research.

The simplest solution to the last-period problem for a pre-retiree is to credibly signal an interest in a *continuing* relationship (McKenzie and Lee, 2010). For example, in my case, I lobbied for an appointment as an Emeritus Professor (which is not automatic at my University). In exchange for access to resources, I agreed to mentor junior faculty, co-author with faculty, assist job seeking students, etc. Authoring books in four different areas (investments, derivatives, corporate finance, and interviewing for jobs) and winning a string of teaching awards made my offer more credible.

If you are, however, unable to negotiate a continuing relationship after you leave, then you may yet have to stand your ground against hardball tactics from last-period parasites. So, be sure to read Mnookin et al (2004), or the summary in PON (2020). Forewarned, forearmed!

11.14 The Triumph of Principles

Let me end on a positive note. Why work so hard on your teaching when faced with so many hurdles (not least of which are the admin boffins who view you as an inanimate line item in their budget)? The answer is simple: Taking the high road described by my interviewees means that when it comes time to move on from your employment, you can do so with your head held high, knowing that you did your job and served your students well.

> "Nothing can bring you peace but yourself. Nothing can bring you peace but the triumph of principles" (Emerson, 1841, para. 50).

Appendix A

Appendix: Letter to Teachers

I sent the following email to a select group of university teachers in the United States, United Kingdom, Australia, Israel, and N.Z.

```
Subject: Introspection > Interviews with
Top Teachers


I am retiring soon.  I had 30 years of
highly-rated university teaching here
and in the U.S., and I want to pass on
whatever teaching advice I can while it
is fresh in my memory.  So, one of my
```

near-term book projects in retirement is to record the practical things I did to make my university teaching effective, memorable, and highly rated relative to my peers' efforts. I have been making notes, and I already have enough raw material for a short book. It should appear in 2021 as a pocket-sized physical edition and as a cheap Amazon eBook.

I do not want to limit myself to my own narrow world view, but I don't know what I don't know. So, to give a broader perspective, I am asking you and other highly-rated university teachers about their teaching.

I am looking for easily transferrable skills, rather than person-specific unique attributes. I am looking for practical teaching tips that make the students happy, challenge them, and that worked for you. I am also interested in tips/advice that increase efficiency and thereby create more time for research.

You do not have to limit your answers to what happens inside the classroom; that's just the tip of the spear.

I have some questions for you. Please answer them in whatever way suits you. Mull them over. Feel free to give long answers or short answers. Feel free to ignore any of my bullet points. Feel free to just say what you think in a stream of consciousness.

- When you were a student, did you have a great teacher who did something special in the classroom? If so, what was it?

- What are the three most important things you do (or do not do) as a teacher that make you a great teacher?

- Do you have a great tip for online/remote teaching that you did not mention yet?

- Did your gender, ethnicity, age, nationality, language, disability (or anything else) create a classroom hurdle that you had to overcome? If so, how did you overcome it?

- Is there an important question I should have asked you, but which I failed to ask? If so, what is that question and what is the answer?

- Do you have any other comments?

I will not associate your specific comments with your name (so feel free to speak plainly). I plan to thank you in the acknowledgements of my book, and to give you a couple of free hardcopies.

Please send me a follow-up email if something else occurs to you later that you should have said here.

Feel free to forward this email to a university teacher you rate very highly; I will be happy to have the additional feedback.

Regards and thanks
Timothy
timcrack@alum.mit.edu

References

Abbadie, Jacques, 1684, *Traité de la Vérité de la Religion Chrétienne*, Chez Reinier Leers: Rotterdam, Netherlands.

Baldwin, Roberto, 2020, "Self-Driving-Car Research Has Cost $16 Billion. What Do We Have to Show for It?," Available here: `https://www.caranddriver.com/news/a30857661/autonomous-car-self-driving-research-expensive/` (dated Feb 10, 2020; downloaded Sept 5, 2021).

Barrett, Lisa Feldman, 2020, "Balancing the Brain Budget," Lisa Feldman Barrett on *The Knowledge Project* with Shane Parrish, Available here: `https://podcastnotes.org/knowledge-project/balancing-the-brain-budget-lisa-feldman-barrett-on-the-knowledge-project-with-shane-parrish/` (dated Sept 20, 2020; downloaded Jul 4, 2021).

Beugelsdijk, Sjoerd, Robbert Maseland, and André van Hoorn, 2013, "Are Hofstede's Culture Dimensions Stable Over Time? A Generational Cohort Analysis," Available here: `https://ssrn.com/abstract=2336893` (dated Oct 7, 2013; downloaded Jul 4, 2021).

Beugelsdijk, Sjoerd, Robbert Maseland, and André van Hoorn, 2015, "Are Scores on Hofstede's Dimensions of National Culture Stable over Time? A Cohort Analysis," *Global Strategy Journal*, Vol. 5 No. 3, (Aug), pp. 223–240.

Bolton, Paul, 2012, "Education: Historical Statistics," House of Commons Library, Social & General Statistics, Standard Note: SN/SG/4252, (27 Nov), 20pp.

Browne, M. Neil and Stuart M. Keeley, 1985, "Achieving Excellence: Advice to New Teachers," *College Teaching*, Vol. 33 No. 2, (Apr–Jun), pp. 78–83.

Buchanan, Thomas, and Edward Palmer, 2017, "Student Perceptions of the History Lecture: Does this Delivery Mode have a Future in the Humanities?", *Journal of University Teaching and Learning Practice*, Vol. 14 No. 2, Available here: `https://ro.uow.edu.au/jutlp/vol14/iss2/4`.

Butler, Alexander W., 2017, "The Marmots of Finance," Episode 33 of *Tea for Teaching*, 2017 Rebecca Mushtare and John Kane, Available here: `http://teaforteaching.com/33-the-marmots-of-finance/` (at the 33:30-mark on the audio).

Butler, Alexander W., 2020, *A Presentation on Presentations*, Rice University, 36pp.

Chan, Melissa, 2016, "Here's How Winning the Lottery Makes You Miserable," Available here: `https://time.com/4176128/powerball-jackpot-lottery-winners/` (dated Jan 12, 2016; downloaded Sept 17, 2021).

Chickering, Arthur W. and Zelda F. Gamson, 1987, "Seven Principles For Good Practice In Undergraduate Education," *AAHE Bulletin*, March, pp. 2–6. Available here: `http://eric.ed.gov/?id=ED282491`.

"Clay," 2021, "Creation of Life from Clay," See, for example, `https://en.wikipedia.org/wiki/Creation_of_life_from_clay` (dated Jun 20, 2021; downloaded Jun 21, 2021).

Coffield, Frank, David Moseley, Elaine Hall, and Kathryn Ecclestone, 2004, "Learning Styles and Pedagogy in Post-16 Learning: A Systematic and Critical Review," Published by the Learning and Skills Research Centre, 182pp.

Crack, Timothy Falcon, 2018, *How to Ace Your Business Finance Class: Essential Knowledge and Techniques to Master the Material and Ace your Exams.* Revised Third Edition (Jul). See the advertisement at the end of this book and `www.Amazon.com`.

Crack, Timothy Falcon, 2020a, *Foundations for Scientific Investing: Capital Markets Intuition and Critical*

Thinking Skills, 10th Edition. See the advertisement at the end of this book and `www.Amazon.com`.

Crack, Timothy Falcon, 2020b, *24 Essential Tips for Selling Print Replica eBooks on Amazon: How to Capture New Readers by Turning Your Physical Book into an eBook*. See the advertisement at the end of this book and `www.Amazon.com`.

Crack, Timothy Falcon, 2021a, *Foundations for Scientific Investing: Multiple-Choice, Short-Answer, and Long-Answer Test Questions*, 7th Edition. See the advertisement at the end of this book and `www.Amazon.com`.

Crack, Timothy Falcon, 2021b, *NYSE Ticker Tape 1867–1994*, Available here: `http://www.foundationsforscientificinvesting.com/ticker-tape-dating.htm`.

Crack, Timothy Falcon, Lynn McAlevey, and Anindya Sen, 2020, "U.S. Stock Returns, the Berry-Esseen Theorem, and Statistical Testing," working paper. Available here: `https://ssrn.com/abstract=3641266` (dated Feb 4, 2020; downloaded Feb 4, 2020).

Crack, Timothy Falcon, Michael J. Osborne, Malcolm A. Crack, and Mark J. Osborne, 2021, "A New Approach to Student and Fisher Using Polynomial Roots," working paper, Available here: `https://ssrn.com/abstract=3598613` (dated Mar 31, 2021; downloaded Jul 7, 2021).

Crack, Timothy Falcon, and Helen M. Roberts, 2015a, "Credit Cards, Excess Debt, and the Time Value of Money: The Parable of the Debt Banana," *The Journal of Financial Education*, Vol. 41 No. 1, (Spring), pp. 117–137.

Crack, Timothy Falcon, and Helen M. Roberts, 2015b, "Credit Card Balances and Repayment under Competing Minimum Payment Regimes," *Review of Quantitative Finance and Accounting*, Vol. 45 No. 4, (Nov), pp. 785–801.

Crouch, Catherine and Eric Mazur, 2001, "Peer Instruction: Ten Years of Experience and Results," *American Journal of Physics*, Vol. 69 No. 9, (Sept), pp. 970–977.

Davis, Tenney L., 1939, "Decorative Bronzes in the George Eastman Research Laboratory of the Massachusetts Institute of Technology," *Journal of Chemical Education*, Vol. 16 No. 1, (Jan), pp. 3–6.

Deming, W. Edwards, 2000, *Out of the Crisis*, MIT Press: Cambridge, Ma. (Originally published 1982.)

Deming, W. Edwards, 2018, "Deming's 14 Points for the Transformation of Management," Available here: https://deming.org/wp-content/uploads/2020/06/One-Pager-14Points.pdf (originally extracted from pp. 23–24 of *Out of the Crisis*). See also https://deming.org/explore/fourteen-points/.

Deming, W. Edwards and Raymond T. Birge, 1934,

"On the Statistical Theory of Errors," *Review of Modern Physics*," Vol. 6 No. 3, (Jul), pp. 119–161.

Dolan, Tim, 2020, *IPEVO Visualizer Software for Document Cameras: Beginners Guide*, `https://www.youtube.com/watch?v=u7Trv-OuBVo`.

Dunn, Rita, Jeffrey S. Beaudry, and Angela Klavas, 2002, "Survey of Research on Learning Styles," *California Journal of Science Education*, Vol. II No. 2, (Spring), pp. 75–98.

Eison, J., 1990, "Confidence in the Classroom: Ten Maximums for New Teachers," *College Teaching*, Vol. 33 No. 1, (Jan–Mar), pp. 21–25.

Emerson, Ralph Waldo, 1841, *Self-Reliance*, appearing in his first volume of collected essays. Available here: `https://www.gutenberg.org/files/16643/16643-h/16643-h.htm`, and here `https://math.dartmouth.edu/~doyle/docs/self/self.pdf`

Epigeum, 2011, "Student attention over an hour," Available here: `https://epigeum.com/downloads/uct_accessible/uk/01_lecturing1/html/course_files/2_30.html` (dated 2011; downloaded Sept 5, 2021).

Falk, Ruma and Clifford Konold, 1999, "The Psychology of Learning Probability," Appearing in Gordon, F.S. and S.P. Gordon (Eds), *Statistics for the Twenty-First Century*, Mathematical Association of America, pp. 151–164.

Feller, William, 1971, *An Introduction to Probability Theory and its Applications*, Volume II, Second Edition, John Wiley and Sons: New York, NY.

Financial Samurai, 2019, "How to Deal With a Micromanager," (May), 5pp., Available here: https://www.financialsamurai.com/how-to-deal-with-a-micromanager/ (dated May 2019; downloaded Jun 2021). Be sure to read both the article and the comments.

Fleming, Neil and David Baume, 2006, "Learning Styles Again: VARKing Up the Right Tree!," *Educational Developments*, Vol. 7 No. 4, (Nov), pp. 4–7.

Furey, William, 2020, The Stubborn Myth of Learning Styles," *Education Next*, Vol. 20 No. 3, (Summer), pp. 8–13.

Gabarro, John I. and John P. Kotter, 1980, "Managing Your Boss: A Compatible Relationship with Your Superior is Essential to Being Effective in Your Job," *Harvard Business Review*, Vol. 58 No. 1, (Jan/Feb), pp. 92–100. Reprinted with minor revisions in 2005, *Harvard Business Review*, Vol. 83 No. 1, (Jan), pp. 92–99.

Graham, Benjamin, 2006, *The Intelligent Investor: A Book of Practical Counsel*, Revised Edition, Harper Collins: New York, NY. (Originally published in 1949, this is Graham's 1973 text annotated by Jason Zweig.)

Greene, Robert, 1592, *The Second and Last Part*

of Conny-Catching, Printed by John Wolfe for William Wright: London. Available here: `http://www.luminarium.org/renascence-editions/greene4.html`.

Halmos, 1974, "How to Talk Mathematics," *Notices of the American Mathematical Society*, Vol. 21 No. 3, pp. 155–158. Available here: `https://faculty.washington.edu/heagerty/Courses/b572/public/HalmosHowToTalk.pdf`

HSPH, 2012, "Food Pyramids and Plates: What Should You Really Eat?," Harvard School of Public Health, The Nutrition Source, Available here: `https://www.hsph.harvard.edu/nutritionsource/healthy-eating-pyramid/` (dated Oct 2012; downloaded Jul 17, 2021).

Husmann, Polly R. and Valerie Dean O'Loughlin, 2019, "Another Nail in the Coffin for Learning Styles? Disparities among Undergraduate Anatomy Students' Study Strategies, Class Performance, and Reported VARK Learning Styles," *Anatomical Sciences Education*, Vol. 12 No. 1, (Jan/Feb), pp. 6–19.

Ingraham, Christopher, 2014, "America's Top Fears: Public Speaking, Heights and Bugs," *Washington Post*, Available here: `https://www.washingtonpost.com/news/wonk/wp/2014/10/30/clowns-are-twice-as-scary-to-democrats-as-they-are-to-republicans/` (dated Oct 30, 2014; downloaded Jul 15, 2021).

Karr, Jean-Baptiste Alphonse, 1849, *Les Guêpes*, Jan. (A self-published satirical magazine printed in Paris, presenting political and literary dissent. The title translates as "The Wasps.")

King, Alison, 1993, "From Sage on the Stage to Guide on the Side," *College Teaching*, Vol. 41 No. 1, (Jan–Mar), pp. 30–35.

Lazear, Edward P., 2004, "The Peter Principle: A Theory of Decline," *Journal of Political Economy*, Vol. 112 No. 1, Supplement, ppS141–S163.

Macey, Jonathan, 2010, "The Demise of the Reputational Model in Capital Markets: The Problem of the 'Last Period Parasites'," *Syracuse Law Review* Symposium: Law and the Financial Crisis: Economic Regulation during Turbulent Times, Vol. 60 No. 3, (Apr), pp. 427–448.

Mason, Robert C., 1983, *Chickenhawk*, Viking Press: New York, NY.

Massa, Laura J. and Richard E. Mayer, 2006, "Testing the ATI Hypothesis: Should Multimedia Instruction Accommodate Verbalizer-Visualizer Cognitive Style?," *Learning and Individual Differences*, Vol. 16 No. 4, (Dec), pp. 321–335.

McDonald, Ewan, 2020, "Why is New Zealand So Progressive?", Available here: `https://www.bbc.com/travel/article/20200518-why-is-new-zealand-so-progressive` (dated Aug 20, 2020; downloaded Sept 1, 2021).

McKenzie, Richard B. and Dwight R. Lee, 2010, "Production Costs and the Theory of the Firm," Chapter 7 in *Microeconomics for MBAs: The Economic Way of Thinking for Managers*, Second Edition, Cambridge University Press: Cambridge, England.

MER, 2021, "Monthly Economic Review: March 2021," New Zealand Parliamentary Library, Research and Information, 8pp.

Mnookin, Robert H., Scott R. Peppet, and Andrew S. Tulumello, 2004, *Beyond Winning: Negotiating to Create Value in Deals and Disputes*, Belknap Press: An Imprint of Harvard University Press.

Mueller, Pam A. and David M. Oppenheimer, 2014, "The Pen is Mightier than the Keyboard: Advantages of Taking Longhand Notes Over Laptop Note Taking," *Psychological Science*, Vol. 25 No. 6, (Jun 1), pp. 1159–1168.

NAR (National Association of Realtors), 2021, "Research and Statistics: Housing Indicators," Available here: `https://www.nar.realtor/research-and-statistics` (dated May 2021; downloaded Jul 16, 2021).

Navarro, Joe, 2019, *Former FBI Agent Explains How to Read Body Language—Tradecraft*, `https://www.youtube.com/watch?v=4jwUXV4QaTw`

NBR, 2015, *Nightly Business Report*, July 29, See the 19:30-mark on the video recording, Available here: `https://www.youtube.com/watch?v=qpEyv-lzfKI` (dated Jul 29, 2015; downloaded Feb 8, 2017).

NYU, 2021, "Grading: Grading System," Available here: `https://www.stern.nyu.edu/portal-partners/registrar/policies-procedures/grading-policies` (downloaded Sept 16, 2021).

Pashler, Harold, Mark McDaniel, Doug Rohrer, and Robert Bjork, 2008, "Learning Styles: Concepts and Evidence," *Psychological Science in the Public Interest*, Vol. 9 No. 3, (Dec), pp. 105–119.

Peter, Laurence J. and Raymond Hull, 1969, *The Peter Principle: Why Things Always Go Wrong*, William Morrow & Co Inc.: New York, NY.

PON (Program on Negotiation Staff), 2020, "10 Hard-Bargaining Tactics to Watch Out for in a Negotiation," Available here: `https://www.pon.harvard.edu/daily/batna/10-hardball-tactics-in-negotiation/` (dated Sept 28, 2020; downloaded 23 Apr, 2021).

Ramsey, Dave, 2021, "The Ramsey Show - Highlights," Available here: `https://www.youtube.com/c/TheRamseyShow/featured`.

Reid, Jennifer, 2006, "Barriers to Maori Student Success at the University of Canterbury," master's thesis, University of Canterbury, 155pp.

REINZ, 2021, "REINZ June Data: House Prices Continue to Rise Across the Country, Defying

Expectations," Real Estate Institute of New Zealand Residential Property Data. Available here: `https://www.reinz.co.nz/residential-property-data-gallery` (dated Jul 13, 2021; downloaded Jul 16, 2021).

Reynolds, David and Zhenzhen Miao, 2014, "How China Teaches Children Maths So Well," *The Conversation.* Available here: `https://theconversation.com/how-china-teaches-children-maths-so-well-32052` (dated Sept 27, 2014; downloaded Jul 19, 2021).

Riener, Cedar R. and Daniel T. Willingham, 2010, "The Myth of Learning Styles," *Change: The Magazine of Higher Learning*, Vol. 42 No. 5, (Aug), pp. 32–35.

Ritchie, Anne Thackeray, 1885, *Mrs. Dymond; A Novel by Miss Thackeray*, Harper & Brothers: New York, NY. Available here: `https://www.loc.gov/item/07041667/`.

Rogowsky, Beth. A., Barbara M. Calhoun, and Paula Tallal, 2015, "Matching Learning Style to Instructional Method: Effects on Comprehension," *Journal of Educational Psychology*, Vol. 107 No. 1, (Jan), pp. 64–78.

Seales, Rebecca, 2017, "Let's Save Maya Angelou from Fake Quotes," BBC News, Available here: `https://www.bbc.com/news/41913640` (dated Nov 13, 2017; downloaded Jul 2, 2021).

Shakespeare, William, 1596, *The Merchant of Venice.*

Shakespeare, William, 1599–1601, *Hamlet.*

Shakespeare, William, 1606, *Macbeth.*

Shaw, George Bernard, 1903, *Maxims for Revolutionists* (Appendix to *Man and Superman*), The University Press: Cambridge, MA. Available here: `https://www.gutenberg.org/cache/epub/26107/pg26107.html`.

Snider, Vickie E. and Rebecca Roehl, 2007, "Teachers' Beliefs about Pedagogy and Related Issues," *Psychology in the Schools*, Vol. 44 No. 8, (Nov), pp. 873–886.

Statista, 2021, "Percentage of the U.S. Population who have Completed Four Years of College or More from 1940 to 2020, by Gender," Available here: `https://www.statista.com/statistics/184272/educational-attainment-of-college-diploma-or-higher-by-gender/` (dated Apr 2021; downloaded Jun 30 2021).

Stephens, Abby, 2017, "The Benefits of Hand-written Versus Digital Notetaking in College Lectures," *Lexia: Undergraduate Journal in Writing, Rhetoric and Technical Communication*, Vol V, 2016-2017, pp. 1–10.

St Louis Fed., 2021, "S&P/Case-Shiller 20-City Composite Home Price Index (SPCS20RSA)," Available here: `https://fred.stlouisfed.org/series/`

SPCS20RSA (dated May 25, 2021; downloaded Jun 14, 2021).

Swift, Jonathan, 1721, *A Letter to a Young Gentleman, Lately Enter'd Into Holy Orders by a Person of Quality*, Second Edition, (Letter Dated Jan 9, 1720). Printed for J. Roberts at the Oxford Arms in Warwick Lane, London. Available here: https://en.wikisource.org/wiki/The_Works_of_the_Rev._Jonathan_Swift/Volume_5/A_Letter_to_a_Young_Clergyman.

Tharapos, Meredith, 2018, "Cultural Intelligence: An Intelligent Approach to Cultural Diversity in the Classroom!," Available here: https://www.talkingaccounting.com/2018/06/24/cultural-intelligence-an-intelligent-approach-to-cultural-diversity-in-the-classroom/ (dated Jun 24, 2018; downloaded Jun 21, 2021).

Tharapos, Meredith, 2019, "Speak Easy: Strategies for Communicating Effectively," Available here: https://www.talkingaccounting.com/2019/03/03/speak-easy-strategies-for-communicating-effectively/ (dated Mar 3, 2019; downloaded Jun 21, 2021).

Torgerson, Shane, 2010, "Meteor Crater Aerial View 2010," Available here: https://upload.wikimedia.org/wikipedia/commons/4/46/Meteorcrater.jpg (dated "9/6/2010"; downloaded Jul 8, 2021).

Twain, Mark, 1893, *The £1,000,000 Bank-Note*," Available here as a pdf file: `https://s3.amazonaws.com/booksatwork/wp-content/uploads/2014/06/Twain-Million-Pound-Note.pdf`.

University of Chicago, 2004, *The Graduate School of Business: Announcements 2004–05*, 136pp.

USCB, 2020, "Income and Poverty in the United States: 2019," United States Census Bureau, Available here: `https://www.census.gov/library/publications/2020/demo/p60-270.html` (dated Sept 15, 2020; downloaded Aug 16, 2021).

USMC, 2012, "United States Marine Corps, Weapons Training Battalion, Training Command, Lesson Plan: Pistol Presentation and Search and Assess, CPP.8 Combat Pistol Program, Revised 10/1/2012," Available here: `https://www.trngcmd.marines.mil/Portals/207/Docs/wtbn/MPMS/CPP-08-Presentations.pdf?ver=2015-06-09-103805-583`, 9pp (dated Oct 1, 2012; downloaded Jun 14, 2021).

Voss, Chris, 2018, "Chris Voss—3 Tips on Negotiations, with FBI Negotiator," Available here: `https://www.youtube.com/watch?v=xQJOylbLYJY` (dated Dec 20, 2018; downloaded Sept 16, 2021).

Wallis, W. Allen, 1980, "The Statistical Research Group, 1942-1945: Rejoinder," *Journal of the American Statistical Association*," Vol. 75 No. 370 (Jun), pp. 334–335.

Whitehead, Alfred North, 1923, "The Rhythm of Education," *Bulletin of the American Association of University Professors (1915-1955)*, Vol. 9 No. 7, (Nov), pp. 17–19.

Whitehead, Alfred North and Bertrand Russell, 1910/1912/1913, *Principia Mathematica*, Vols. 1/2/3, Cambridge University Press: Cambridge, England.

Willingham, Daniel T., Elizabeth M. Hughes, and David G. Dobolyi, 2015, "The Scientific Status of Learning Styles Theories," *Teaching of Psychology*, Vol. 42 No. 3, (Jun), pp. 266–271.

Wilson, Marc, Maree Hunt, Liz Richardson, Hazel Phillips, Ken Richardson, and Donna Challies, 2011, "Āwhina: A Programme for Māori and Pacific Tertiary Science Graduate and Postgraduate Success," *Higher Education*, Vol. 62 No. 6, (Dec), pp.699–719.

Wittrock, Merlin C., 1990, "Generative Processes of Comprehension," *Educational Psychologist*, Vol. 24 No. 4, (Oct–Dec), pp. 345–376.

Wong, Bang, 2011, "Points of View: Color Blindness," *Nature Methods*, Vol. 8 No. 6, (Jun), p. 441. Available here: `https://www.nature.com/articles/nmeth.1618.pdf`.

Index

24 Essential Tips for Selling
Print Replica eBooks on Amazon:
How to Capture New Readers by Turning
Your Physical Book into an eBook
Timothy Falcon Crack

PhD (MIT), MCom, PGDipCom,
BSc (HONS 1st Class), IMC

This 54-page eBook gives more than two-dozen essential tips accumulated over years of turning self-published physical print books into "print replica" eBooks sold on www.Amazon.com. (What did I learn the hard way? What did I wish I had known before I published eBooks? What are the biggest trip-ups you need to watch out for?) A print replica eBook uses a simple pdf-formatted text block. So, there is no messing around with unfamiliar EPUB or MOBI formatting, HTML code, or reflowable eBooks (i.e., where the book reorganizes itself when the reader resizes the text). If you are not selling your books as eBooks, then you are missing out on customers and the royalty income they provide!

www.Amazon.com (Kindle)
timcrack@alum.mit.edu

How to Ace Your Business Finance Class:
Essential Knowledge and Techniques to
Master the Material and Ace Your Exams
Timothy Falcon Crack

*PhD (MIT), MCom, PGDipCom,
BSc (HONS 1st Class), IMC*

A pocket-sized book for students (or instructors) in a first university finance class. I use 25 years experience teaching this material to explain carefully the stumbling blocks that consistently trip up students. Chapters titles: Foundations, Financial Statements, TVM I (One Cash Flow), TVM II (Multiple Cash Flows), Inflation and Indices, Bonds and Interest Rates, Equities and Dividend Discount Models, Capital Budgeting I (Decision Rules), Capital Budgeting II (Cash Flows), Capital Budgeting III (Cost of Capital), Capital Budgeting IV (A Paradox), The CAPM and Interest Rates, Risk and Return, Market Efficiency, Capital Structure, and Dividends.

www.Amazon.com (Paperback)
www.Amazon.com (Kindle)
timcrack@alum.mit.edu

Heard on The Street:
Quantitative Questions from
Wall Street Job Interviews
Timothy Falcon Crack

*PhD (MIT), MCom, PGDipCom,
BSc (HONS 1st Class), IMC*

A must read! Over 235 quant questions collected
from actual job interviews in investment banking, investment management, and options trading. The interviewers use the same questions
year-after-year, and here they are—with solutions! These questions come from all types of interviews (corp. finance, sales and trading, quant
research, etc.). The questions come from all levels
of interviews (undergrad, MS, MBA, PhD). The
latest edition also includes 260+ non-quant actual interview questions, and a revised section on
interview technique. Questions from **traditional
corporate finance** interviews are indicated with
a bank symbol in the margin (71 of the quant
questions and 192 of the non-quant questions).

Pocket Heard on The Street
Timothy Falcon Crack

PhD (MIT), MCom, PGDipCom,
BSc (HONS 1st Class), IMC

These two pocket-sized editions fit in your pocket or purse, and are easy to read on the subway, bus, train, or plane! They are a carefully curated selection of the best questions from the full-sized edition of *Heard on The Street*. The red-covered edition has 75 quant questions, with detailed solutions. The yellow-covered edition has 20 brain teasers, 30 thinking questions, and over 100 non-quantitative questions. The brain teasers, and more than half the thinking questions have detailed solutions. The quant questions in the red edition usually require math/stats, but the brain teasers and "thinking questions" in the yellow edition usually require little or no math; the thinking questions are in between.

www.Amazon.com (Paperback)
www.Amazon.com (Kindle)
timcrack@alum.mit.edu

Basic Black-Scholes:
Option Pricing and Trading
Timothy Falcon Crack

PhD (MIT), MCom, PGDipCom,
BSc (HONS 1st Class), IMC

Extremely clear explanations of Black-Scholes option pricing theory, and applications of theory to trading. Based on award-winning teaching at Indiana University. The presentation does not go far beyond basic Black-Scholes because a novice need not go far beyond Black-Scholes to make money, all high-level option pricing theory extends Black-Scholes, and other books go far beyond Black-Scholes without the firm foundations given here. Includes Bloomberg screens, expanded analysis of Black-Scholes interpretations, and downloadable spreadsheets to forecast profits and transactions costs, and to explore option sensitivities (the Greeks).

---

www.Amazon.com (Paperback)
www.Amazon.com (Kindle)
timcrack@alum.mit.edu

Foundations for Scientific Investing:
Capital Markets Intuition and
Critical Thinking Skills
Timothy Falcon Crack

*PhD (MIT), MCom, PGDipCom,
BSc (HONS 1st Class), IMC*

A firm foundation for thinking about and conducting investment. It helps to build capital markets intuition and critical thinking skills. Every investor needs these skills to conduct confident, deliberate, and skeptical investment. This book is the product of 25 years of investment research and experience (academic, personal, and professional) and 20+ painstaking years of destructive testing in university classrooms. The integration of finance, economics, accounting, pure mathematics, statistics, numerical techniques, and spreadsheets (or programming) make this an ideal capstone course at the advanced undergraduate or masters/MBA level.

www.Amazon.com (Paperback)
www.Amazon.com (Kindle)
timcrack@alum.mit.edu

Foundations for Scientific Investing:
Multiple-Choice, Short Answer, and
Long-Answer Test Questions
Timothy Falcon Crack

*PhD (MIT), MCom, PGDipCom,
BSc (HONS 1st Class), IMC*

This book accompanies *Foundations for Scientific Investing*. It provides 700+ class-tested questions (600+ multiple-choice questions and 125 short-answer questions), plus the long-answer questions already appearing in *Foundations for Scientific Investing*). Suggested solutions to the multiple-choice and short-answer questions are given. The multiple-choice questions may also be useful as a test bank for instructors in any advanced investments class.

---

www.Amazon.com (Paperback)
www.Amazon.com (Kindle)
timcrack@alum.mit.edu

PUBREF:20220202:15:54.616,982.OU